TEN MEGATRENDS
CHANGING OUR LIVES

YOUNG SOP AHN

Contents

Introduction

Since time immemorial, different time periods have presented humanity with different opportunities and risks. However, the opportunities and risks this century in particular is presenting to us are unique. It is undeniable that we are living in the most critical century in human history. The contemporary world is undergoing a series of revolutions. Rapid advances in science and technology are key drivers of the revolutions. They are dramatically transforming every aspect of our life: economy, politics, international relations, generational relations, education, role of intellectuals, human-technology relationships, personal privacy, human life-span, and workforce demographics. The revolutions are disruptive at a societal level but also at global level. Apart from the revolutions, our planet is going through changes that will alter the life of everyone and everything around the world. Climate change poses a fundamental threat to the places, species and people's livelihoods. In short, this century is already posing unprecedented challenges for all of us.

John Maynard Keynes, one of the most influential economists of the twentieth century, wrote in 1937: "The idea of the future being different from the present is so repugnant to our conventional modes of thought and behavior that we, most of us, offer a great resistance to acting on it in practice."[1] The world has since changed beyond recognition. Constant global changes may be considered natural, but they continue to have unprecedented positive and negative effects on our lives. Concerning the negatives in particular of inexorably advancing technologies, Stephen Hawking warned that we cannot know if humanity will be destroyed by them.[2] Touching on climate change, the late visionary physicist also said humankind may be heading for an apocalyptic catastrophe on earth and called for humans to colonize the moon and Mars within the next century as an insurance policy against this doomsday scenario.[3] This warning may sound too radical but provides us with food for thought.

We can come to anticipate the impacts these changes will have on our lives by analyzing megatrends, or events which occur over a certain period of time that influence all the faces of our life. In an ideal world, looking into the future would be an exact science, and we would be able to forecast where these global changes are taking us and learn how best to prepare for the consequences. This is not the case, of course, especially in this mind-blowing century in which our future looks more uncertain than ever. Exploring megatrends that are occurring now is perhaps the closest we can come to figuring out what comes next.

In more detail, probing into what may happen tomorrow was not so challenging in the past as it is now. Today, this task should deal with a world system which is becoming far more convoluted and volatile. However, the good news is that global organizations and thinkers have steadily expanded their efforts to uncover megatrends, although they recognize that perfect knowledge about where the world is heading is unfeasible and at least very hard to attain.[4] They are determined to improve our understanding of upcoming challenges and aid us in making plans to deal with them. They have also been encouraged by the fact that their ability to prognosticate what is coming to us has been steadily improving, enhancing our capabilities to do well in the days ahead, both individually and unitedly as a society.[5] As a result, the number of experts from various disciplines who are joining the study of megatrends is growing, albeit slowly.[6]

I have maintained that the key snag impeding our efforts to accurately and timely uncover megatrends does not necessarily lie in the difficulty involving the effort but in our own desertion of the endeavor per se to undertake this task. My motivation to write this book was this: I happened to be reminded of the famed observation by George Orwell, who remains best remembered for authoring the cult classics, *Nineteen Eighty-Four* and *Animal Farm,* that

> a writer's subject matter will be determined by the age he lives in—at least this is true in tumultuous, revolutionary ages like our own—but before he ever begins to write he will have acquired an emotional attitude from which he will never completely escape. (J. Meyers, *Orwell: Life and Art* [Chicago: University of Illinois Press, 2010], 67)

At the same time, the books that renowned futurists, such as Alvin Toffler, John Naisbitt, and Patrick Dixon, authored in the 1980s–90s to show what our future world would be like had greatly impressed me.[7] At that time, advancing information technologies were reshaping our society as the term, "information revolution," signifies. Computers were not only increasing in number but also getting faster, cheaper, ubiquitous, and connected to the Internet rapidly in schools, businesses, public offices, homes, and so on. I could immediately sense that the information age was inexorably progressing, profoundly changing our lives.

This perception inspired me to try to foresee new megatrends to emerge in the decades ahead—that is to say, the trends that would be very different from those the thinkers in times past dealt with. By this time, I had acquired a compelling "emotional attitude" from which I could never get away. Trying to sharpen my foresight into new megatrends on one hand and scrutinizing relevant studies concerning this on the other, I have been carefully watching for the last twenty years what megatrends are playing out. The key point is that I have continued and updated my research on surfacing megatrends for a long time, which has enabled me to author this book in this critical era of promises and perils.

This book consists of ten chapters, each dealing with one megatrend. I have written this book for not only academics but also general readers, in particular, who are anxious to know how dominant megatrends will change their day-to-day lives. In other words, the prime goal of my book is to educate the public in general on how the world is changing and to have them prepare for their future. I should admit that my book, like the books Naisbitt, Toffler, and other thinkers have written, is academic in nature, and the tone of this text will reflect this. However, to best meet my key aim here, which is to serve the intellectual need of general readers, I have done my best to write this book in an easy-to-follow, entertaining, and enlightening manner, which I term the "3E principles of writing for all readers." I have made every possible effort to avoid the trap of getting locked in silos of excellence in which experts communicate with their peers only. For example, I've tried to explain the basic concepts of the new terminologies that have emerged because of, say, advancing technologies.

Reflecting this concern, my book can be considered nonfiction that easily reads like interesting narrative nonfiction. I have tried my best to meet this requirement especially because I have found that existing articles and reports on megatrends lack the effort to this end. I have also tried my best to look at megatrends in a fresh and stimulating perspective. For this reason, all the articles and reports on megatrends mainly for strategic thinking for government policy makers[8] are of secondary consideration in this book.

To discover the ten megatrends outlined in this book, I have scrutinized over seven thousand reports and articles on websites alone. However, I would like to admit that different authors could craft their own world view and offer their own megatrends. Whatever may be said about my book, I cannot emphasize the following enough. I've invested a lot over the last two decades to author a book that everyone should read and will hold the reader's interest from start to finish. I invite my readers to provide feedback, as it would be of great help to my subsequent writings on how our lives are changing.

Young Sop Ahn

CHAPTER 1

Civicracy

1. What's wrong with representative democracy?

Little Billy said, "My father plays the piano in an opium den." His teacher, greatly shocked, called Billy's father.

"Yes, that's what I told him. I lied," Billy's father replied. "But how can I tell my eight-year-old kid that his father is a politician?"

British parliamentarian Rory Stewart started his TED (Technology, Entertainment, Design) Talk with this quip in 2012.[1] Honored in 2008 as one of the seventy-five most influential people of the twenty-first century chosen by *Esquire* magazine, Stewart noted that 84 percent of the British said that politics was broken. He said that people anywhere in the world looked at politicians as being somewhere between a snake, a monkey, and an iguana. Earlier in 2010, David Cameron, then leader of Britain's Conservative Party, remarked during his own TED Talk how deep the problems with British representative democracy ran. He went as far as to quip that scientists were thinking about replacing rats in their experiments with politicians. Asked why, the scientists answered, "Well, there's no shortage of politicians, no one really minds what happens to them and, after all, there are some things that rats just won't do."[2]

The US democracy is doing no better. Polls have shown that US politics is failing. Congress approval remained low at 13 percent and 16 percent in 2016 and 2017, respectively.[3] Congressional approval dropped to an all-time low of 9 percent in late 2013, according to a *CBS News/New York Times* poll.[4] The 2013 Harvard Public Opinion Project found that a majority (52%) of eighteen- to twenty-nine-year-old Americans would replace every member of Congress, if given the chance.[5] Seasoned journalist Bob Schieffer wondered in 2013 in one of his takes for *CBS*'s *Face the Nation*, which he then moderated, if the United States was still qualified to tell others how to run their countries.[6]

As for the US presidency, Donald Trump seemed to be heading toward an unknown fate as of September 2018, with the odds of his impeachment being discussed widely. The *Atlantic* reported in late 2017,

> We have never had a president so ill-informed about the nature of his office, so openly mendacious, so self-destructive, or so brazen in his abusive attacks on the courts, the press, Congress (including members of his own party), and even senior officials within his own administration. (J. Goldsmith, "Will Donald Trump destroy the presidency," *Atlantic* [October 2017], available at: https:// www.theatlantic.com/, accessed December 31, 2017)

President Trump's approval rating already dropped to 37 percent in the second week of 2018.[7] In September 2018, *CNN* and other polls showed Trump's approval rate was falling further.[8]

The United States, despite its status as the world's strongest country, has an awful dark side. For example, it has the world's highest incarceration rate and the largest number of people in prison.[9] The US society has lost its balance due to, say, the huge, widening wealth and income gap between the rich and the poor. "The top 1 percent controls 42 percent of U.S. wealth."[10] Also, "the top 1 percent takes home nearly a quarter (24 percent) of the national income, and owns half of the country's stocks, bonds and mutual funds."[11] The United States had the world's largest deficit of US$484.1 billion in current account balance as of 2015,[12] and the world's highest government budget deficit of US$530 billion estimated in 2016.[13] A high and growing federal debt will weaken the US economy over the long term and hurt Americans.[14] The United States was also one of the world's top 10 countries with largest national debt versus gross domestic product (GDP) in 2018, with a national debt standing at US$ $19.23 trillion in 2018.[15] Besides, continuing controversies over moral and social issues involving abortion, immigration, gender discrimination, race inequality, even the recent resurgence of the white supremacist ideology, and so on have been troubling the US society. Some analysts argue that the United States will continue to decline due to the weakening of its political energies.[16]

Survey after survey of the US public sentiment toward politics has confirmed that the country's citizens' disillusionment toward their political delegates keeps growing. US citizens' political apathy is deepening due to the lack of their representatives' efforts to remedy the deep-seated problems the country has faced for a long time.[17] This indicates that the people want to do away with the bulk of the political establishment. President Donald Trump seemed to have capitalized on such anti–political establishment sentiment among the US public. Before he won the 2016 US presidential election, Iowa GOP chairman Jeff Kaufmann attributed the success of Donald Trump in the Republican presidential race for the White House to a "hunger for an outsider."[18] The business tycoon was an independent (2011–12) before he announced in June 2015 his candidacy for president as a Republican. *USA TODAY* reported in February 2016 shortly after Jeb Bush dropped out of the Republican race for president, that the year 2016 was "not the year for an establishment figure." "Bush's presidential bid ran afoul of the antiestablishment 'outsider' politics that have dominated the 2016 campaign and produced the phenomenon of Donald Trump."[19]

Former US president Barack Obama was also nearly an outsider to Washington politics, which he often called poisonous. Obama had served less than two years as US senator when he announced his candidacy for US president on February 10, 2007. Michelle Obama too has expressed her great distaste for Washington politics. On October 25, 2016, the *Washington Post* looked back into a 2014 *New York Times* report about the then First Lady[20] that said, "She loathes Washington's toxic politics."[21] Michelle Obama's passionate speech supporting Hillary Clinton as Democratic presidential nominee at the Democratic National Convention of 2016 almost stole the show. While the First Lady was campaigning alongside Clinton as the most potent uber-surrogate on the campaign trail, her speech and charisma were so impressive that her popularity skyrocketed, overwhelming Clinton's. The number of Americans who were hoping Michelle Obama would race for the White House one day soared. However, "Michelle Obama has spoken openly about her distaste for political vitriol and often recalls asking why her husband wanted to expose himself to the barbs of political life at all."[22]

Globally, most representative democracies are problem ridden. Between 2007 and 2011, Belgium experienced a political crisis of no government for as long as 541 days, the longest such record in modern political history. The prolonged crisis was due to the failure of the Belgian political establishment to meet the demand of the Belgian population for state reform. In France, Emmanuel Macron was elected new president of France in a landslide victory on May 7, 2017. However, the political future of the youngest ever French president remains uncertain. A significant number of French citizens took to the street in anticapitalist protests.[23] Prior to the French election, a bizarre but provocative and "cool" civic campaign called Obama17 was started in February 2017 to make Barack Obama the next French President. The campaign began circulating a petition for the former US president, who is very popular across the world, to be allowed on their country's ballot during the upcoming French presidential election, which was apparently "running into an issue many Americans can identify with: voting against a candidate instead of for one."[24] An organizer of Obama17 admitted that the campaign was ultimately a joke, but its inspiration reflected the key issue of present-day French politics: "We want to show that people are fed up with the politicians here," the campaign organizer said.[25]

Young democracies are generally revealing graver problems than old democracies. Spain's political crisis has been deepening. The country which returned to democracy four decades ago suffered more than three hundred days of political paralysis before it could get a government in late October 2016. Most Spaniards deeply distrust their corrupt government and political establishment, and another round of political crisis can happen anytime.[26] In Brazil, President Dilma Rousseff was impeached for illegally manipulating government accounts and was removed from office on August 31, 2016. In less than one year after Rousseff was removed from office, Brazilians staged protests around the country to call for new President Michel Temer to step down after graft charges.[27] Pew studies found in 2014 that 78 percent of Brazilian respondents and 83 percent of those in India regarded dishonest political leadership as a grave issue.[28]

According to a 2017 Freedom House report, Jamaica and El Salvador are among the free, democratic countries of the world.[29] However, Jamaica is notorious for high levels of crime and violence and has had one of the highest murder rates in the world for many years. Many of the top ruling elites of the Caribbean country are educated at top universities in the United States and the United Kingdom, such as Harvard, Princeton, and Oxford, but considered corrupt and incompetent. The situation is about the same in El Salvador. This country has been tormented by one of the highest homicide rates in the world. The most well-known gangs called maras are largely responsible for the extremely high murder rate. The gang's activities range from drug, arms and human trafficking; assault; extortion; identity fraud and theft; illegal gambling and immigration; kidnapping; money laundering; and people smuggling to prostitution, racketeering, robbery, and vandalism, for all of which malfunctioning politics is largely to blame. The Central American country has drawn international attention for numerous injustices involving unlawful police killings, missing children, rendering organized labor illegal, and so on. Such a sad reality is deepening the public distrust of the political establishment in developing democracies.

Since democratically elected governments are not working across the world, democracy appears to have intrinsic flaws. Jorge Soto, a member the Global Agenda Council on the Future of Government of the World Economic Forum (WEF) says that

> the global economic crash in 2008 was a potent catalyst for the erosion of public confidence in political institutions and processes. Citizens now place more faith in private companies than in their own government leaders, and even then, they don't particularly trust the private sector, with the latest Edelman Trust Barometer showing global trust in business at 58% and trust in government sunk to 44%. (J. Soto, "The weakening of representative democracy," *Outlook on the Global Agenda 2015* [2015], available at: https://www.weforum.org/, accessed February 26, 2015)

Soto's analysis of "the weakening of representative democracy" was trend no. 5 among the top ten trends facing the world in 2015 that a WEF report dealt with. "As our governments have grown, their mechanisms have been plagued by decades of factional alignment, dynasty and deep corruption."[30] Due to the Internet, the public can identify with people having the same values and fears, exchange ideas, and build relationships faster than ever before. Our governments are nineteenth-century institutions with twentieth-century mind-sets, only to fail to communicate with twenty-first-century citizens who are reluctant to recognize their value.[31]

For example, people are calling for tighter gun control across the world more fiercely than ever nowadays. In the United States, their protest amounts to rejecting the Second Amendment to the US Constitution, an institution dating back to the late eighteenth century when their sociopolitical conditions were so insecure that the citizenry deemed it necessary to organize a militia system, to participate in law enforcement, to safeguard against tyrannical government, to repel invasion, to suppress insurrection, and so on. Nevertheless, many political representatives are still getting elected with the support of lobbyists trying to protect outdated institutions for their own immediate interests. People's delegates are elected and reelected only to pursue short-term agendas. It is natural that people see their political system as broken. Recent years have shown that citizens' patience has reached its limit, "taking their grievances to the streets and through mass demonstrations."[32]

With representative democracy in trouble overall, a lot of odd, challenging expressions, such as democracy 2.0, postdemocracy, neo-democracy, alternative to democracy, democracy that needs to be rebuilt, and so on have emerged.

2. Is Communist China's one-party system superior to democracy?

The most outright challenge to Western representative democracy lately is perhaps Eric Li's claim that Communist China's one-party system is superior to democracy. The Chinese venture capitalist in Shanghai admired "the adaptability, meritocracy, and legitimacy of the Chinese authoritarian one-party system."[33] Arguing that China sees its current form of government, or any political system for that matter, "merely as a means to achieve larger national ends,"[34] he said Western democracy has become "boring." His TED talk praising the Chinese system received about 2.5 million views as of January 2018, generating more than five thousand comments—many of them supportive. A poll conducted in 2013 by Pew's Global Attitudes Project found 88 percent of Chinese citizens said their national economy was doing well, more than in any of the other 38 countries surveyed, including the United States in which only 33 percent of the respondents said their economy was doing good. In China, 66 percent perceived progress in their lives in the last five years, according to the poll.[35] A 2018 Edelman Trust Barometer survey also found that "about 84 percent of the surveyed Chinese people said they have trust in the government, beating the rates in all other countries measured."[36]

Born in Shanghai in 1968, at the height of the Cultural Revolution, Li moved to the United States while young and was once a believer in the American Dream. Educated at the University of California at Berkeley, he found his way into the campaign of US businessman Ross Perot in the 1992 US presidential race. Prior to this, he had worked in private industry for Perot. When Perot lost, he returned to China. In February 2012, Li wrote an op-ed in the *New York Times* titled, "Why China's Political Model Is Superior."[37] He concluded that history does not bode well for US-style democracy.[38] His argument in favor of Beijing's opacity and policy against freedom of speech is provocative and interesting since Western democracies are apparently failing to function.

Many Chinese, especially the incumbent Chinese political leadership, must have extolled his views. They must have also been buoyed when a World Bank study said China had overtaken the United States as the world's largest economy based on purchasing power parity (PPP) at the end of 2014. Besides, none could entirely rule out the possibility that Beijing would be able to replace Washington as the world's top superpower. For instance, data released on June 30, 2015, by the Pew Research Center supported this prospect.[39] Nonetheless, it would be rash of any analyst to jump to the conclusion that Li made a well-advised case. It has been established that authoritarian political systems, if not all, have a few short-term advantages over democracy, such as efficiency in policy making and implementation, and cheap labor-based economic competitiveness owing to oppressed or illegitimatized labor unions.

When the economies of the Asian "gang of four"—South Korea, Taiwan, Singapore, and Hong Kong—were growing fast, three of them except Hong Kong had authoritarian political systems. Their authoritarian rule, however, unraveled over time in South Korea and Taiwan. As for Singapore, Freedom House ranks the small city-state of some 5.4 million as a "partly free" country.[40] However, Singapore's representative democracy is a unicameral parliamentary political system that has three branches of government and allows multiple political parties. The World Justice Project (WJP) Rule of Law Index ranks Singapore among the top countries in the world surveyed for their performance in the criteria of "Constraints on Government Powers, Absence of Corruption, Open Government, Fundamental Rights, Order and Security, Regulatory Enforcement, Civil Justice, and Criminal Justice."[41] The country was also ranked ninth in the human development index (HDI) the United Nations Development Programme (UNDP) released in 2018, compared with China's eighty-sixth,[42] and has made progress in the freedom index at least since the onset of this century. Singapore's PPP-based per capita GDP was over US$93,905 and ranked third in the world as of 2017, according to the World Bank.[43] It is also the world's no. 1 and no. 2 in terms of ease of doing business,[44] and economic freedom,[45] respectively.

Since democratization, South Korea and Taiwan have still enjoyed relatively robust socioeconomic development. For example, South Korea was the world's no. 1 in terms of information and communication technologies (ICT) development index, compared with China at no. 81[46] and was ranked eighteenth in HDI in 2016. Taiwan boasts one of the world's highest PPP-based per capita GDP exceeding US$48,000 and that of South Korea stood at some US$38,000 in 2016.[47] By all accounts, the three countries are among the world's highest in terms of various socioeconomic and human development indicators.

Another remarkable example is Japan. The Japanese have enjoyed Western-style democracy all the way since the end of World War II. Japan, which used to be among the poorest countries in the world, registered an economic miracle that lasted half a century from the end of the World War II to the finish of Cold War. Chalmers A. Johnson, late professor at the University of California at Berkeley, who published in 1982 a best-selling textbook, *MITI and the Japanese Miracle*,[48] believed the official bureaucracy of Japan, notably the then Ministry of International Trade and Industry (MITI), had played a defining role in the miraculous growth of the Japanese economy. The expert in Japanese affairs, while discrediting the communist-type command economies, suggested that the US economy should learn a lesson from the Japanese model of collaboration between the state and big businesses.[49]

Did the Japanese government's active intervention in its economy continue to contribute to Japan's economic development? The Japanese economy, which the rest of the world then envied, began to unravel over time. It suffered slow growth and melted down largely due to the after-effects of the Japanese asset price bubble and domestic policies, intended to wring speculative excesses from the stock and real estate markets, and the subsequent global slowdown in 2000. However, the Japanese economy vigorously bounced back after 2005. The Ministry of Economy, Trade and Industry (METI), known for its liberal atmosphere, was created in 2001 when the MITI was dissolved and merged with other agencies as its power waned. Since 2005, the Japanese economy has surpassed the growth rates of the United States and the European Union. According to the International Monetary Fund (IMF), Japan was the third largest economy in the world in 2016 in terms of nominal GDP, following the United States and China.[50] Social sciences are not exact sciences. Nevertheless, social scientists do their best to scientifically validate their views and assumptions through rigorous research efforts. Their scientific findings often prove incorrect, though. The experiences of quite a few countries illustrated so far demonstrate that Eric Li's case for Chinese one-party system cannot be scientifically substantiated.

Joseph Nye, professor at Harvard University, emphasizes in his book *Is the American Century Over?* that worrying about the decline of the United States goes through cycles—cycles that include, say, the latest Great Recession and the downturn of the economy.[51] Nye notes that in both hard power, such as military and economic power, and soft power, such as diplomacy and appealing culture, which is the ability to get what one wants through traction rather than through coercion or payment, the United States is enjoying an overwhelming lead over all other countries. He suggests that it will be many unknown years before the United States could ever cede its role as the world's most powerful nation and adds that China will not equal the United States in overall power for several unknown decades to come, if at all this can ever happen.

Japan seems to be putting into practice Nye's view. Japan has developed a concept dubbed "Cool Japan" as a form of soft power that aims to make Tokyo a cultural superpower.[52] In a similar vein, Fareed Zakaria, host of *CNN"*s *Fareed Zakaria GPS*, said in his commencement address at Harvard University in 2012, "There is no equivalent of Harvard in

China or India, nor will there be one for decades, perhaps longer."[53] By this remark, he obviously implied that China is unlikely to be equal to the United States in most aspects of national strength, especially in terms of soft power, for decades to come or forever.

Furthermore, if Eric Li had based his argument for the "superiority" of the Chinese authoritarian political system over Western democracy primarily on the rapid economic growth China has achieved since Deng Xiaoping's embrace of capitalism and market economy, he should have found a critical contradiction in his argument. He should have paid more attention to the relationship between capitalism and democracy. Capitalism basically equals the free market that in turn promotes political freedom, which is the heart of Western-style democracy. As a shrewd politician, Deng Xiaoping knew too well of this linkage between economic and political freedom, but he had to stop the evils of communism and introduce free market economy for the future of China. In other words, he could not but take the alternative that communism in China would remain in name only and be eventually replaced with Western-style democracy. Deng declared "one center (economic development) and two basic points (reform and opening to the outside world)" at the thirteenth Communist Party Congress in 1987.[54] It has long been established that economic development and opening of a society generally result in transition to democracy.[55]

Besides, Eric Li must have overlooked the value of soft power, which cannot develop well in any oppressive political system. He also needs to realize that, speaking in terms of economic performance alone, China's GDP has been trending down in recent years, reflecting contradictions in its economic policies rooted in the so-called "socialist market economic system"—a misnomer—and this general downtrend is expected to continue for an unknown period to come.[56]

The People's Republic of China is pronounced in Chinese as *"Zhonghua renmin gongheguo,"* which signifies a flowery country in the center of the world. In retrospect, China, contrary to what its name symbolizes, had gotten a cold reception from the international community for a long time, at least since the First Opium War (1839–42). It was only around the time when China had managed to become a member of the

World Trade Organization (WTO) in 2001 that Beijing began to draw international recognition as a potential economic power.

Despite its impressive economic growth recorded in the last few decades, Chinese sense of inferiority toward the outside world, which had grown at least from the days when its vulnerability was revealed in the two Opium Wars and its defeats in the two Sino-Japanese Wars, remains solid in Chinese psychology. Chinese political leaders seem to be capitalizing on that sentiment to boost the economic growth–based legitimacy of the one-party rule. In other efforts to secure political legitimacy, Chinese leaders seem to have learned a lesson from former Singapore's leader Lee Kuan Yew. They appear to be committed to an anticorruption campaign as Communist Party General Secretary Xi Jinping formally announced in November 2012. The corruption that has persisted in China has increased in tandem with its economic rise. The WEF points out that "in China, 90% of people surveyed by Pew said the corruption was a problem."[57] The highly publicized anticorruption drive of China is reminiscent of the Corrupt Practices Investigation Bureau initiated by Lee Kuan Yew. Thanks to the anticorruption campaign and the impressive economic growth, Lee Kuan Yew was able to consolidate the performance-based legitimacy of his three-decade authoritarian rule, even earning the title, "Father of Singapore."

Shortly after the 2016 Davos forum, the *Wall Street Journal* touched on political implications of the declining Chinese economy. The newspaper reported to the effect that there was a rise in criticism that the political leadership of China was losing control of its economy.[58] The Chinese economy was projected to slow down in 2018–19, as exports decelerate, according to the Organization for Economic Cooperation and Development (OECD).[59] The key point is that it is hard to establish that the Chinese regime type has the intrinsic capacity to enable its economy to enjoy an enduring prosperity especially in this innovative age in which human potential cannot be fully developed without individuals' freedom to choose, which democracy allows. As for the issue of corruption alone, it is worth remembering the view of US entrepreneur George Lucas: "Power corrupts, and when you're in charge, you start doing things that you think are right, but they're actually not." The essential point is that China needs to promote democratic resilience to facilitate fundamental reforms to enhance its international competitiveness before it is too late.[60]

As socioeconomic indicators turn for the better, public demand for democracy rises as a rule. For this reason, China's suppression of human rights can be viewed as a ticking time bomb that can go off anytime, as it once did in the Tiananmen Square in 1989. A gigantic country like China, whatever uniqueness its government-civil society relationship may have had throughout its history, is bound to be pluralistic as time passes. It needs institutions of checks and balances required to moderate competing opinions and interests. One-party authoritarian rule, especially in the most populous country in the world, cannot perform single-handedly the multiple roles of the executive, the legislative, and the judiciary, which work independently of each other in a democracy. The Chinese rule cannot accommodate different interests to win public support on a long-term basis, whatever efforts it may make to have a clean and merit-based government. Respect for democratic values is not something unique to the West or some special nations but inherent in all human beings living across the globe.

3. Civicracy is inherent in democracy

The view that democracy should be rebuilt is contradictory.[61] Democracy is founded on a set of universal values, such as freedom, justice, equality, and fairness. As a set of values, democracy does not need to be rebuilt; for example, honesty as a value does not need to be renovated. Democracy is not simply a project of real politics, but a political goal universally valued. The phrase, "the weakening of representative democracy" can be misleading since democracy as a set of values cannot fail. The phrase does mean falsehearted representatives have made democracy a counterfeit. Winston Churchill once observed "democracy is the worst form of government, but it is better than any other type of government we have ever tried." Churchill's observation should be interpreted as a warning that no political system in real politics can be perfect, as all political systems are susceptible to be run by wrong leaders and representatives of people. Russians are known to be the least enthusiastic about democracy globally, "but even there, more agree than disagree that it is the best system."[62] The main problem with representative democracy today is that it seems to have become "the worst form of government," thanks to wrong representatives. Most establishment politicians have made representative democracy flagging. As Rory Stewart remarks, "they are regarded by the public as something of poisonous or whacky animals."[63] "Voters have been revolting against no-choice politics by choosing the unthinkable: Brexit, fringe political parties, rejecting the Italian reform referendum, Trump."[64]

Luckily for representative democracy, the politics of this century is becoming increasingly open and transparent with the rising capacity of concerned citizens to act as political watchdogs. For instance, the trend of using social media as a political watchdog is intensifying rapidly.[65] It's not difficult to imagine how amazing the development of all web-based services informing how politicians are performing their jobs will be in a decade or so. There will be a millionfold improvement in what we can get expect from computing in 2030 for the prices of today.[66] With the advent of hyperfast computing, the influence of social media on politics and government will not only be much more powerful but also lead to a much more responsible behavior on their part.[67]

Former British prime minister David Cameron explained how the Missouri Accountability Portal (MAP), for instance, is working.[68] The MAP has empowered citizens to examine the transparency of their state government. In the past, only the government could hold the information about how it ran public affairs, and only a few elected people could try and grab that information and question it and challenge it. Today, people in the State of Missouri can search, analyze, check, and question every single dollar their state government spends.[69] Such a governmental practice supports the prospect that the time-honored principles of democracy, "government of the people, by the people, for the people," will never perish from the earth, as the sixteenth president of the United States, Abraham Lincoln, emphasized in the Gettysburg Address on November 19, 1863.

Probably in a decade or so, even the MAP will be considered an outdated instrument for citizens' supervision of their government, as new technologies, such as incredibly fast computing, emerge. The undemocratic politics practiced by undemocratic politicians in the name of representative democracy are being remedied, thanks to an increasing number of concerned citizens who are going to involve themselves ever more aggressively in public affairs for the enduring survival and health of representative democracy.

Against this backdrop, "civicracy"—a compound word of "civic" and "-cracy" (meaning rule or government) that I coined—is rising. "Civicracy" means active participation on a massive scale by citizens in politics in representative democracies to overhaul "show business for ugly people" as US political commentator Paul Begala mockingly defines politics. It has emerged to come to the aid of representative democracy in practice. Wrong politicians are to blame for "the weakening of representative democracy," and they must be ousted from politics. The essential point here is that democracy and civicracy are basically the same, as both represent the same end or value—that is to say, the rule of, by, and for the people. Civicracy in the capacity of democracy as a value is becoming a reality since citizens of this era are becoming more enlightened and concerned about the future of representative democracy in which they wish to live.

Some may challenge this view by noting that not all citizens are informed, honest, and responsible toward their society. In other words, they may say all citizens are not and cannot be perfect. This notion sounds plausible, but it neglects the fact that most people love and pursues virtues and want to lead their lives based on them. For this very reason, they want to live in a democracy. Many citizens may be innocent, but they are not stupid. Innocent citizens have often elected dishonest politicians as their representatives. In this respect, representative democracy has procedural flaws. Due to these flaws, corrupt, cunning politicians have been able to cheat honest voters and tolerated, even colluded with, dishonest citizens like the mafia and encouraged them to prosper. The prime goal of most politicians has been to get elected or reelected to public offices using whatever ways and means they could. They abused the people's civic duty to vote in violation of the true spirit of representative democracy. After all, they failed to be role models for citizens to trust and follow.

The United States' election of Donald Trump as president in 2016 can be considered in the context of civicracy. *Fortune* reported on November 7, 2016, "Donald Trump is the most disliked and least trusted nominee ever measured."[70] An "innocent" voter called Andrea living in Florida said, "I cried when I left the polling location because I don't like Trump at all. I was deeply saddened to vote for him. His personality, his mannerisms and his inexperience repulse me. I wish there had been another conservative choice without simply throwing away my vote. I know if I travel outside of the U.S., I will be deeply disliked because of him."[71] Trump's words, actions, frequent and voluble tweets, and so on have steadily given rise to public controversy since his election as US president. A lot of criticisms have arisen not only in the United States but also in the rest of the world that Trump is not presidential[72] or was a wrong choice[73] made by none other than US citizens. The image of Uncle Sam has suffered as "publics across the world question Trump's leadership," according to a Pew Research Center survey.[74] Not a single day has passed without controversy involving Donald Trump since his election as US president.

Regardless of whatever has happened in Trump's presidency and right or wrong choices of presidents or other political delegates by citizens, civicracy is going from strength to strength. Civicracy does not progress in a linear fashion. It cannot but sustain trials and errors, like all other things under progress on this planet. Civicracy has yet to become fully grown. Also, civicracy, even when it matures, cannot be perfect since it is run by human beings, who are innately prone to making mistakes. This nature of civicracy leads us to look at the election of Donald Trump as US president from a different angle. In that election, the key message of US citizens to US politics was clear: US political establishment needs change, and US citizens can change it. During the election, polls showed that Americans wanted neither Hillary Clinton nor Donald Trump as their president.[75] This means that Americans voted for "change," not for either of the two candidates.

Civicracy does not give an unconditional yes to outsiders and an unconditional no to establishment politicians. Civicracy has essentially the capacity to tell right from wrong. Honest and faithful establishment politicians, if any, will be able to survive civicracy, but wrong outsiders will have no chance to live to tell the tale as civicracy advances. Also, citizens in civicracy do not necessarily look for flawless saints and angels as their representatives. They are, if anything, realistic rather than idealistic. Former US president Barack Obama commands great respect and admiration at home and abroad. Most Americans agree that Obama accomplished a lot and led a scandal-free presidency over his eight-year tenure in the White House and would go down as one of the best US presidents,[76] but few would consider him a "flawless saint."

On the face of it, the 2016 South Korean political scandal may be considered just another example of a corruption scandal that often involves a country's top leader. To briefly describe the scandal, President Park Geun-hye had been accused of colluding with her close private friend and confidante Choi Soon-sil, who had no official government position and had not even gone through security clearance, to take bribes and extort donations from big businesses. The National Assembly of South Korea impeached Park on December 9, 2016, and on March 10, 2017, the Constitutional Court of Korea ruled to uphold the impeachment to remove Park from office. When media coverage of the scandal began, a series of nationwide protests by millions of South Koreans calling for Park's immediate resignation took place. However, the South Korean scandal showed at least three seemingly small but significant features that have special implications for growing civicracy.

First, the protesters avoided business days and rallied on weekends only. Second, the civil disobedience was peaceful, orderly, and festive; it was dubbed "an honorable civil revolution" from the international society.[77] Third, a lot of volunteers did their best to make sure the demonstrations were nonviolent and collected rubbish littered in the streets around the Gwanghwamun square and the Blue House (equivalent to the White House) in Seoul after the protests. Protest leaders used on social media with the hashtag #democleanup to coordinate postdemo street cleaning. The "honorable civil revolution" was considered no small sign that civicracy is maturing in South Korea.

The South Korean scandal had another important implication for civicracy. Choi Soon-sil is the daughter of Park Geun-hye's late "mentor" Choi Tae-min, who was an associate of Park Geun-hye's father, Park Chung-hee, the soldier turned dictatorial president of South Korea, assassinated in 1979. Choi Tae-min was a fortune teller and founder of "a shamanistic religious cult that melds Christianity and Buddhism and other practices." He was likened in a leaked US State Department cable to a "Korean (Grigoriy) Rasputin,"[78] who infiltrated the court of the last Russian czar, Nicholas II, as a self-proclaimed holy man, and wielded unusual power over the czar until his assassination by irked royals.[79] Park Geun-hye who has been well-known for her mulishness may have been under Choi Tae-min's shamanic influence, as a *Washington Post* article implies.[80] According to the *Washington Post* report on the mystic aspect of Park's scandal,

> Across Asia, people in power, both in business and politics, lean on the advice of an array of mystics. In South Korea, myriad prominent executives employ fortune tellers to help determine their professional and personal affairs. (I. Tharoor, "South Korea's president is hardly the only leader to turn to mystics and shamans," *Washington Post* [November 2016], available at: https://www. washingtonpost.com/, accessed November 2, 2016)

Choi Soon-sil "seems to have advised Park on everything from her wardrobe to speeches about the dream of reunification with North Korea."[81] An important implication the South Korean scandal has for civicracy is that citizens can never fully understand the mental state of their prospective political leaders and are thus prone to make mistakes when they vote. As if supporting this notion, some renowned US psychiatrists and mental health experts said, "We believed Trump's mental state presented a danger to the public and felt we had a duty to warn them."[82] Whether the doctors' beliefs are right or wrong, the two "mental" cases teach us that a primary goal of civicracy does not lie in ousting wrong politicians from office but in trying its best to elect right ones in the first place.[83] Considering that no able psychologist, let alone general citizens, can understand exactly the psychic state of a politician, there seems to be a long road ahead for civicracy before it can be flawless or reach full maturity. Nonetheless, the future of civicracy looks bright.

Speaking additionally of US president Donald Trump in the context of civicracy, representatives of the House Al Green and Brad Sherman initiated in June 2017 formal efforts to impeach Trump. The scope of special counsel Robert Mueller's investigation into Russian interference in the 2016 US presidential election, which began May 17, 2017, reportedly included potential obstruction of justice by Trump and others.[84] Before the special counsel's office wrapped up its Russia investigation on March 22, 2019, Trump's lawyer Rudy Giuliani said on August 24, 2018, that Americans would "revolt" if Trump impeached "for political reasons."[85] What Giuliani intended to mean by "revolt" was unclear. It needs to be made clear, however, that civicracy, which pursues a set of values inherent in democracy as already indicated, does not favor any civil disobedience that disregard law and order as it aims to protect democracy after all even if, say, polls show majority of Americans support the impeachment of Donald Trump.[86] It supports a fair and just legal process that will bring wrong politicians to justice or clear innocent politicians of alleged wrongdoings. It seeks a peaceful, lawful transformation of real politics.

Representative democracy as a political system may be likened to a computer system. However excellent the computer system may be, if its operator—that is, the people's representative in this analogy—is not good at running the system, it will never work as intended. Civicracy is working relatively well in some countries, as shown in the democracy index that measures every year the state of democracy, which means the functionality or health of a country's democracy. In 2017, Norway ranked first among the top ten in the index followed by Iceland, Sweden, New Zealand, Denmark, Ireland, Canada, Australia, Finland, and Switzerland.[87] All these countries were also among the top twenty in the corruption perceptions index (CPI) in 2016 that Transparency International has published since 1995.[88] These countries are praised as examples for other countries to follow, and citizens across the world are being informed of how their political systems work.

Historically, democracies have increased worldwide over the last two hundred years.[89] In this progress, civicracy has been getting stronger. Looking ahead, the empowered public will be able to ask politicians to disclose, say, on websites every single dollar they raise from corporations, lobbyists, individuals, and so on and how they spend the money. They will be able to watch closely the link between, say, corporate contributions and corporate interests. They will also be able to demand that politicians make public all the details of their political activities, including the bills they have introduced or are going to introduce and their concrete results. Citizens and civic groups, often or always, in collaboration with a few good watchdogs like Benjamin Lawsky,[90] New York's aggressive banking regulator who was campaigning to clean up Wall Street, will forcefully support and use organizations like "Friends of the Internet" as opposed to "Enemies of the Internet." Nowadays, citizens are more convinced than ever that politicians' irregularities, ineptitude, and betrayal of public expectations are greatly due to their pursuit of personal, factional, and partisan interests instead of the public good.

Governments levy taxes on citizens. Citizens in all democracies of the world today seem inclined and eager to ask their governments to faithfully abide by the maxim, "He who pays the piper calls the tune." They know part of their tax money is used for the welfare, honors, privileges, and even pomposity of their political representatives. This may prompt them to consider a teacher-student relationship. Students pay tuition as they learn from their teachers. Imagine, however, a hypothetical situation in which teachers learn from their students. In that case, teachers should pay tuition to their students. If the private sector, often referred to as the citizen sector, has little to learn from the public sector, which includes elected officials, but the public sector has a lot to learn from the private sector, such as innovative spirit, the merit-based fulfillment of duties, entrepreneurship, and so on, the public sector should pay tuition to the private sector. However, what about our reality? Citizens are financing the well-being of politicians in traditional inertia.

Civicracy is redressing this unfairness. The Occupy movement, which began on September 17, 2011, in New York City's Wall Street in the Financial District, can be considered as an example reflecting this trend. The Occupy Wall Street (OWS) movement first used the "socioeconomic" slogan, "We are the 99%." The Occupy movement developed into a sociopolitical movement against not only social and economic inequality but also against the lack of a functioning democratic leadership around the world.[91] The *Washington Post* reported that the Occupy movement, which was described as a "democratic awakening" by US philosopher Cornel West in late 2011, was difficult to distill to a few demands.[92] For politicians, the Occupy movements must have been one of the most frightening warnings of civic challenges to their survival in politics. In practice, on October 12, 2011, Los Angeles City Council became one of the first governmental bodies in the United States to adopt a resolution stating its informal support of the movement. In October 2012, the Executive Director of Financial Stability at the Bank of England stated the protesters were right to criticize and had persuaded politicians and bankers "to behave in a more moral way."[93] In South Korea, something of "Occupy Yeouido" ("Yeouido" symbolizes South Korea's National Assembly as it is located in Yeouido, Seoul) and "Occupy the Blue House" actually occurred in the wake of the "Park Geun-hye-Choi Soon-sil Gate." Civic activism is awakening across the world, as citizens begin to believe that their actions can be a powerful influence for positive change. Globally, 76 percent of adults (78 percent in the United States) agree with this belief.[94]

The forthcoming movements of civil disobedience are expected to focus more strongly on salvaging representative democracy from the ropes. Citizens today can organize easily outright resistance against dishonest politicians in a reshaped form of the OWS. It is always possible that "Occupy Capitol Hill," "Occupy the White House," "Occupy Westminster," "Occupy Yeouido," and other Occupy movements happen.

Forthcoming public protests will of course follow democratic rules and principles, advancing civicracy.

As civicracy advances, the Internet and social media will also challenge the anomalies of multimedia corporate conglomerates that own a variety of mainstream media. They are supposed to function as key watchdogs to disclose and prevent misconduct by politicians. If they fulfill this role, they will be friends of social media. However, the reluctance of titanic media groups to support the cause of the Occupy movement has been one of the prime reasons that had discouraged the momentum of the movements. Complaints that the media wasn't paying attention to the substance of the protests and their larger purpose persisted.[95] The growing power of the Internet and social media has now opened a way for civil resistance to do what the for-profit media establishment is often doing for its own interests rather than the public good. Social media may overshadow the conventional corporate media soon as criticisms that the conventional media is failing to act as one of the four pillars of democracy because they remain inactive or even impede political and social renovations are increasing. Mainstream media, for its own survival, will have to better perform its original mission to serve public interest.

Nonetheless, as Soto notes, social media should not be considered as a panacea for all the existing political and other problems. He worries that "as powerful as the online world may be, a social media–like structure for democracy, where everybody shares and discusses their opinions at once, would simply lead to anarchy."[96] However, as civicracy grows mature, citizens are expected to use social media responsibly to find the best answers to the problems their society faces.

Civicracy functions as the most potent self-protective mechanism for democracy. Since the heart for genuine service to the public should be the principal basis for politicians to continue in politics, politicians will be compelled to take the initiative to search for the methods to form a framework for civil society–government cooperation in which citizens will be able to debate a variety of important issues with their representatives. In this framework, citizens should not regard themselves as "genuine" problem solvers. They should still respect governments and politicians, if they continue to prove themselves worthy of public trust, so that they can position themselves to articulate the issues faced by society, not their solutions.[97] Indeed, civicracy equals this structure.

4.   Civicracy is likely to mature sooner than expected

To recap, civicracy is neither an alternative to democracy nor a modified structure of this. On the contrary, civicracy only contributes to materializing authentic democracy. Democratically elected governments are obliged to honor citizens' reasonable opinions and calls as vital catalysts to renew themselves. Most democratically elected governments today are not qualified to remind their citizens of the well-known remark US president John F. Kennedy made during his inaugural address on January 20, 1961: "Ask not what your government can do for you, ask what you can do for your government." If they fail to thoroughly renovate themselves so that they change the prevalent public perception that politicians and public officials are serving mainly their personal benefits, disregarding public interest, they will soon face grave consequences.

The public of this century is not myopic and is able to see much farther. On June 5, 2016, Swiss voters overwhelmingly rejected in a referendum a proposal to introduce a guaranteed unconditional basic monthly income of US$2,555 for adults and US$668 for each child. Opponents of the proposed measure said that disengaging the link between work done and money earned would be bad for the future of their country, as it would increase the number of the unemployed.[98] Some may say that the Swiss can afford to refuse the offer as they live in one of the most affluent, happiest countries in the world, with per capita GDP (PPP) of US$59,150 and a low level of income inequality. Nonetheless, the result of the vote is considered a powerful indicator that the Swiss are now enlightened enough to anticipate what short-sighted measures will do to their future. Citizens of civicracy should look to the Swiss as a role model. Politics of this century demands politicians faithfully serve such an enlightened public.

Impressive signs are surfacing that show that even in some authoritarian countries with vibrant economies civicracy is growing. There was a coup attempt in Turkey[99] on July 15, 2016, but it lacked public backing. Turkish social media played a significant part in the failure of the coup attempt. All the four preceding coups succeeded in the twentieth century. The authoritarian rule of Turkish President Recep Tayyip Erdogan has violated human rights and has drawn international criticism for the last fourteen years. Nevertheless, Turkish citizens had apparently determined that the fifth military coup in their nation was anachronistic and should not be repeated in their country. The clear and unambiguous pro-democracy coalition played the most decisive role in the failure of the coup attempt.[100] Despite conflicting analyses about the reasons for the coup failure, the key message to the world from the hundreds of thousands of Turks who rallied against the coup and for democracy was obvious. It was that the Turkish should decide their own fate through legitimate process. On April 16, 2017, Turkish citizens voted in a constitutional referendum to replace Turkey's parliamentary system with a presidential one. However, with authoritarian Erdogan in power, the political future of Turkey remains uncertain. "The country has been a test of what happens when democracy is put together with political Islam."[101] No matter what happens, the Turkish political development underway has another important implication for civicracy. It is that civic commitment to democracy is continuing to grow in the developing world, too, even if the road ahead of civicracy is expected to be not so smooth in Turkey and elsewhere.

In the last analysis, it wouldn't be well advised to say that we are now being drawn further away from democracy, despite a lot of concerns about "the weakening of representative democracy." To be more precise, it would be better advised to say that civicracy is becoming the rule and will be mature enough for authentic democracy to stand firm as a rock, not weakening democracy per se but weakening and ousting wrong political representatives, within the next couple of decades or perhaps sooner than expected.

Chapter 2

The Triumph of Wisdom

1. Human stupidity is not infinite

Consider a hypothetical joke. The United States had become the world's second superpower trailing China. However, Washington could invent an almighty weapon that would enable the United States to scare all other countries and to exercise absolute hegemony over the world. Having known this, China's top leader came to the White House. The Chinese president asked the US president to give him the secret to develop the omnipotent weapon. The US chief executive did so without hesitation. The Chinese leader left, rejoicing in his good fortune. He knew the secret for the development of the invincible weapon he obtained could empower China to continue to enjoy its supremacy over the world. A few days later, however, the Chinese president came back to Washington and returned the secret to the US president. "I've been thinking," the Chinese leader said, "I know how valuable the secret is, but I want to give it back to you in the hope that you can give me something even more precious. Give me what you have within you that enabled you to give me this most important secret. Give me what you have within you that enabled you to give me this top secret with no reluctance."

Hearing this, the US president responded, "I want to, but unfortunately I can't, because what you want to get from me this time is neither a classified document nor a tangible object, but something invisible. That is the United States' hope for world peace and prosperity. I thought if Beijing determined that China could obtain any military secret from the United States, China would feel there is no need for an arms race with Washington. I believed that China would be convinced that Washington had no intention whatsoever to enter a war with Beijing, which would be of no avail to either of us. Furthermore, I thought you would be able to use China's military budget to feed your people better and to increase your charitable activities for poor countries instead. As a result, world peace and prosperity could be promoted to the interest not only of our two nations but also of the whole world."[1]

Different analysts have suggested different views on the process of world development. However, they have agreed at least since the days of Aristotle's *Rhetoric*[2] that all recorded stories of societal progress reflect how much wisdom, which is usually defined as the ability to think and act using knowledge, experience, understanding, common sense, and insight, human beings have been able to demonstrate. Naturally, they link their analyses and interpretations of past events with human wisdom or stupidity. In fact, all recorded major events, including the two world wars, have been the products of good or bad judgments that the key players involved have made.[3]

Thinking of this, let's look at Sino-American relations. Relations between the United States and China have extraordinary implications for the future of global security and peace. Would China ever declare a war against the United States or vice versa? In other worlds, would it ever be possible that either China or the United States could be silly enough to use up all their opulence someday in the future suddenly? Common sense tells us the answer is no. The two countries would rather follow the saying that goes, "When prosperity comes, do not use up all of it at once."

However, the answers from pundits are mixed. John Mearsheimer, a professor of political science at the University of Chicago and a *New York Times* best-selling author, says that there is a greater possibility of the United States and China going to war in the future than there was of a Soviet Union–NATO general war during the era of the Cold

War.[4] Quite a few analysts characterize Sino-American relations as a dualism: adversarial and cooperative. If the United States and China remain fundamentally opposed to each other, their present-day cooperation in various areas should be considered a marriage of convenience that could break up anytime. Their adversarial relationship could lead to another catastrophic world war.

Looking back, few experts could foresee World War I or World War II approaching. Michael Horowitz, a professor of political science at the University of Pennsylvania, says that prominent authorities tried in 1900 to predict what the world would look like twenty years into the future, but they missed the catastrophic event, World War I.[5] Horowitz continues that world-class authorities in 1930 also missed the rise of Adolf Hitler and World War II. The key warning of this expert in international affairs is that the world is so complicated and volatile that few can predict how the years will unfold going forward.

World history has recorded right and wrong predictions. A prediction that another world war is likely to break out could be as wrong as its opposite. Still, our ability to predict the future correctly has come a long way since the days of the two world wars.[6] Didier Sornette, a world-famous analyst of forthcoming occurrences and a professor in the Swiss Finance Institute, observes that even the most extreme future events are knowable and predictable.[7] Those who repudiate a Sino-American war scenario suggest that such a gloomy scenario must have been seduced into a wrong belief. Their message to the world can be summarized like this: don't worry; another world war will never happen for sure.[8]

While a large-scale Sino-American war cannot completely be ruled out,[9] we have every reason to believe such a conflict to be realistically impossible.[10] Hitler might have been very intelligent but displayed very little wisdom. Barry Schwartz, professor of psychology at Swarthmore College, remarks,

> The good news is you don't need to be brilliant to be wise. The bad news is that without wisdom, brilliance isn't enough. It's as likely to get you and other people

> into trouble as anything else. (B. Schwartz, "Our loss
> of wisdom," TED, available at: http://www.ted.com/,
> accessed February 27, 2009)

Mearsheimer and other analysts who argue that "a war between the U.S. and China is more likely than recognized now"[11] seem to think much of the past tragedies caused by brilliant but unwise leaders like Hitler and past failures to predict events like the two world wars. However, they seem to be ignorant of the fact that human beings have learned well that their follies—like Hitler's stupidity, for example—have been responsible for man-made catastrophes (e.g., the two world wars) and have therefore subsequently tried to and continue trying to prevent a repeat of such calamities. They also seem to need to update their views of the modern-day world structure, which has become so complex and interconnected that a suicidal global conflict has become quite an impossibility. Among others, they should not overlook the fact that human wisdom can adapt to changing realties based on increasing knowledge and experience.

After World War II, which resulted in an estimated fifty to eighty-five million fatalities, a ruined Germany could rise again as a world power. The country learned firsthand the dreadfulness of a man-made calamity that was simply the outworking of the stupidity and reck-lessness of one of its own citizens, Hitler. Germans have learned that barring unpredictable natural and accidental disasters, all large-scale mishaps and tragedies have been outright manmade—that is to say, have resulted from human stupidity. As the German experience shows, wisdom is largely made, not born as is often perceived. Germany was not the only country that has grown in wisdom because of past mistakes. The Cold War did not develop into an actual war owing to increased human wisdom that resulted in self-control on the part of the then world leaders to avoid a repeat of the two world wars.[12] Furthermore, for the major world leaders of post–World War II period, past errors were an important lesson with which they were able to advance world peace.[13] China's sovereign leader Deng Xiaoping and the last leader of the Soviet Union Mikhail Gorbachev can be cited as notable examples.

Deng is considered "the architect" of a new brand of socialist thinking, combining, albeit in a contradictory expedient, the Communist Party's socialist ideology with the pragmatic adoption of market economy, as indicated in chapter 1. His famous maxim that says, "It doesn't matter whether a cat is black or white, if it catches mice it is a good cat," has been able to rescue China from the ruins of communism and elevate the country to one of the most powerful countries in the world.

US president Ronald Reagan's policy toward the Soviet Empire that aimed at facilitating a more secure and peaceful world might have played a significant part in the collapse of the Soviet Union.[14] However, the "evil" empire "certainly collapsed of its own weight."[15] In other words, Gorbachev's wise decision to stop past errors, such as the Brezhnev Doctrine, was manifested in his throwing in the towel under a collapsing economic system in favor of a bid for a de-escalation of the arms race[16] and resulted in the dissolution of the Soviet Union. Gorbachev then adopted the policies of glasnost (openness) and perestroika (reforming the economic and political system). As a result, a new chapter in the world order came to take shape. In terms of nominal GDP, China and Russia are the second and the twelfth largest economies in the world, respectively, according to 2017 IMF estimates.[17]

Ancient Roman politician and lawyer Marcus Cicero said, "Any man can make mistakes, but only an idiot persists in his error." US policy circles generally seem to believe that global leaders today like to take such advice more seriously than ever. They believe a Sino-American war is unlikely as it would be against their counsels and unwise.[18] Steven Pinker, Pulitzer prize–winning professor of psychology at Harvard University, suggests that we are currently heading toward a more peaceful world. "Today we may be living in the most peaceful era in our species' existence," he says. Pinker elaborates that we are enjoying the longest period of some seventy years of the most peaceful world after World War II.[19] This means that humankind generally has become more well versed in the value of wisdom over time and capable of avoiding the catastrophic damage of foolish events like world wars. According to Nicholas Kristof, a *New York Times* columnist, the year "2017 was probably the very best year in the long history of humanity."[20]

We have every reason to appreciate Albert Einstein's warning that human stupidity is infinite. However, if we don't believe humans can reduce their stupidity we could not but expect a gloomy future for humanity. Fortunately, as thinkers indicate, we are witnessing that human wisdom is rising, and human folly is decreasing in this century.

2. "Structural" wisdom

Many still argue that there is a long road ahead of us before we could ever see an overpowering victory of wisdom over silliness. It is true that we are still witnessing a lot of foolhardy acts committed by humans. Unconventional warfare in Yemen and Syria and dictators and terrorists in trouble spots have been prime sources of serious concern among peace-loving people. Reportedly, the regime of Syrian leader Bashar al-Assad used chemical weapons against its own people. Various Islamist militant groups, notably as the Islamic State of Iraq and Syria (ISIS), are carrying out indiscriminate terror attacks in Europe, the Middle East, Africa, and other parts of the world. North Korea's nuclear brinkmanship and US president Donald Trump's possible use of force against North Korea has raised the specter of nuclear war,[21] endangering world peace and security. Besides, a variety of outrageous underground activities against humanity at national and international levels are going on. This dark side of the world may prompt many of us to question the view that the general world peace we have enjoyed for the last seven decades is the outcome of increasing human wisdom.

Refuting the notion that human wisdom has been growing, antinuclear activists have been blaming nuclear scientists, especially the first nuclear pioneers engaged in the Manhattan Project, for the unending nuclear threats to world peace.[22] However, the general global peace we are witnessing today has grown with "the paradox of progress."[23] The scientists who led the Manhattan Project, for instance, started the research and development of nuclear weapons not to destroy world peace but to demolish the breakers of world peace—namely, the evil leaders of Nazism, fascism, and Japanese militarism and their ideas themselves. The nuclear bombing in 1945 against two Japanese cities, Hiroshima, and Nagasaki, killed more than 100,000 people and injured some 130,000. The human cost was horrible. Nevertheless, all the nuclear scientists who participated in the Manhattan Project, with no exception, have deeply been committed to world peace. Glenn T. Seaborg who joined the project had made great contributions to the Limited Test Ban Treaty, the Nuclear Non-Proliferation Treaty, and the Comprehensive Test Ban Treaty. Seaborg, former chancellor of the University of California at Berkeley, advised ten US presidents from Harry S. Truman to Bill Clinton on how to reduce and eventually eliminate all nuclear weapons on earth. He also repeatedly emphasized peaceful applications of nuclear energy. The Nobel laureate who was once listed in the Guinness Book of World Records as the person with the longest entry in *Who's Who in America* wrote in 1970 in his book titled *Peaceful Uses of Nuclear Energy,*

> It is a compilation of remarks, and excerpts of remarks, that I [Seaborg] have made in recent years in an effort to bring to the public the story of the remarkable benefits the peaceful atom has to offer man. (G. T. Seaborg, *Peaceful Uses of Nuclear Energy: A Collection of Speeches* [Oak Ridge, TN: U.S. Atomic Energy Commission, Technical Information Division, 1970], 1)

Human wisdom has yet to grow enough to accomplish a truly secure and peaceful world. However, the wisdom that the world has so far accumulated from increasing knowledge and experience has motivated major global leaders to bear and demonstrate a greater responsibility toward world peace. The closely integrated, complex global system of this era, especially, is bringing home to global leaders the repeated calls for lasting world peace from renowned pundits and statesmen, such as the twenty-eighth president of the United States, Woodrow Wilson,[24] and Nobel Peace Prize–winning US statesman Frank B. Kellogg, who observed,

> Certain it is that a great responsibility rests upon the statesmen of all nations, not only to fulfill the promises for reduction in armaments, but to maintain the confidence of the people of the world in the hope of an enduring peace. (F. B. Kellogg, A Banquet Speech at the Nobel banquet delivered at Grand Hotel, Oslo, Norway, on December 10, 1929)

The pundits' advice as well as the historical lessons that have taught humans to learn from the errors of the past is not all that stops another world war from transpiring. Think of a wide variety of global issues the world must handle collectively, such as climate change; terrorism; the dearth of food, water, and energy; cybersecurity; the negative effects of advances in science and technology; and so on. The world at large is "structurally" forced to keep making collaborative efforts to find solutions to these problems. The world's most powerful actors, including the United States, the advanced nations of Europe, China, Japan, and Russia are compelled to lead these efforts simply because such problems are their own problems. Another world war directly clashes with the vital interests of the world's great powers. This era is different from that of Hitler who started a conventional war, as he was confident of winning it. All of us know too well that a large-scale war today will produce no winners but losers. Even the rabble-rousers of rogue states in the world's most fiery trouble spots,[25] such as the brutal tyrant Bashar al-Assad of Syria and North Korean leader Kim Jong-un, must have learned enough by now that it would certainly kill none other than themselves in case they provoke a war of global consequences. US president Donald Trump and Kim Jong-un had a historic summit on June 12, 2018, in Singapore. Trump and Kim signed a document committing to "work towards the complete denuclearization" of the Korean peninsula. It is too early to tell whether "the complete denuclearization" will happen, but the joint declaration at least indicates that Kim Jong-un may have realized by now that his dynasty's six-decade-long nuclear development program has only ruined the country and put his regime's survival at risk.

The more complex, volatile, and challenging global problems become, the more prudence global actors need to demonstrate to ensure their own survival. On September 28, 2015, then US president Barack Obama emphasized at the United Nations General Assembly the importance of working together with Russia and other countries to prevent a third world war and to establish world peace and said that the United States would be willing to work with any country to make our global community secure and peaceful.[26] It is often the case that political leaders make ceremonial remarks underscoring world peace as merely speakers, not as doers. It is unclear at present if Chinese president Xi Jinping has really learned the value of peace. It is thus uncertain whether he made the following remarks truthfully. However, given the global reality that requires the stability of the world more than ever, we have little reason to underestimate his remarks as lacking authenticity. President Xi underlined the basic principle about how world affairs should play out in the years ahead. Xi Jinping called on September 22, 2015, for better relations with the United States, warning that conflict between the two nations could have only a disastrous outcome, in a keynote speech on the first day of his state visit to the United States. "Should they enter into conflict and confrontation, it would lead to disaster for both countries and the world at large,"[27] he asserted.

In brief, the ever-changing, complicated, interconnected world structure is playing a focal part in making the world more secure and peaceful. As a result, we are living in a world of "structural" wisdom, by which it is meant that the closely interlocked world structure has made it impossible for any country to threaten global peace. Few would dispute that advancing globalization has made the world literally a "global village." Herbert Marshall McLuhan, a Canadian philosopher and communication theorist envisioned this as early as 1962. As it were, all of us as global villagers will be on the same boat forever.[28]

Specifically, what might happen if a war breaks out between China and the United States? The Chinese American community is the largest overseas Chinese community outside of Asia. According to the 2010 census, the Chinese American population numbered approximately

3.8 million. Also, some 330,000 Chinese students studying in US colleges outnumbered their peers from the top four countries combined that followed China as of 2016.[29] Since 2009, Chinese direct investment in the United States and Europe have increased sharply, and developed economy–bound flows are poised to grow heavily through 2020, according to Rhodium Group estimates.[30] Also, an assessment of outward foreign direct investment calculated by the Rhodium Group shows that Chinese firms are now operating in at least forty of the fifty states of the United States and have investments across a wide range of US industries.[31] Many other data show Sino-American economic cooperation and other exchanges have been growing rapidly. China regained its crown over Japan as the United States' biggest overseas creditor in June 2017, with its holdings of US debt standing at US$1.15 trillion, compared with Japan's US$1.09 trillion in the same month, according to a *CNN* report.[32]

The Trump administration declared the "America First" trade policy for Americans to compete fairly with the Chinese and win on a level playing field, labeling Beijing a currency manipulator. Quite a few analysts noted that there's a significant chance the Trump administration could set off a trade conflict with China.[33] In fact, the war officially began on July 5, 2018. However, considering the fundamental nature of US-China economic cooperation, it is unlikely that the two great powers will continue an intensive trade war that would be of no avail to not only the two largest economies in the world but also to the rest of the global economy. In 2017, US exports to China totaled over US$130 billion, making it the third-largest export market for US goods behind Canada and Mexico.[34] Quite a few economists note that a US hardline trade policy toward China may be to China's benefit and the United States' loss.[35] In July 2018, when the trade conflict formally started, 56 percent of American voters thought the situation was bad for U.S. jobs.[36] Worldwide, close economic cooperation between the world's two largest economies is crucial to the stability and prosperity of the global economy.

However, the view that the US-China trade conflict is undesirable is one thing and the warning that China needs a thorough economic reform is quite another. The Chinese economy has begun to unveil the problems inherent in the socialist market economy unique to China. Ian Armstrong, a senior analyst and editor at *Global Risk Insights*, notes that China's recent economic struggles would mean a serious reexamination of existing policies by Beijing. He says,

> The Chinese economy has not had a smooth summer. Between the general slowing of economic growth, the recent plummet of the stock market, and the subsequent devaluation of the renminbi, the "Chinese dream" is now appearing more elusive than initially anticipated. There is now more reason than ever to re-evaluate the existing policies out of Beijing (and China's political system that produces such policies), including those that only indirectly influence the economy. (I. Armstrong, "Forecasting China's anti-corruption campaign," *Global Risk Insights* [2015], available at: http://globalriskinsights.com/, accessed August 30, 2015)

Other analysts warn the upcoming several years will be a critical period for China. A report released in March 2016 by the Wharton School of the University of Pennsylvania says,

> China's economy continues its decline. That fall underscores the Chinese government's announcement last week lowering its economic growth target for 2016 to between 6.5% and 7%, compared with 6.9% last year. ("Trouble ahead: What's next for the Chinese economy?" The Wharton School of the University of Pennsylvania [2016], available at: http://knowledge.wharton.upenn. edu/, accessed March 9, 2016)

The report added that ratings agency Moody's also said that it had lowered its outlook for Chinese government bonds from "stable" to "negative."[37] Earlier, in the Davos forum held in January 2016, the biggest global economic worry centered on China, as its economy was slowing down, and its debt levels were swelling, which could cause serious market turmoil worldwide.[38]

The WEF's report on Global Risks 2017 repeated the same concern about the decline of the Chinese economy as it noted in the preceding year: "China is in a gradual slowdown as its economy transitions from an investment-led to a consumption-led growth model."[39] The *Herald Sun*, an Australia-based morning tabloid newspaper, also reported in October 2016 that "Ratings agency Standard & Poor's has delivered a stern warning on China's growing debt pile, declaring the rate of growth in the nation's corporate debt unsustainable."[40] Recent studies from China's domestic institutions confirm the same. Surveys conducted by Peking University and others show gloomy prospects for the Chinese economy. They also note severe socioeconomic gaps, including worsening inequalities in income, access to education and health, and so on.[41] More recently a *Forbes* story says, "China is set to lose its 'emerging market' status as growth continues to decline."[42] Davos 2019 also foretold China's economy will keep decelerating.

The ominous prospects for China's economy are no good news for the United States and the rest of the world. *Business Insider* reported in June 2015 that "China's economic slowdown isn't just bad for China. It's bad for everyone who trades with China."[43] This article confirms once more that China and other global actors, including the United States, are riding in the same boat, as they are interconnected more closely than ever. Seen from the perspective of global progress, it would be simply silly if any country desired to be the world's no. 1 on the back of its competitors' economic setbacks, whether they are due to domestic policy failures or external impacts. Hundreds of the world's largest US companies, including Berkshire Hathaway, JPMorgan Chase, Wells Fargo, Bank of America, Apple, AT&T, Citigroup, ExxonMobil, and General Electric, are operating in China. Of the top twenty world's biggest public companies in China, twelve are US companies as of May 2017.[44] More than 110,000 Americans are living in China today. The relationship between the two countries is complex and dynamic.

Global issues, existing or potential, such as financial crises, international terrorism, climate change, positive and negative impacts on humans of advancing technologies, protection of intellectual property rights, global economic inequality, and arms reduction, inevitably require closer collaboration between all countries for sustainable development of the world. Recently, some analysts have begun to talk about a revival of nationalism in the wake of Brexit, Trump's "America First" policy and ban of immigration from so-called shithole countries, and so on, but globalism and nationalism always march in sync to each other rather than against each other.

This prospect realistically rules out a major economic conflict between the two largest economies, let alone a major military clash. Let's assume a Sino-American conflict develops in the South China Sea. Would they be level headed enough to use only conventional weapons on a limited scale? The United States and China have been known to own 4,804 and 250 nuclear warheads, respectively. Dropping just one Castle Bravo device–level nuclear bomb[45] on either of the two nations would be horrible enough—cities leveled, populations vaporized, the global economy paralyzed, and a great part of the world uninhabitable. Hypothetically, what would happen if the two nuclear countries used all the nuclear warheads they have today against each other? Such a war would usher in the apocalypse. In 2012, graphic designer Maximilian Bode noted,

> There are an estimated total of 20,500 nuclear warheads in the world today. If the average power of these devices is 33,500 kilotons, they are enough to destroy the total earth landmass. (S. Biddle, "How many nukes would it take to blow up the entire planet?" Gizmodo [2012], available at: https://gizmodo.com, accessed April 5, 2012)

Wisely, humankind has tried to reduce the danger to its own survival. "The number of nuclear weapons in the world has declined significantly since the Cold War."[46] From a high of 68,000 nuclear weapons in 1985, there were some 14,900 nuclear weapons in 2017, according to the Federation of American Scientists.[47]

3. Rising wisdom will enable humanity to continue enjoying peace and prosperity

Let's look at more data that supports the prospect that human wisdom will prevail over stupidity. Throughout world history, humans have generally recognized the value of wisdom to enhance their standards of living.[48] Humankind has seen constant economic progress despite intermittent difficulties. Up until April 2009, the IMF had said that a global annual real GDP growth rate of 3 percent or less was "equivalent to a global recession."[49] According to this measure, there were six global recessions between the 1970s and the early twenty-first century: 1974–75, 1980–83, 1990–93, 1998, 2001–2, and 2008–9. The most noteworthy in these recessions is the financial crisis of 2007–8, also known as the Global Financial Crisis, by far the worst of the six postwar recessions, both in terms of the number of countries affected and the decline in real world GDP per capita.

While recognizing such recurring global economic problems, we need to look at a bigger picture—that is, how the global economy has grown since the beginning of recorded history, which begins with the accounts of the ancient world around the fourth millennium BC and coincides with the invention of writing. According to the *World Factbook*, the US Central Intelligence Agency (CIA) released in October 2015, the gross world product (GWP), the combined gross national product (GNP) of all countries in the world, was estimated to stand at US$0.01 billion in 1,000,000 BC rising to US$0.09 billion in 300,000 BC. J. Bradford DeLong, professor of economics at the University of California at Berkeley, estimated the total GWP in 1990 US dollars for main years between 1,000,000 BC and AD 2000. Around the fourth millennium BC, it reached US$0.77 billion. In AD 1, it was US$18.5 billion, and it took more than one millennium to double the amount, and the global economy was growing 0.11 percent a year around that time.[50]

[51] It was from 1955 that the global economy began to grow at 4–6 percent a year. Since then, the global economy has registered robust growth, and in 2000, the GWP rose to US$41,016.69 billion. This means that the global economy had grown more than twenty-two hundred

times by the year 2000 since AD 1. Also, the GWP has seen an over seventyfold increase up to 2014 since 1900. Equally stunning is the fact that the GWP has almost doubled in a time span of only fourteen years (2000–2014) in this century. As of 2014, it stood at US$77,868 billion.[52] This striking economic performance of the modern times has been able to make our world a much richer place to live overall. Because of the remarkable economic growth between 1990 and 2015, the percentage of the world's population living in extreme poverty fell from 37.1 percent in 1990 to 10.7 percent in 2017.[53] China has become one of the best performers in poverty reduction and wealth increase of its population. The average Chinese person is ten times richer today and lives for twenty-five years longer than he or she was fifty years ago.[54]

Not only in politics and economics but also in other areas, human wisdom is growing. It is weakening oppressive institutions, such as sexism, racism, ableism, ageism, and so on. As for sexism, for example, the number of experts, including psychologists, who argue that we must be naïve or stupid to talk about sex differences in intelligence or indeed sex differences in anything has been steadily increasing.[55] It would be silly if anyone believed males have a monopoly on wisdom. Increasing empowerment of women represents one evidence that shows that the wisdom of humankind is expanding. The empowerment of women is expected to continue to usher in deep social changes in the next few decades. Most impressively perhaps, the societal status of women is changing in the Arab world, where females have throughout history experienced severe discrimination and have been subject to restrictions of their freedoms and rights.

In October 1983 *U.S. News & World Report* already reported on how the role of women was changing in the Arab world. It said that greater opportunities for education at the university level were being made available to women in many countries in the region. The report continued,

> In Egypt, women serve in Parliament and the cabinet. Recently a woman was named director of the national television stations—a very powerful position in the

Mediterranean country. In Jordan, there has been tremendous economic development, which has had a great impact on the status of women. In just a decade, women have won the right to vote and run for election. ("The role of women is changing in the Arab world," *U.S. News & World Report* [1983], available at: https://www.usnews.com/, accessed October 10, 1983)

Even in Syria, a country under dictatorship, the minister of culture is a woman.[56] Queen Noor al-Hussein of Jordan announced that Jordan now had a woman minister of social development and four women on the National Consultative Council, the equivalent of Congress.[57]

The historical development since the mid-twentieth century of women's right to vote in the Arab world has been remarkable. Beginning with the women's right to vote on a universal and equal basis in Lebanon in 1952, other countries in the region, including Egypt, Tunisia, Mauritania, Algeria, Morocco, Libya, Sudan, Yemen, Bahrain, Jordan, Iraq, Kuwait, Syria, and Oman, have followed suit. On December 13, 2015, the conservative Islamic kingdom Saudi Arabia also elected the first woman named Salima bint Hazab al-Otaibi to public office as she won a seat on the municipal council in Mecca. From 2011, Saudi Arabia has taken steps for women to exercise the right to vote and to have a bigger public role by making it possible for them to run as candidates for public offices, sending more women to university, and encouraging female employment. In late September 2017, Saudi Arabia announced that it would now also allow women to drive. The Saudi government's decision is expected to boost Saudi Arabia's economy.[58] The positive signals emerging from the Arab world strongly indicate that the traditional and religious obstacles that have so far shackled women's rights and liberties are decreasing globally.

Although it is conceded that humankind will certainly confront new tests that are even now emerging and might prove to be hard to deal with in the upcoming decades of growing uncertainty, many analysts believe that human wisdom will keep growing enough to rise above these unexpected challenges. Anticipating this, leadership programs, for example, to train young people to meet new challenges with wisdom are increasing in the United States and in other parts of the world. Herschel V. Jenkins High School in Savannah, Georgia, introduced in mid-2015, a leadership skills program in which students could learn how to come together; communicate effectively and constructively; build up inspiration and vision; strengthen spiritual, mental, and emotional capacities; and create a sustainable and prospering society.[59] Similar programs to train young people as future leaders of wisdom to play key roles in preparing for forthcoming problems are increasing rapidly in many parts of the world.

The totalitarian Soviet Empire collapsed due to its own contradictions. Likewise, radical Islamic terrorists will fall because of their own contradictions. They are killing their fellow Muslims. Internal power struggle between Islamic extremist terror groups has been intensifying. Terrorism-sponsoring countries, and leaders of rogue states like Kim Jong-un of North Korea and Bashar Hafez al-Assad of Syria will also fall due to their own contradictions built in their unhumanitarian political systems vulnerable to internal explosions like the Arab Spring and mounting international pressure that aims at bringing such tyrants to justice. In this context, the aftermath of the US war in Iraq, which started in 2003 and ended in 2011, draws extra attention. The war succeeded at least in overthrowing the dictatorship of Saddam Hussein, although it has been under fire from an array of sources both inside and outside the United States. Most encouraging perhaps is that for the fifteen years since the war, democracy in Iraq has been, if anything, evolving as a moderate success, if not as a utopia, with coalitions across ethnic and religious lines.[60]

A lot more aspects of growing human wisdom across the world can be suggested, besides world peace, the empowerment of women, and expanding freedom as illustrated above. For example, the power of compassionate wisdom is growing to promote such values as empathy, kindness, social responsibility, harmonious and caring human relationships, and a greater sense of well-being and purpose.[61] With humans getting overwhelmed by all the suffering in the world today, 74 percent of adults globally agree that they wish they did more to help people in plight, and the number of such people is increasing.[62] Outside the religious realm, compassionate wisdom is going from strength to strength as a global movement for spiritual enhancement.

Even if the years ahead are expected to see a rapid rise in new problems, it is undisputed that human history written so far has been characterized by the ultimate triumph of wisdom over folly. In the last analysis, our future will show how human wisdom continues to grow, promoting world peace and prosperity.

CHAPTER 3

Informal Education

1. Classic and modern-day legends of informal education

No human being begins to grow without informal education. All "infants start learning informally from (or before?) birth, mainly through interaction with the mother or other caregivers."[1] US educational reformer John Dewey contended in the late nineteenth and early twentieth century that informal education was the basis for all formal education.[2]

The extraordinary success of Steve Jobs in the digital world may well lead us to wonder if formal education really goes well with human potential. Jobs gave an important advice to his audience during his commencement speech in 2005 at Stanford University. Jobs said his decision to drop out of college after six months was one of the best decisions he had ever made in his life. He added that the minute he dropped out he could stop taking the required classes that didn't interest him and begin dropping in on the ones that looked far more interesting, such as a course in calligraphy.[3]

The pioneer of the personal computer revolution continued that Reed College, which he attended at that time, offered perhaps the best calligraphy instruction in the country. The course was very interesting to him but did not give him any hope of any practical application in his life, but ten years later, when he was designing the first Macintosh computer, it all came back to him, he said. He noted that since Windows just copied the Mac it was likely that no personal computer would have had the wonderful typography that they do today.[4] If Jobs had been able to take same quality courses in calligraphy and others through informal education, he must have preferred them to dropping in on the courses at Reed.

The visionary brought our attention to his bitter experience of getting fired from Apple, the company he himself had founded. He said to the effect that his "public failure" in Apple was also one of the best blessings of experience-based informal education that could have ever happened to him. He remarked that after getting kicked out of Apple, he was free from the heaviness of being successful and could enter one of the most creative periods of his life. During the difficult period after the dramatic flop at Apple, he must have attended an informal school that might well be dubbed "University of Suffering and Challenge (USC)." He went on to say, "Remembering that you are going to die is the best way I know to avoid the trap of thinking you have something to lose."[5] He emphasized, "Death is very likely the single best invention of life."[6] Few would have trouble figuring out that this belief Jobs had acquired must have come from the informal education he had received through USC. When we regard USC as an institution of informal education for training the spirit of challenge, perseverance, and other mental assets, the scope of informal education is immensely expanded to include the disciplining and steeling of one's mind and nerve. Considering that the success of most great people is mostly dependent on the state of their mind and spirit with few exceptions, the value of USC can never be underestimated. Jobs must have acquired the grit to overcome sufferings and hardships, and even the fear of death.

Formal schools have been criticized for their failure to develop our potential. The type of mental strength that Jobs acquired can hardly be expected from formal schooling. In sum, the "Father of the Digital Revolution" was largely an upshot of informal education. His childhood supports the criticism of formal schools. Jobs had difficulty working in a traditional classroom and tended to resist authority figures. He frequently misbehaved and was suspended a few times. His childhood and youth were damaged with frustrations over formal schooling. During his formal schooling years, he was regarded as a troublemaker, even a social outcast. Nonetheless, Job's father did not give up on the future of his son. He taught his son how to build things in his home garage to pass along his love of mechanics. By the time he was ten, Jobs was deeply involved in electronics and befriended many the engineers outside his brick-and-mortar school. He acquired most of his knowledge in electronics and engineering, which he liked, through informal education, including self-teaching.[7]

History has lengthened the list of success stories of informal education. According to a *Forbes* survey, almost two-thirds of the world's billionaires made their fortunes from scratch, relying on fortitude and determination, neither on prestigious college diplomas nor on good genes.[8] Most of these rags-to-riches people could not afford college or even primary school education. Even so, they did not disregard the importance of education itself. Many of them found their way into an educated personality through education outside of brick-and-mortar schools, depending heavily on self-teaching. They studied at home late at night and at Sunday Schools or free schools in the community. They would borrow books from libraries, often miles away from their homes.

Well-known classic examples of great legends who worked their way through a high level of learning that played a decisive role in their achieving miraculous levels of success include Andrew Carnegie, John D. Rockefeller, Benjamin Franklin, Abraham Lincoln—you name it. Andrew Carnegie and John D. Rockefeller were rags-to-riches billionaires who had acquired remarkable expertise in their fields of specialty and demonstrated extraordinarily forward-thinking capacity. Andrew Carnegie had mostly taught himself. The Scottish American industrialist, known as the "Steel King of America," led the enormous expansion of the US steel industry in the late nineteenth century and built a leadership role as a philanthropist for the United States and the British Empire. Carnegie wrote several books and numerous articles based on his unusual inspiration, practical knowledge, skills, and experiences. Of what he had learned outside formal education and demonstrated in practice, his deep commitment to the responsibility of business for society would perhaps be the most impressive. In the book he wrote in 1900, *The Gospel of Wealth,* he emphasized that those with great wealth must be socially responsible and must use their assets to help others.

US business magnate John D. Rockefeller had little education beyond high school. His net worth in terms of a percentage of the US GDP in 1937 when he died would place him as the wealthiest known person in recent history, overwhelming that of Bill Gates, Warren Buffett, or Sam Walton. Like Carnegie, Rockefeller made himself one of the most respected philanthropists in history. Even though he himself had received no college education, he founded or helped found a lot of leading institutions for higher education, including the University of Chicago. There is no denying that his practical ideas about doing business and philanthropic activities have had enormous intellectual and humanitarian impacts on a huge number of people across the world.

Outside the financial world, Benjamin Franklin, who is particularly famous for his omnipotence as an author, statesman, inventor, and so on was self-taught. Franklin, one of the Founding Fathers of the United States, remains the most famous multitalented figures in US history. He once said that an investment in learning pays the best interest. Given the fact that he depended upon self-teaching for his wealth of knowledge, he must have thought that the type of education, formal or informal, didn't matter and that what mattered most was the practical knowledge one needed to achieve goals.

Abraham Lincoln is an icon of arduous self-teaching. Overcoming various hardships, he had made his career an amazing success. Lincoln was an avid reader throughout his life. The reason that Abraham Lincoln's Gettysburg Address has had such enormous impact on the hearts and minds of so many people across the world is that his message to the public was not just knowledge but also fortitude to triumph over all kinds of sufferings and adversities. Such character enables a person to be truly eloquent, audacious, and appealing to their audience. Lincoln's popular speech from deep down inside his heart became a universal endorsement of the principles of nationalism, republicanism, equal rights, liberty, and democracy. In other words, his courageous, lucid, to-the-point, and enticing speeches would have been impossible without his informal education at USC.

The *Huffington Post* compiled a slideshow "18 Successful Home-School Alums."[9] Of the eighteen, Pearl S. Buck and Serena Williams are particularly remarkable. Buck, the winner of the Nobel Prize in Literature and the Pulitzer Prize, started getting homeschooled at the age of six by her mother and private tutors. Her parents were religious missionaries in China, and Buck was taught by her mother for half of the day, and a Chinese tutor for the other half. Buck received formal education after she moved back to the United States in 1910 at the age of eighteen, but her early home schooling no doubt played a key role in making her the first US woman Nobel laureate in literature.[10]

Celebrated tennis player Serena Williams is a modern-day success story of informal education. She is regarded by most commentators, players, and sportswriters as the greatest female tennis player of all time. However, it has become obvious by now that she had learned during her childhood that without proper education in a range of subjects she might not become a truly legendary tennis player. She began her home schooling in her preteen years at the age of three due to an intensive focus on tennis training. In addition to English as her mother tongue, Williams speaks conversational French, and knows some Spanish and Italian. She has learned foreign languages outside formal schools. The tennis superstar coauthored with Beard Hilary, an award-winning writer, a book about "life and how to play it."[11] It is uncertain if Williams was self-taught to be good at writing. Nonetheless, it is certain that as an exemplary homeschooler, her unusual experience qualified her enough to coauthor a book with a prominent writer. Some may tend to look at celebrities coauthoring with famed writers negatively as if they were ghostwriters. But such critics are missing a crucial point. Many celebrities like Williams and Jobs are unusual thinkers as USC graduates and more than qualified to coauthor with any eminent writer. She is also known to be in the process of writing a story line for a TV show.

In addition, the wide range of Williams' charitable activities across the world that require not only hands-on experience but also expert knowledge, for which many universities offer postgraduate courses, would have been difficult to carry out without her informal education on philanthropy. The impressive philanthropic activities Williams has performed provide us with an opportunity to get a fresh view that the self-taught person tends to be more empathetic toward the struggles of others than the elites from well-to-do families and prestigious schools. "They feel an obligation to do what is in their power to combat these struggles because they view the problems and the hurt that comes with them as their own."[12] Empathy is a crucial trait of philanthropists.[13] The following study by the *Chronicle of Philanthropy* can be considered validating this view.

> In 2011, the wealthiest Americans—those with earnings in the top 20 percent—contributed on average 1.3 percent of their income to charity. By comparison, Americans at the base of the income pyramid—those in the bottom 20 percent—3.2 percent of their income [and even then] they do not itemize deductions on their income-tax returns. (Quoted in K. Stern, "Why the rich don't give to charity," *Atlantic* [April 2013], available at: https://www.theatlantic.com, accessed May 5, 2013)

The study continues,

> Last year, not one of the top 50 individual charitable gifts went to a social-service organization or to a charity that principally serves the poor and the dispossessed. (Quoted in K. Stern, "Why the rich don't give to charity," *Atlantic* [April 2013], available at: https://www.theatlantic.com, accessed May 5, 2013)

As for educational aid, the wealthy prefer to support prestigious colleges and universities, such as Harvard and Columbia.[14] Revealing her deep commitment to the importance of education for the poor, Williams has set up the Serena Williams Foundation that aims to provide the highest quality education available for underprivileged youth around the world.[15] The key point is that in educational charity alone, informal education has triumphed over formal education.

The success stories about legendary personalities raise a legitimate question. What would have happened to the aforementioned and other self-taught legends if they were born to well-to-do families and their parents had forced them to get into prestigious schools so that their kids could find well-paid conventional professions, such as becoming lawyers, doctors, government officials, business managers, and so on? How to define a successful life is surely a philosophical question hard to deal with. Even so, it is certain that it would have been difficult if all the great people we briefly discussed above could become such icons of inspiring success if they had been born into wealthy families and taken the traditional educational routes their parents might have forced them to take.

Leading international organizations, including the United Nations Educational, Scientific and Cultural Organization (UNESCO), has recognized the importance of informal education for individual, social, economic, and political development since the late twentieth century. UNESCO anticipated in 1997 that informal education would play a key role in the development of all countries in the world in the twenty-first century.[16] Advances in informal education is accelerating in this century, especially since it must be the focus in addressing a wide range of emerging issues of global society, such as literacy, income generating skills, risks and benefits of new technologies, poverty reduction, and economic productivity, according to Ananda Paudel, undersecretary of the Ministry of Education of Nepal.[17]

2. Informal education is gaining rapid momentum

All the old and new dramatic stories about the triumph of informal education demonstrate how, when, where, and what we have been "forced" to study may have little significance toward practical purposes. They underscore that it matters the most whether we have studied what we liked to learn, following our own hearts and whether we have been able to build up our capabilities to achieve our own goals. Learning can no longer be divided into a place and time to acquire knowledge (school) and a place and time to apply the knowledge acquired (the workplace).[18] Repeatedly, it comes out undisputed that education per se, formal or informal, is important. Education is not all about learning skills to earn a living either. John Dewey said that "Education is not preparation for life; education is life itself." Dewey's notion implies that learning never stops throughout our life-span.

The development of human society has paralleled the progress in the opportunities for quality education. Traditional schools make the mainstream of education yet. However, few would dispute that formal schools, however upgraded or renovated, will not be free from superfluous, inflexible, and ineffective bureaucracy. On the other hand, most experts agree that informal education can meet the ever-widening variety of educational needs in a timely, flexible, and inexpensive fashion. Pointing out the failings of formal education, they have begun to question how formal schools will contribute to the development of individuals and their societies in the days ahead and even how long they will be able to last.[19]

Despite the variety of problems formal schools have faced, there are relative strengths and weaknesses of formal and informal education. Even so, stories about the victory of informal education keep increasing. It is also impressive that many deficiencies with traditional education are being remedied by informal education. It also seems that the ideal of universal education is literally being universalized, largely thanks to the speedy development of informal education. Furthermore, specialists in education note that traditional schools are prone to squeeze the creative potential of their kids.[20] Their criticisms of formal education are not limited to its inadequate capacity to identify and encourage students' potential creativity. Formal schools may also kill the true spirit of the quest for pragmatic learning and self-improvement as opposed to the armchair knowledge that students acquire at the ivory tower.

Informal education continues to find new directions, correcting long-lasting problems with traditional education. Informal education itself is also changing fast in its form and substance. In terms of its role, weight, impact, strengths, the technology it uses, the ways it is administered, and other features, informal education of this century has become very different from that of the past as follows.

First, informal education has become a necessary tool of education today for all of us. The traditional discussion of education that centers on how to improve school education has failed to make much meaningful headway because it is hard to rectify deep-rooted problems with formal schools, including bureaucratic barriers. Humans are intrinsically capable of self-correction. Informal education has now become one of the most critical catalysts for transforming education. Informal education of the past was usually considered an alternative to formal education that people under special situations, including those suffering economic difficulties, were unable to access. This formulation still holds in part.

However, education of this century demands that we be creative, inspirational, and constructively adventurous to succeed. If we are unimaginative, boring, and routine, we will fail in whatever we are planning to do. As far as formal schools throttle our potential creativity, we don't need to make a fool of ourselves. If so, what is the most important secret to receive the kind of education that will work for our futures? The answer is simple. We should study basic subjects, such as reading, writing, and arithmetic, and then the courses that interest us, the ones offered by a variety of institutions for informal education. Ideally, the courses for informal education need to be delivered through various avenues by popular intellectuals who can teach us with ease, interest, and passion and facilitate our quick and easy understanding of the subject material. The need for popular intellectuals will be discussed in detail in chapter 5.

Second, advances in technologies, including ICT, are providing limitless educational opportunities. The expanding availability of the Internet has become vital to education, as it provides almost unlimited possibilities for learning. The Internet, as a powerful means of informal education, embraces all interested people, including curious kids, employees of various workplaces, the underprivileged, and the handicapped. The huge variety of self-teaching resources on the Internet has become a powerful aid, if not a panacea, for a self-paced, free online study of what people like or need to learn outside formal schools. Informal education provides education recipients with far more control over the learning process than formal education.

Diversifying digital media for educational purposes provides us with not only the information and knowledge for our immediate educational needs but also a way to teach ourselves. YouTube-like video streaming for various guides for self-tutoring keeps increasing and are becoming more exciting and easier to understand. We can also get formal education through informal educational methods, even earn formal college degrees or certificates (cost varies depending on the courses). Increasingly top-notch formal institutions of higher education, such as the Massachusetts Institute of Technology (MIT), Harvard, Yale, and Stanford, are offering real-time lectures taught by world-class professors, entrepreneurs, and legendary figures, with some courses being eligible for college credit.

For instance, a massive open online course provider called edX was created in May 2012 by joint efforts of MIT and Harvard.[21] It doesn't matter if we're sitting in a college classroom or on a subway or jogging in a park wearing our earphones when we listen to the lectures. In greater detail, informal education doesn't bother us with lectures we miss, normal work duties we perform if employed, instructors we don't like, uncomfortable and even intimidating school environments, inflexible seating arrangements, conventional norms, rigid and outdated school rules and regulations, and many other unpleasant and useless things we wish to avoid, besides the time required to go to school, the expensive tuition, and the fixed schedules of the classes we wish to attend. For the disabled who have difficulty commuting between home and school, and often find formal school settings unfriendly to them, the educational resources available on the Internet are their essential supporters.

Third, as new knowledge and skills for practical purposes emerge, and rapidly so, we should be able to fulfill our educational needs to our satisfaction. Informal education can meet this demand. If we've finished formal education at an advanced level like a PhD, but desire to continue to update our knowledge and skills, we can depend on informal education providers that vary in teaching experiences and techniques and content expertise. Most college and postgraduate degree holders employed in the workplace don't need to return to brick-and-mortar schools to update their expertise nowadays. Our present-day reality says that we should update our knowledge and skills regularly or perish. Nowadays we cannot claim that we are still practically well-educated simply because we've earned a college or postgraduate degree. In many cases, a formal college degree or certificate we may have earned only a few years ago does not guarantee our survival as an employee or expert unless we keep updating our knowledge in a timely fashion. Advancing informal education helps us overcome this problem.

As Accenture Research found, two-thirds of US college graduates say they need further training and instruction to enter the workforce.[22] This does not necessarily mean they must go to graduate schools to earn advanced degrees. Nor does this necessarily mean that those who graduated from college a few years ago are too underqualified to occupy or keep decent positions at workplaces. The truth is that the knowledge and skills we use today will become obsolete very soon. One of the key features of continuing scientific and technological innovations lies not so much in continuity as in speed. Everything surrounding us is changing so fast, but most schools and teachers simply cannot catch up with this change. Many schools and teachers are teaching their students what is already outdated. Already in 2003, a Parliamentary Council of Europe report said, "the Parliamentary Assembly recognizes that formal educational systems alone cannot respond to the challenges of modern society and therefore welcomes its reinforcement by non-formal educational practices."[23] In short, the fast-changing world is bringing home to us the importance of continuing education.

Take fast-changing kid science, for example, for basic understanding of how the knowledge of today is being discarded next morning. Kids learned before 2006 that there were nine planets—Mercury,

Venus, Earth, Mars, Jupiter, Saturn, Uranus, Neptune, and Pluto—in the solar system. No planet used to be known to exist outside it. Since then, astronomers have spotted over eight hundred planets around other stars (and thousands more "candidates"). Pluto was demoted to a dwarf planet in 2006. Today, the International Astronomical Union (IAU) recognizes five dwarf planets—Haumea, Makemake, Eries, Pluto, and Ceres—and scientists believe there may be dozens or even more than a hundred dwarf planets awaiting discovery. The first three IAU-recognized dwarf planets were discovered in 2005. In addition, US astronomers, including Mike Brown, consider an additional six trans-Neptunian objects to be "nearly certainly" dwarf planets.[24] *CNN* also reported in January 2016 that astronomers in the United Kingdom, the United States, and Australia found the galaxy's largest solar system, which is in an orbit around its star seven thousand times the size of Earth's orbit around the sun.[25] Recently, scientists confirmed that Albert Einstein rightly predicted the existence of gravitational waves a century ago. They have finally spotted these elusive ripples in space-time (meaning the three dimensions of space—length, width and depth—and one dimension of time). The physicists with the Advanced Laser Interferometer Gravitational-Wave Observatory disclosed that their twin detectors had heard the gravitational "ringing" produced by the collision of two black holes about four hundred megaparsecs (1.3 billion light years) from Earth, according to a report *Nature* released in February 2016.[26]

Of course, our knowledge has continuously improved. What matters today is that the short life-span of knowledge is growing shorter much faster. Not only astronomy and physics but also all other sciences including ICT, health technologies, and so on, reveal the same. Harvard mathematician Samuel Arbesman calls this phenomenon "the half-life of facts."[27] A half life means the amount of time it takes for half of a substance to undergo some specified process. For example, the half life of a drug is the amount of time it takes before half of the active elements are either eliminated or broken down by the body. The half life of knowledge from all disciplines is getting increasingly shorter in this century.

Numerous other examples demonstrate how fast existing knowledge is getting outdated today. The computer programming language theory, which is a branch of computer science, may last only two to eighteen months these days. The changes in theory used to be discussed usually in a ten-year interval from the 1950s to the 1990s.[28] Something like this can be said of social sciences too. International relations, economics, and business have become too volatile nowadays for top-notch pundits to look one or two years ahead. For example, how many experts could predict Brexit (the United Kingdom's withdrawal from the European Union) would happen before the British referendum on the country's EU membership was held on June 23, 2016? Analysts also predicted that there would be significant changes in relations of the United States with China, North Korea, Russia, and other countries under the Donald Trump Administration.[29] However, they failed to offer any reliable, concrete evidence to support the changes on the basis of existing theories, with some saying, "Trump is an enigma wrapped in mystery."[30] As for economics, world-class economists have made wrong predictions more frequently than in the past, only to demonstrate near-sightedness and incorrect validations for their assumptions. For instance, just on the eve of the global financial crisis of 2007–8, the IMF reported in the 2007 *World Economic Outlook*, "Overall risks to the outlook seem less threatening than six months ago."[31]

Equally notable in the context of the speed of existing knowledge becoming obsolete and the importance of informal education to fill the void is the fact that almost all knowledge contained in many books about, say, online transactions has permanently expired, even though they were published only a couple of years ago. Increasingly, college textbooks that were published just a few years ago are being removed from campus bookstore shelves, as much of their content consists of outdated knowledge. Under the circumstances, perhaps the only and the most convenient, dependable door for learners to open to update their knowledge is informal education that transmits the latest knowledge in a timely fashion.

3. The future of formal education

We can still produce Tommy Wilsons today. Christopher Eisgruber, president of Princeton University, noted in his commencement address in 2014[32] that Tommy Wilson, an 1879 Princeton graduate, was adrift after earning his degree and failing as a lawyer. Wilson went back to school, earned a PhD in political science, dropped his first name in favor of his middle name, Woodrow, and became a Princeton professor, the University's president, and then the twenty-eighth president of the United States. Ambitious students' pursuit of advanced or professional degrees at the postgraduate level at traditional universities is of course not undesirable. Keeping up with something inside the box does not necessarily mean losing out to looking for something outside the box "to use the cliché."[33]

Informal and formal education are not antonyms of each other, and the two often supplement each other, as noted already. Growing digital classrooms at traditional schools is a major educational feature of our time. The number of faculty members at traditional universities who take courses online according to their needs are increasing at a striking pace.[34] After all, traditional schools matter. Considerable truth is recognized in what Christopher Eisgruber considered important as stated in the speech, such as in-class experiments at brick-and-mortar schools that seem impossible or difficult to conduct online. It is also true that experts at traditional schools are developing new frontiers in science, technology, economic development, corporate management, public administration, and so forth.

With that said, it's been quite some time since scientific experiments in cyberspace began. More sophisticated scientific and technological explorations, experiments, and training that have been conducted in traditional classrooms and labs are being performed in cyberspace today. Many are also predicting that advancing artificial intelligence (AI) technology is expected to bring revolutionary changes to all aspects of education via the Internet. For example, the dominance of AI in the banking sector is growing. Some experiments performed through the Internet are producing incredible results.[35]

Education is being reshaped to provide us with not only innovative knowledge and skills but also the stimuli to awaken our potential creativity. The traditional belief that an exalted degree from a postsecondary school amounts to a lifetime guarantee of our success is only partly correct today and is expected to continue to wane. A prestigious degree can still put our career over the edge and yield a bigger paycheck. According to Life on the Buy Side, an Internet site for aspiring money managers, there is a well-known formula that is guaranteed to work when it comes to breaking into Wall Street. The first advice in the three-point formula is to attend a target university, especially a good business school.[36] However, this traditional principle has begun to conflict with reality.

Increasingly Wall Street outliers who have never gone to business schools are joining the list of the highest-paid fund managers. As early as 1996, Loren Pope, author of *Colleges That Change Lives*, quoted a *New York Times* report of 1994 that "a quarter of Harvard's class of 1958 had lost their jobs, were looking for work, or on welfare, just when their careers should have been cresting."[37] Rising today is the number of employers who don't really care about our alma mater or even our college specialty. They don't appreciate our college grade point average (GPA) either. As if they are looking for homeschooled legendary doers, they do care about what we can practically do for the targeted work their companies and organizations specialize in.[38] During job interviews, they care about our capacity for imagination, diligence, devotion, enthusiasm, thinking big and outside the box, and a pioneering spirit. Facing unparalleled economic pressures due to advances in technology, shifting major sources of economic growth, and the ensuing business uncertainty that some call "the new normal,"[39] companies are forced to find new markets or to radically change business strategies in ways that require new training for their employees. Their definition of "new training" implies employees' imagination, vision, passion, motivation for innovative planning, zeal to update knowledge and skills, and so on.

Realistic employers today are different from their predecessors. They are watching closely the characteristics of knowledge and training evolving toward the future, as they are closely connected with the prospects for their businesses. Companies operating in declining markets are desperately looking for innovative people and are eager to urgently train their employees to survive and remain competitive with other firms. Most of them know well that formal education across the world has faced serious challenges and crises. It is natural that today's employers want their employees to depend heavily on informal education so that they can get what the companies need as fast as possible.

Schools, for their part, have been aware of this reality. For example, the engineering-centered Ajou University located at the outskirts of the Seoul metropolitan area in South Korea announced in June 2016 that it had introduced a revolutionary grading system, the so-called Blue Semester,—meaning "the innovative semester"—which allows students to perform any creative, practical work of their own choice to earn a grade, such as designing a new type of automobile according to their own imagination, ideas, and concepts, a way different from the conventional grading system that requires students to listen to professors' lectures or participate in professor-led experiments and debates according to rigid schedules to get credits and grades.[40] Quite a few major universities in the country have adopted similar evaluation systems, and the number of such schools is increasing worldwide. Innovative universities across the world don't really care about so-called teaching methods since they know well the methods themselves create their own stereotypes and suppress students' independent imagination. As a result, students attending such schools are looking toward informal education to find what they need. This century of fusion of disciplines also requires us to understand complex systems.[41] Our conventional major in a certain field of interest at a formal school is being valued less and less as demonstrated by the forward-looking employers as mentioned above.

Business employers are witnessing that the number of the graduates from prestigious schools who are getting nowhere is increasing these days. Also rising is the number of employers who question even the moral value of top-notch schools. They particularly pay attention to the fact that top-class schools do not necessarily produce moral leaders of society. They note that Ivy League schools' grade inflation, for example, is anachronistic and will only hurt students' futures, and point out other drawbacks in their current educational goals and practices. The *Economist* reported that these first-rate schools are perhaps trying to hide something.[42]

News media negatively reacted to the shocking 2012 Harvard cheating scandal that involved approximately 125 students.[43] Harvard students claimed that collaboration like note sharing and consulting teaching fellows had been widespread. However, their claim had only exacerbated the image of Ivy League students among their prospective employers as well as the public. According to some critics, "they've only gone from dishonesty to more dishonesty."[44] Such condemnations fueled once again speculations among not only educational specialists but also general citizens as to how the fate of famed traditional schools will unfold as time goes by. The key concern here is that the good grades we may earn thanks to cheating on exams or grade inflation would in no way make us an able and innovative or the moral leader our society needs and only ruin our career. Distinguished schools have been failing to educate their students as personalities morally responsible for their society. Many of the students don't fit the name of their schools.

A high level of moral responsibility for society has been practiced more often by the people who have been informally educated. In addition to the legendary self-taught philanthropists as already mentioned, Irish singer and songwriter Paul David Hewson, better known by his stage name Bono of U2, is an eye-catching personality as a philanthropist. Even though he just finished secondary school and never attended college, Bono has become one of the world's best-known philanthropic performers and has earned an honorable nickname, "the moral face of fusion philanthropy." For his impressive charitable activities, Bono succeeded remarkably in enlisting powerful allies comprising religious, media, business, and political as well as philanthropic leaders, including former US president Bill Clinton. Bono has been spearheading new organizational networks that bind global humanitarian relief with geopolitical activism and corporate commercial enterprise. Among his major philanthropic initiatives is Product Red aimed at raising money for the Global Fund to Fight AIDS, Tuberculosis, and Malaria in the poorest countries of Africa and elsewhere. In November 2007, *NBC Nightly News* honored Bono as someone "making a difference" in the world. On December 11, 2008, Bono was given the annual Man of Peace prize awarded by several Nobel Peace Prize winners in Paris. Bono has been known to love to read books whenever possible to teach himself.

Looking ahead, most traditional schools will have to struggle to improve not only the quality of their curriculum, faculty, and facilities that relate to students' employment opportunities but also the moral aspects of their education. They have known for long enough that there has been no shortage of claims that education in traditional schools in the United States and many other countries has declined not only scholastically but also ethically. In "a world that is more dangerous than ever before,"[45] the importance of morality for the well-educated as well as celebrities in achieving a sustainable society at national and global levels cannot be overemphasized. It may be incorrect to say that informal education produces more moral citizens than formal education. Still, we must take note of the fact that many experts are saying formal schools are failing in this respect.

Also, rapid increase in life expectancy in all aging or aged societies has made informal education an essential for the elderly to adapt themselves to a knowledge-based society. The last half century has been amazing in this regard. "Not only can learning during the later stages of life bring happiness, wellbeing, and a connection to the wider community for those studying unceasingly, it can also reduce dependency on welfare."[46] More elderly people want to receive informal education at, say, community learning centers, in pursuit of many factors related to their happiness, such as intellectual pastime, self-realization, social participation, better performance in the workplace, and so on.

Although Nola Ochs earned her bachelor's degree at the age of ninety-five at a formal school, her impressive story has important implications for informal education with special respect to human beings' intrinsic desire to learn, and the expanding educational needs for the aged. She became a Guinness World Record holder as the world's oldest college graduate and was named the 2007 Kansas Woman Leader of the Year. The elderly has the same eagerness for continuing education, enhancement of self-esteem, and earning a living as do their younger counterparts. Nowadays it has become unthinkable for them to dispense with informal education for such pursuits.

The roles of human beings are becoming increasingly specialized and diverse. A special consideration in this context is that specialists do not necessarily need to be identical to academics, who are supposed to have a high-level ability to think, understand, and perform researches proficiently as customarily defined, although the two words "specialist" and "academic" are often used as synonyms. It is admitted that academics are well educated and indulge in studying and other activities that involve careful thinking and mental effort. Some of them may find popular movies less interesting than studying grammar, logic, and rhetoric, which are called trivium, or a systematic method of critical thinking used to derive factual certainty from information perceived with the five senses—sight, sound, taste, smell, and touch. On the other hand, there are specialists in nail art, bakery, interior construction, popular entertainers, cartoonists, decorative painters, fashion designers, movie directors, professional athletes, and so forth. The crucial question here is this: Do they need to earn advanced academic degrees from schools as most academics do? The answer is no.

Trying to predict the future of formal education, many experts have argued that despite a lot of strengths of informal education, education needs, among others, physical spaces where human beings as sociological animals can meet and communicate with each other. They claim that students should better understand each other through face-to-face communication and other forms of personal contact in various events and occasions that school settings offer. According to them, they also need to mingle with people from diverse backgrounds, circumstances, nationalities, and so on, on school campuses.[47]

Former president of Harvard University Lawrence Summers once said to the effect that globalization of Harvard would be a blessing but "Harvardization" of the globe would be a disaster. School campuses no doubt serve such requirements. To understand human life, we may use various media, such as photos, videos, newspapers, books, information on the Internet, and so on. They will help but not suffice. We can never understand places, cultures, or people to our satisfaction without personal contact with and exposure to them. However, critics respond that the spaces where we can develop human relations are not limited to college grounds only. Human relationships, they contend, can be cultivated throughout our life from early days onward, not only in schools but also in, say, family life, playgrounds, parks, social events, various gatherings, libraries, workplaces, religious institutions, and in many other places. They recognize that diverse opportunities and places have been important resources of informal learning for numerous world-famous, humanity-driven, well-rounded personalities.[48]

The prospects for traditional schools are rather bleak, if anything. The ability of informal education to provide humans with quality education will become more prominent especially with the relentless progress of relevant technologies. For the public, this is good news. More humans will be able to access various types of contents through informal education. AI and robots are posing serious challenges to formal education. Richard Susskind, president of the Society for Computers and Law in the United Kingdom and author of *The Future of the Professions*, expects that within decades traditional professions will be dismantled as most, if not all, professionals, such as doctors, pharmacists, lawyers, accountants, consultants, journalists, the clergy, and so on, will be replaced by less-expert people, new types of experts, and high-performing systems, thanks to AI and robots in an Internet society.[49] This prospect suggests once again that the current educational landscape will undergo drastic changes in the coming decades. Traditional medical schools, law schools, business schools, schools of public administration, theology, journalism, and other institutions for professional education are very likely to either disappear or be radically transformed.

Yuval Noah Harari, a lecturer at Hebrew University and author of the international best seller, *Sapiens: A Brief History of Humankind*, offers another interesting view about the shifting educational environment. He observed in 2016 that AI had already begun to outperform humans in many areas, and there's no guarantee we would be able to keep up as this continues. Ian Sample, science editor of the *Guardian*, presents Harari's argument:

Children alive today will face the consequences. Most of what people learn in school or in college will probably be irrelevant by the time they are 40 or 50. If they want to continue to have a job, and to understand the world, and be relevant to what is happening, people will have to reinvent themselves again and again and faster and faster. (I. Sample, "AI will create 'useless class' of human, predicts bestselling historian," *Guardian* [2016], available at: https://www.theguardian.com/, accessed May 23, 2016)

With the megatrends in education as noted by Susskind, Harari, and other gurus unfolding, informal education will continue to evolve in an array of ways to meet changing educational needs. Overall, the whole business of education, formal or informal, has already entered a pivotal period of amazing changes and adaptation to new realities. The key point, however, is that education will change in the years ahead, informal education will continue to be indispensable and play a key role in the process of this global transformation, as all humans will have to struggle continually to keep up and reinvent themselves to last and prosper in the forthcoming decades.

CHAPTER 4

Innovative Teens

1. Innovative teens on the rise

Nelson Mandela, the late president of South Africa and "Father of the Nation," called education "the most powerful weapon with which you can change the world." This notion sounds more convincing today than ever before when we see the rise of innovative teens. The teens of the contemporary era called Generation Z, to use the cliché, are accessing education differently as compared to the teens of Generations X and Y and contributing to transforming the world.[1] Laurie Penny, an English columnist and author, notes that today's teens are "smarter, tougher, and braver"[2] than their cohorts of preceding generations.

The story about legendary dancer Dame Gillian Barbara Lynne, born in 1926, was written not in the present but in the past century. Still, her story has important implications for what is happening today and will happen tomorrow. The childhood of Gillian Lynne was not smooth. Her story reminds us of the astounding creative potential inherent in all kids that Sir Kenneth Robinson believes is killed in schools. Lynne was regarded as hopeless when she was an elementary schoolgirl. Her school wrote a letter to her parents. "We think Gillian has a learning disorder." Luckily for her, a doctor found out her potential talent to become a dancer. The doctor said to her mother, "Gillian isn't sick; she's a dancer. Take her to a dance school."[3] After she quit the school, Gillian worked hard and her way through to become a renowned British ballerina, dancer, choreographer, actress, and theater director.

A little girl was in a drawing lesson. She was six and at the back, drawing. The teacher had been saying that this little girl hardly ever paid any attention during the class, but in this drawing lesson she did. The teacher was fascinated, went over to her, and asked, "What are you drawing?" The girl said, "I'm drawing a picture of God." The teacher said, "But nobody knows what God looks like." And the girl said, "They will in a minute." This story too implies children basically have potential creativity, which is, however, easily ignored or even crushed in schools as Sir Robinson, an educational advisor and author of worldwide fame, highlights.[4] His notion reminds us of the well-known remark Maria Montessori, the Italian physician and educator, made in 1936: "Early childhood education is the key to the betterment of society."

These thought-provoking stories will be able to lead us to the following conclusion with ease. We should do our best to encourage kids to find their potential creativity, which is killed in school, but elsewhere can be discovered and developed to make them good dancers, painters, writers, poets, designers, musicians, illustrators, cooks, sportspersons, and so on. In other words, if we wish to become a successful personality, we should discover first our latent creativity in a specific field on which we can concentrate with great interest.

Digital media has increasingly reported about the rising number of incredible teens and their success stories. Mainstream media are also striving to be the first in touting such teens, and reports of teen legends who have made millions of dollars are emerging far more frequently than before. In November 2012 the *Atlantic* featured an article titled "Young people have the power to change the world."[5] Since 2015, *TIME* magazine has featured a list titled "The 30 most influential teens" every year."[6] "To determine *TIME*'s annual list, we consider accolades across numerous fields, global impact through social media and overall ability to drive news," said the weekly in November 2017. In 2016, *Fortune* reported "18 under 18" innovative entrepreneurs.[7] These are only a few examples of numerous such stories that say young teens today are putting adults to shame, "changing industries and ultimately changing the world."[8] Is this new phenomenon or "new normal" happening as adults encourage their kids to be more creative than ever before? The answer is yes and no. Why? To find the reason, let's read on, looking at more examples of such teen legends.

Nick D'Aloisio, born in London in November 1995 to Australian expatriates, is a British entrepreneur and computer programmer. He looks like any other kid, goes to school, and has cool hair, but has become a legend or a bona fide geek idol for every youngster with digital dreams. The self-taught programmer created a smartphone app in his spare time. He got his first computer at the age of nine and used that to make movies. Nick learned how to code using *C for Dummies* and online videos. He created his first app in 2008 at the age of twelve, and had to submit it under his father's name, since he was four years too young to meet the app store's minimum age of sixteen. After that, he developed a new app every summer break until 2011, when the then-fifteen-year-old developed Trimit, the forerunner to Summly. The application is used as an effective tool to condense big text content into a small summary text.[9]

The popularity of Summly was explosive. Nick had gotten tech luminaries and venture capitalists to slobber all over themselves to wheel and deal with him. He, at just fifteen years of age, was recognized as the youngest person to receive a round of venture capital in technology from Hong Kong's legendary rags-to-riches billionaire Li Ka-Shing. In March 2013, his Summly news app was sold to Yahoo for a reported US$30 million, making D'Aloisio one of the youngest self-made millionaires ever. Yahoo also gave him a position in the company. Running with celebrities and appearing all over television and the Internet, he, currently a student at Oxford University, led the Yahoo News Digest team, which launched at the 2014 Consumer Electronics Show, an electronics and technology trade show of worldwide fame. On November 12, 2013, the ambitious entrepreneur was also honored in *TIME* magazine's "Time 100" as one of the world's most influential teenagers.

BBC reported in October 2015 that a teen made a revolutionary robot arm. The teen named Easton LaChappelle came up with a truly remarkable robotic limb. His brainwave came when he was bored in class. One day the young US inventor realized he wanted to do something extraordinary with his life. Soon enough, at the age of sixteen, he decided to start the self-imposed challenge and went to a local supermarket and bought a simple game called Mindflex, which allows players to control a ball using the power of their mind. He took the game apart, seeing how different movements were linked to brainwaves, and translated this into his robotic arm.[10] Even more surprising is that he is a self-taught specialist in prosthetics or as prosthetist. He made his first mechanical hand and kept improving the design with 3D-printed parts. An encounter with a seven-year-old girl at a science fair, whose prosthetic arm cost US$80,000 (and would need to be replaced when she outgrew it), inspired him to turn his prototype into a real and affordable piece of technology.[11]

When Aidan Dwyer was out strolling in some woods, an idea popped into his head. "My design is like a tree," the then thirteen-year-old boy told *CNN* in late 2011, "but instead of having leaves it has solar panels at the ends (of the branches)." The teenager inventor was one of twenty-four recipients of the 2011 Young Naturalist Award from the American Museum of Natural History. His idea on revolutionizing the solar power industry was widely acclaimed. Although critics challenged Dwyer's power calculation, which they argued was flawed, most, including even some of the critics, admired his extraordinary imagination. Dwyer, on his own part, has persevered and accepted the flaw in his experiment. Later, he began working to change his experiment to include data on currents. Dwyer was thirteen years old in 2011 and self-taught. During a 2011 conference of PopTech, a respected nonprofit organization focused on innovation, he said he was confident that he could change the world. He has had friend requests on Facebook from venture capitalists, which he said he had declined.[12] Whether or not he will eventually make a solar breakthrough, it is remarkable that the imaginative teen has already surprised the world.

Thomas Suarez, another US boy inventor, told *ABC News* in April 2012, "I've made a lot of money for a kid." The thirteen-year-old youngest iPhone app developer made himself CEO of CarrotCorp, which he founded at the tender age of twelve. He won a Tribeca Disruptive Innovation Award, along with notables like Twitter's cofounder Jack Dorsey and filmmaker Edward Burns. On July 14, 2014, the boy wonder, now fifteen, claimed to have designed a 3D printer that is ten times faster and more reliable than anything on the market.[13]

Teenagers' revolutionary achievements are happening not only in the technology world but also in an array of other quests, including business, education, sports, entertainment, social activism, life sciences, you name it. In medicine, Angela Zhang at age seventeen briefed US President Barack Obama on her award-winning research about a cancer-fighting nanoparticle at the White House Science Fair in February 2012. President Obama told her he hopes she cures cancer.

> Zhang, from Cupertino, California, launched her science career after successfully cold-calling her way into a Stanford University lab at 14, but she had to prove her enthusiasm before she could earn a place on a research team. That meant spending hours reading research review articles after school each day. "I remember looking at my first article—all of the words were English, but I didn't understand any of them in conjunction. I spent a lot of time just patiently Googling each word." ... Her determination paid off. She found herself part of a bona fide research team, under the careful eye of a Stanford grad student. (M. Cirincione, "Cancer-fighting Harvard student looks to a future in STEM," *U.S. News & World Report* [2015], available at: https://www. usnews.com/, accessed May 12, 2015)

Chang's story is just another example of a contemporary teen's extraordinary challenging spirit that goes on and on.

Jack Andraka has made a breakthrough in detecting pancreatic cancer at a trivial cost in its early stages when survival rates are at their highest. This cancer is so aggressive and deadly that often by the time it's normally diagnosed it's already spread to other parts of the body. Over 85 percent of all pancreatic cancers are diagnosed late, when someone has less than a 2 percent chance of survival. *CBS 60 Minutes,* which the *New York Times* calls "one of the most esteemed newsmagazines on American television," devoted some fourteen minutes to an interview with the "boy wonder" scientist. Jack beat out fifteen hundred contestants and won in 2012 the grand prize at the Intel International Science Fair. Like a modern-day Rocky, the self-described science geek took the stage and US$100,000 in prize money at the age of fifteen with pure, unadulterated adolescent joy. In 2013 alone, then US president Barack Obama invited the exceptionally accomplished boy to the White House four times. His idea has made him a star speaker at leading medical conferences and institutes in many parts of the world, including the renowned Royal Society of Medicine in England.[14]

Maddie Ziegler, born in 2002, is best known for dancing as pop star Sia's alter ego on tour and in smash-hit videos like "Chandelier" and "The Greatest." This Pittsburgh native who has been called the "first digital dance star" has ambitions beyond the dance world. In 2016, she, at the age of fourteen, launched her own clothing line, Maddie, and voiced a character in the upcoming animated movie, *Ballerina.* Another fourteen-year-old celebrity Logan Guleff appeared on *The Today Show* at the age of nine to demonstrate a recipe he submitted to JIF's Most Creative Sandwich Contest. Since Guleff won the 2014 MasterChef Junior champion, he has become a rising star in the culinary world. In 2016, he was named Southern Living's Best New Southern Cook and earned a spot on *Fortune's* "18 under 18" list.[15]

Many celebrated figures were born into and brought up in special circumstances favorable to developing their creativity at a young age. For instance, Facebook cofounder Mark Zuckerberg was born in 1984 into a comfortable, well-educated family and began to learn computer programming from his father when he was in his early teens. This means that he began to change the world when he was a young teen. Facebook, founded in 2004 when Zuckerberg was nineteen years old, is now the world's largest social network, and its monthly active users were over 1.94 billion as of March 2017. Zuckerberg's net worth was estimated to be US\$63.3 billion as of May 2017, and he was ranked as the fifth richest person in the world in a *Forbes* report.[16] Zuckerberg was also ranked tenth on the *Forbes* list of "The world's most powerful people 2016."[17] On May 25, 2017, he gave the commencement speech for Harvard University, the school he dropped out of after his sophomore year.

Unlike Zuckerberg, many other teens were born into ordinary or poor families or even to the poorest ones in the poorest countries but are still surprising the world. Kelvin Doe, a child from a poor district of Freetown in the capital city of Sierra Leone, which is one of the poorest countries in the world whose per capita nominal GDP was US\$623 in 2017 (IMF estimate). In Freetown, the lights will only come up once a week; with electricity so intermittent, he was unable to stop his insatiable curiosity to understand and build his own electronics. "Among the various things he managed to build from scrap parts are a battery to power lights, a multi-channel audio mixer, a hand-powered generator, and an FM Radio transmitter."[18] As his inventiveness became widely known, Doe was interviewed on local television, and his fame skyrocketed when he took part in a local youth-oriented innovation challenge organized by David Sengeh, a PhD student at the MIT Media Lab. Soon after this, Doe became the youngest person in history to be invited to the Visiting Practitioner's Program at MIT. His story has since gone viral, inspiring millions. It has been seen by more than ten million people. Subsequently, he also guest-lectured undergraduates at Harvard.

Laurence Rook, a thirteen-year-old boy born into a low-income family in Croydon in south London, invented in 2011 a doorbell that calls the householder if nobody answers the door. Rook said he got thinking about his invention after his mother missed several deliveries. The doorbell technology calls up a person's cell phone, allowing the homeowner to talk to whoever's waiting on that porch. He said,

> It started over a year ago when my mum was expecting a
> parcel to be delivered. It was the second or third delivery,

> and instead of leaving a slip saying, "please come to this post office and collect your parcel," I thought "why don't they call you?" and from there I thought of the idea of putting a phone inside the doorbell so you can talk to them. ("Croydon boy Laurence Rook invents phone-linked doorbell," *BBC News* [2011] available at: http://www.bbc.com/, accessed June 7, 2011)

Scarcely had the young teen invented the phone-linked doorbell, he received orders worth up to US$322,500 for the product.[19]

Malala Yousafzai, a Pakistani activist for female education and the youngest-ever Nobel Prize winner, began to be well known across the world for human rights advocacy for education and for women, when she was a young teenager. The eleven-year-old advocate of promoting education for girls wrote a blog under a pseudonym for *BBC* detailing her life under Taliban occupation, their attempts to take control of her hometown called the Swat Valley, and her views on education for women. The summer of 2010, journalist Adam B. Ellick made a *New York Times* documentary about her life as the Pakistani military intervened in the region. The then thirteen-year-old education activist rose in worldwide prominence, giving interviews in print and on television.

In the afternoon of October 9, 2012, Yousafzai boarded her school bus in the northwest Pakistani district of Swat. A gunman asked for her by name, then pointed a pistol at her and fired three shots. One bullet hit the left side of her forehead, traveled under her skin through the length of her face, and then went into her shoulder. After the attack, she remained unconscious and in critical condition, but later her condition improved enough for her to be sent to the Queen Elizabeth Hospital in Birmingham, England, for intensive rehabilitation. In a 2011 interview with *CNN*, Yousafzai made remarks full of plain wisdom and determination that appealed strongly to a wise mind—that part of each person that can know and experience truth. "I have the right of education. I have the right to play. I have the right to sing. I have the right to talk. I have the right to go to market. I have the right to speak up." When asked during the interview why she risked her life to raise her voice, she replied, "If I didn't do it, who would?" She declared decisively, "I shall raise my voice."[20]

Some may regard Yousafzai's remarkable courage as exceptional. However, specialists in social change are paying unusual attention to the fact that the number of teens who are playing critical roles in transforming the world are rising at an unprecedented speed. Kid entrepreneurs are increasing, and teenagers' do-it-yourself revolution[21] and rebellion against the traditional power structure of schools[22] are gaining momentum. In terms of ingenuity, entrepreneurship, independent work and audacity, kids of today born around the year 2000 are different from their parents and grandparents in terms of the capacity for social innovation.

Many are naturally wondering why this century is producing more of such amazing kids. At this point, we need to remind ourselves of the question raised at the beginning of this chapter and its answer—yes and no. Most people will hardly argue that our parents and teachers today are encouraging their kids more vigorously than before to be creative, innovative, entrepreneurial, courageous, and so on and not to be constrained by school education, even when they recognize that a few of them are getting more tolerant of kids' seemingly unrealistic undertakings. Such being the case, the answer is yes and no.

2. Kids of today enjoy different educational and social milieus

Are today's kids smarter than their seniors were in their younger days due to, say, Darwinian evolutionary change? To the contrary, many analysts refute Laurie Penny's notion that today's teens are "smarter" and contend that children of the early twentieth century were smarter than today's kids. To substantiate their arguments, they have cited, for example, a general examination to test eighth-grade students in Bullitt County school system of the State of Kentucky in the United States in 1912, which ignited a debate over the intelligence of present-day children. A question of principal importance is whether an increase or decrease in kid's intelligence has something to do with their innovative ability that leads to successful life. A disturbing observation is when someone you think is more stupid than you is more innovative than you and succeeding in various aspects of life more than you.[23]

However may the debate unfold, experts argue that modern-day kids are different from their counterparts of the past, not in conventional intelligence, but in the ability to think critically, to think in an original way, to challenge the status quo, and so on.[24] For one thing, kids' intelligences of the past century were largely gauged in terms of the ability to answer memory-based questions like "What is a personal pronoun?" "Who first discovered America?" "Define connective tissue," and so on.[25] Today's kids may be performing more poorly in memorized answers with specific words. Some experts claim the skill for rote memorization is important.[26] At the same time, most analysts emphasize the importance of the ability to think critically and creatively as much as that of memorization skills.[27] Increasingly, specialists underscore the importance of the former more.[28]

Another difference in today's children is that they are coming into their classes already knowing their ABCs and writing their names. Many can even read. It is true that today's kids are generally better off, as nutrients and growth factors related to the standard of living regulate brain development during fetal and early postnatal life. In other words, nutrition and intellectual development are believed to have a significant correlation. Some studies have in fact shown that people have gained three to five intelligence quotient (IQ) points every ten years, a phenomenon called "the Flynn effect." However, we need to recall that IQ has been subject to a lot of criticism. Some scientists contend that IQ fails to act as an accurate measure of intelligence in its broadest sense since it fails to account for certain critical areas that are associated with other dimensions of brainpower, such as creativity, curiosity, or emotional aptitude. Still others disregard IQ entirely. The controversial IQ category was removed from the Guinness World Records in 1989/1990.[29]

Even if we admit children of Generation Z have the advantage of the Flynn effect, this benefit must be responsible for only a tiny part of the miraculous achievements that world-shattering kids are making these days. Many contend that the most important factor that is contributing to their success is new educational and social milieus of this century that enable the kids to develop their potential curiosity and imagination more conveniently and effectively. Shelly Bima, mom of a three-year-old and an eight-year-old, living in Minneapolis, said, "There's more to learn, there's more avenues, they have more activities and programs."[30] A dad of three kids aged three, eight, and eleven said they are especially more tech savvy. Kids nowadays are more proficient than adults in the use of technology, such as mobile computing. The present-day world has become much smaller, more convenient, more motivating, and more economical, due to technological innovations. It may be deplorable that the guarantee of an affordable place at university that allowed you to continue your education is no longer available to most people. College fees have tripled; benefits have been slashed; and financial schemes applicable to students, such as the Education Maintenance Allowance in some parts of the United Kingdom, have been canceled.[31] Nonetheless, it is common sense that the computer and the Internet have brought revolutionary changes to the way in which we gain new information and knowledge as mentioned in chapter 3.

As every aspect in our daily life requires the use of computers, the computer market has been growing at lightning speed and computer-related products and services are competing to become not only more serviceable, exciting, and economical but also more user-friendly to all, including kids. In this respect, children are more blessed than adults. Children learn foreign languages much faster than adults. Similarly, children learn not only how to use a computer but also computer programming languages and web development skills much more quickly than adults and even their teachers. The entire audience burst out laughing when Thomas Suarez said jokingly in the said TED talk, "These days, students usually know a little bit more than teachers with the technology. Sorry."

Computer programming or software engineering has generally been perceived to be reserved only for smart people. The current reality shows this perception is wrong. Even though computer coding is something that most people of average intelligence can do with a small amount of effort, a priori misconception creates a myth bubble around what it really requires and isolates the whole activity.[32] Computer programming is not rocket science. Most people still think it too difficult for them to even try to do it, only to give computer coding an inaccurate face.[33] A priori misconception about all levels and aspects of computer training is only preventing more Thomas Suarezs from emerging. It is noteworthy that the three towering computer giants—Apple cofounder Steve Jobs, Microsoft cofounder Bill Gates and Facebook cofounder Mark Zuckerberg—never majored in computer science or engineering at college. We need to call to mind that these three titans too began learning or using the computer or computing-related devices at young ages at home and at other places outside school classrooms. Elementary school children, who can read, write, and have basic math skills, can become computer programmers in a short span of time, if they are willing to learn computer languages. The fact that even little kids attending kindergartens can do it right now must be one of the most decisive evidences that prove computer coding is in no way too complicated or a hard skill. The Internet also provides young teens with a variety of tutorials about, say, how to be well versed in writing computer software. The tutorials themselves are also becoming more user-friendly. This helps curious children become fast learners about the computer.

Pat Wyman, college professor and best-selling author of *Amazing Grades: 101 Best Ways to Improve Your Grades Faster* notes that

> the fact that students can learn by reading, watching videos or listening to audio enables them to learn in the way that suits them best and technology allows students to become better critical thinkers as they put all the data they learn together for research projects. (P. Wyman, *Amazing Grades: 101 Best Ways to Improve Your Grades Faster* [Las Vegas: The Center for New Discoveries in Learning, 2012])

Children are enjoying using computers and mobile devices wherever they happen to be. In schools, libraries, stores, coffee shops, homes, and other places, a lot of new neural pathways carved out by the computer can quickly help children enhance their ability to think critically and creatively. "The computer is the best study resource that is full of information, offers unlimited avenues of undertaking and analysis of the desired results."[34] The information from the Internet is unlimited unlike conventional modes of learning such as textbooks or off-line tutorials from teachers. Advancing technology enables kids to learn new things spontaneously and in multiple modalities. In short, young learners of the twenty-first century use all available learning modalities, as they interact with technology, Wyman suggests.[35] Young teens get not only general information but also advanced knowledge about the computer they need through Internet probing and communication with their peers who frequently gather in study, hobby, and general interest groups.

Teen scientists and inventors working outside the realm of computing also use Internet-related services and products, such as social networking services, and join the forces that are changing the world. With their number rising steeply and technologies keeping on advancing fast, teen scientists and inventors who can adjust themselves to the advances in technologies in a timely fashion will continue to write incredible legends undreamed of in the past. Our social and educational milieus are rapidly changing in favor of such kids. In other words, the atmosphere that encourages children in doing what they like to do is progressing fast. Parents and teachers are becoming more tolerant of such kids.

The success story of Jack Andraka, for example, is the product of not only his own efforts and digital blessing but also social support. When he was thirteen, a close family friend, who was like an uncle to him, died of pancreatic cancer. When the disease hit so close to home, he knew he needed to learn more. Jack went online to find answers. Jack's journey from suburban Baltimore high school freshman to the world of cancer research thus began at age fourteen.[36] Probing the Internet, he found a variety of statistics on pancreatic cancer, but he was shocked when he found modern medicine for detecting pancreatic cancer was still using a sixty-year-old technique. Also, he found it was extremely expensive despite its gross inaccuracy that missed 30 percent of all pancreatic cancers. He began to think about a sensor that could diagnose the fatal disease at the early stage. The sensor had to be inexpensive, rapid, simple, sensitive, selective, and minimally invasive. He decided to go online to what he calls a teenager's two best friends, Google and Wikipedia.[37]

He suspected that when doctors were looking for pancreatic cancer, they were looking at the bloodstream, which was already abundant with tons and tons of protein, and they were looking for a miniscule difference in just this one protein. That seemed to him next to impossible. Investigating through the Internet, Jack found an article that listed a database of over eight thousand different pancreatic cancer–related proteins. He now decided to make it his new mission to go through all these proteins and see which ones could serve as a biomarker for pancreatic cancer. His first task was to discover the protein that would have to be found in all pancreatic cancers at high levels in the bloodstream in the earliest stages. The task was too overwhelming for a teenager to carry out without a lab and other key resources. At one time, when he was reading stealthily a medical journal during class, his teacher snatched it out of his hand as if he had *Playboy* magazine. Undaunted, however, he plugged and chugged his way through the gargantuan self-imposed assignment but came to the verge of losing his sanity at one point. Luckily for Jack, on the four thousandth try, he eventually found the protein.[38]

When Jack finally prepared a test protocol for his theory and sent it out to two hundred top cancer specialists, all but one turned it down. Dr. Anirban Maitra, then a professor at Johns Hopkins University and a renowned expert in pancreatic cancer, got Jack a corner in his lab. He said,

> Jack Andraka is fabulous. I've been delighted and honored to have him in my lab. He sent me a nice write-up on his lab plans and research, very interesting coming from a 15-year-

old boy. You've got to be able to give people a chance. I'm fortunate to have answered his email. ("Physician-scientist Anirban Maitra brings leading expertise and passion for results to pancreatic cancer research leadership role at UT MD Anderson," MD Anderson [News Release] [2013], available at: https://www.mdanderson.org/, accessed April 4, 2013)

Such a broad-minded, encouraging personality who is always ready "to give people a chance" must be among the best type of academics the educational environment of this century needs.

After school and on weekends, Jack's mother would drop him off at the lab, where he learned basic lab techniques and worked on developing his cancer test. Andraka's parents, like all other parents, wanted him to be well prepared for getting into a college but still tolerated and supported his apparently impossible research. Andraka said his parents had him use his home's basement for his "lab," which always remains so jumbled that they were reluctant to know about what went on down there.[39] Tolerant and progressive teachers, parents, neighbors, and society as a whole are encouraging curious, creative youngsters to be audacious to open new frontiers to the unknown world.

Andraka's success story highlights that social support and generosity matter heavily for young teens today: they play a key part in producing amazing kids. Fortunately, teens today have parents, relatives, teachers, friends, and neighbors who are tolerant of them and encourage their freedom to become curious, freedom to inquire, freedom to go entrepreneurial, their courage to let go of certainties, you name it. They are more permissive and supportive to their kids' seemingly impossible ambitions and dreams than their predecessors.

As for the business arena, Juliette Brindak is a US businesswoman and cofounder and chief executive officer of the tween social networking site, Miss O & Friends. When Juliette was only ten, she began drawing a group of made-up characters she called "cool girls," including a primary character named "Miss O." At sixteen, she launched Miss O & Friends, inspired by her earlier drawings. She could enlist her mother and father to help put the site together with their combined graphic and business skills. Her sister Olivia Brindak also helped her inspiration for the site. Miss O & Friends became an instant hit with fellow tweens who began visiting the website by the hundreds of thousands. "Miss O & Friends" earned Juliette money through advertising revenue and was ranked the third largest girls-only website in 2011 by *Inc. Magazine.* The site now generates ten million unique visitors per month, is worth an estimated US$15 million, and continues to rely on word-of-mouth and very little conventional advertising for success.[40]

Like Jack Andraka, Juliette Brindak, Aidan Dwyer, and Thomas Suarez were all able to succeed with the help and support of the people close to them. They have encouraged the curiosity, freaky ideas, and entrepreneurial spirit of wonder kids all the way. Aidan's parents backed up his research when he wondered why tree branches look alike. Thomas decided to make an app when he was only nine years old and has since received generous help from his parents, friends, teachers, neighbors, and even the people at the Apple store.

One special fact about these teen legends is that they are not necessarily child prodigies. Various lists of child prodigies show none of them belong in this category.[41] Realizing the fast-changing educational milieu, "an increasing number of countries see fostering creativity and critical thinking as the next educational challenge,"[42] observes Stephan Vincent Lancrin, senior analyst and project manager of the OECD and the Center for Educational Research and Innovation.

Increasingly, renowned sages and educators nowadays warn of the pitfalls in school education, which may strangle children's creativity. Schools, however prestigious, do not actively try to motivate students to look for and exhibit their creative potential. Stacia Garland, a national award-winning teacher who worked with unconventionally gifted children for sixteen years says,

> Creative children are more likely to demonstrate the following qualities: daydreaming, wanting to work alone, sharing bizarre thoughts and conflicting opinions, and on top of this, these children may not be motivated by

grades. None of these are qualities which are appreciated in the traditional classroom. (S. Garland, "Identifying the creative child in the classroom," Exquisite Minds [2012], available at: http://www.exquisite-minds.com/, accessed September 2, 2012)

Garland is a member of the Florida Association for the Gifted, Gifted Association of Missouri, and the National Association for Gifted Children. Experts today worry most that kids who are creative and have potential ingenuity almost with no exception are very likely to fall victim to the conservative educational and social setting, unfriendly to what they like to learn or do. They agree with the observation by Paulo Coelho, a Brazilian poet and writer: "Everybody has a creative potential and from the moment you can express this creative potential, you can start changing the world." One of the desirable realities of our times is that even if many traditional schools remain unchanged or are changing at a slow pace, an increasing number of young teens are fighting for their own rights to break the status quo.

3. Increasing numbers of innovative teens are putting outdated thinking to shame

Nowadays most parents are being told that an unparalleled number of teens are becoming miracle workers in various occupations. Nevertheless, many of them are still stuck in the conventional mode of thought. They still believe that diplomas from select expensive schools only can guarantee their kids' successful future. According to a *TIME* magazine report, the average annual cost of private high school was US$13,030 as of 2014.[43] An earlier report by *Huffington Post* said that a so-called independent school cost upward of US$136,000 for grades nine through twelve.[44] At high-status universities, nearly half of the student body comes from expensive secondary private schools. Even though the number of parents who question whether the money is worth it is increasing, most parents are still trapped in this outdated way of thinking, failing to embrace a new paradigm for themselves. Even in the most advanced, powerful country in the world, the United States, many parents who are struggling to get by, are willing to spend a big chunk of their meager income for their children's education at costly private schools.

George Vanisi living in Hawaii earns just US$16,000 a year as a mason contractor but must cover all of his seven-member family's expenses, including medical bills related to his wife's heart problems. And yet, Vanisi was until recently also spending money on private school tuition for two of his children. Although the school grants discounts for siblings and offers other forms of financial aid, even the cost of the discounted tuition was a crushing burden to him. So Vanisi worked out a deal with the school to pay his sons' tuition through in-kind masonry and other on-site contracting work. Many other parents in the United States too like to go to great lengths to keep their children out of public schools, which have long been blamed for their failure to offer quality education.[45] This is understandable since US public schools have been under criticism for their failure to encourage students to fulfill their creative potential.

Most parents living outside the United States remain much more retrogressive. The *Wall Street Journal* reported in June 2013, that "for Chinese parents obsessed with the success of their offspring, the latest must-have experience of their kids is a summer program at a prestigious Western school."[46] Few would dispute the usefulness of educational experiences in different regions, cultures, and school settings. Even so, the central question is that whether exposing Chinese children to Western schools would truly stimulate them to think creatively. Otherwise, their mere short-term experience in such a school is unlikely to lead them to the kind of success that will be relevant to upcoming challenges.

South Korean parents would also like to "go to the ends of the earth" just to get their children into prestigious colleges at home or abroad. They coerce their kids into doing anything possible to that end. This "educational tyranny" has stifled for many decades the creativity of potential whiz kids of South Korea.[47] In Japan, the so-called *Kyoiku mamas,* a Japanese pejorative term meaning "education mothers" have also been relentlessly driving their kids to study to get into prestigious universities at the cost of their children's physical and character development, emotional well-being, inborn curiosity and creativity, and other mental assets that education should normally cultivate.[48] Many Japanese children complain of school phobias and even kill themselves. These stories remind us of Einstein's famous observation: "Everybody is a genius. But if you judge a fish by its ability to climb a tree, it will live its whole life believing that it is stupid." Now is the time when Chinese, South Korean, and Japanese parents should rethink if they are coercing their children, who are "fishes," to climb trees. They also need to realize that today's children comprise perhaps the last generation who might follow their instructions deferentially and fag away in a lab to get the right answer.

Regardless of how such parents are thinking and what they are trying to do for their children, playing out before our eyes is an extremely unusual era in which young students are teaching their teachers, and distinguished PhD degree holders are learning expertise from imaginative autodidacts with no college education, who typically assume nonconformist attitudes as curious and creative teens. Most will bet dollars to donuts that all parents who fail to catch up with this accelerating trend prevailing across the globe will surely suffer a devastating failure in leading their kids to fulfilling their full potential. Luckily, the public awareness of this pitfall is obviously mounting as teenagers' remarkable success stories keep increasing.

Finally, parents of Generations X and Y may need to recollect, for example, the early life of one of their heroes, Kurt Cobain, the lead singer of the grunge band Nirvana, considered "the flagship band" of Generation X. Although the legendary musician died in 1994 at the age of twenty-seven, many of his fans and associates symbolically insist the forward-looking Cobain has never been dead because the cultural icon for them would never age, would always be relevant, and always be beautiful.[49] During his high school days, Cobain's father forced him to be a wrestler, which he despised, and his mother gave him a choice: find a job or be banished from home. His greatest success came through their 1991 major-label debut, *Nevermind,* and his band Nirvana entered the world of mainstream pop music. Nirvana has sold over twenty-five million albums in the United States alone and over seventy-five million worldwide.[50] In 1991, Cobain said that "I, or we as a band, never really spent time learning other people's songs. We're from the learn-as-you-play school. We're still in it."[51]

> Over the next decade and beyond, if we are to solve the most pressing issues of our time, we need to tap into the dynamism of youth movements and young social entrepreneurs, for they have the potential to disrupt inertia and be the most creative forces for social change. (B. Osotimehin, "Young people have the power to change the world," *Atlantic* [2012], available at: https://www. theatlantic.com/, accessed November 12, 2012)

In the last analysis, the roles, and achievements in all levels of society of innovative teens will be getting greater in the decades ahead.

C H A P T E R 5

Popullectuals

1. Why popullectuals are more valued in this century

On October 13, 2016, Bob Dylan won the Nobel Prize in literature for "having created new poetic expressions within the great American song tradition."[1] Dylan, a US songwriter and singer, has been influential in pop music and culture for more than five decades. His selection as a Nobel laureate is "perhaps the most radical choice in a history stretching back to 1901"[2] when the prize was first awarded. The Swedish Academy said: "Dylan has the status of an icon. His influence on contemporary music is profound."[3] Some might argue that the pop musician, a college dropout, is not an intellectual. This is a wrong notion. The Nobel laureate is not simply an intellectual but also a "popullectual," a compound I've has coined to mean "popular public intellectual," which is a phrase conventionally used in the academia, but the meanings are different. The difference will be elaborated later in this chapter.

Earlier, in May 2016, Angelina Jolie was appointed as a visiting professor at the London School of Economics (LSE), one of the most prestigious universities in the United Kingdom. The Hollywood's highest-paid actress said, "I am looking forward to teaching and to learning from the students as well as to sharing my own experiences of working alongside governments and the United Nations."[4] The actress, well known for her humanitarian efforts, continued that she hoped educational institutions elsewhere would follow suit. Reactions from the academia to her appointment as an LSE faculty member were not so friendly.

The *Independent* reported in May 2016, that criticisms of her appointment range from a total swindle and a desperate marketing ploy to academic snobbery at its worst. According to the British online newspaper, the British reactions were unfriendly to "the appointment of a world-renowned public speaker to a visiting role at an international higher education institution." The denunciations included "the cult of celebrity continues to flourish," "a mockery to those who value education," and "this sort of thing devalues academic completely."[5] Critics say that the cult of celebrity continues to flourish in the academia.

University professors are intellectuals. Therefore, it is reasonable for us to question in the first place whether the humanitarian actress is qualified to be an intellectual before agreeing or disagreeing with such criticisms. It is not easy to define what an intellectual is since its concept is too broad to define unambiguously. Authoritative dictionaries generally define the word as follows: "a person possessing a highly developed intellect." It may help our understanding of this concept if we were to look at some of its synonyms with assorted nuances. They include highbrow, learned person, academic, bookworm, people of letters, bluestocking, thinker, brain, scholar, genius, polymath, mastermind, rocket scientist, celebrity, and so on. These terms may indicate that a clear-cut, succinct definition of the intellectual is next to impossible. The central question is whether Bob Dylan and Angelina Jolie are tantamount to intellectuals qualified to be university faculty members.

If we remind ourselves that the educational milieu of today is very different from that of the past, it is not so difficult to understand why universities are trying to attract celebrities into their classrooms. They seem to be doing so not as a marketing maneuver but to meet the changing intellectual demand of the times. Nowadays more of us are rethinking the role of education or academics in our lives. The Academy Award–winning actress and political campaigner told the *Guardian*, "It is vital we broaden the discussion on how to advance women's rights and end impunity for crimes that disproportionately affect women, such as sexual violence in conflict."[6] This observation by the special envoy for the United Nations High Commissioner for Refugees (UNHCR) suggests that the contents of the topics she will discuss at LSE will be based on her unusual hands-on experiences. Angelina Jolie is expected to be an amusing professor at LSE after all.

US writer Robert C. Savage once said, "Most people are willing to pay more to be amused than to be educated." His observation has important implications for how to educate people especially when emerging problems are much more complex and difficult to handle. The *Guardian* reported already in May 2009 that according to a study conducted by Sandi Mann, senior lecturer in occupational psychology at the University of Central Lancashire in England, "almost 60% of students find at least half their lectures boring—with about 30% claiming to find most or all of their lectures boring."[7] If learning could be as amusing as watching funny movies, it would be able to access a far greater number of people. The UNHCR goodwill ambassador is qualified to be a popullectual, as she is expected to be an amusing, popular professor able to access a great number of people, inside and outside the university community.

The compound "popullectual" may sound strange to readers, but we already have a lot of popullectuals. Speaking of the academia alone, the number of "popular public intellectuals" in the customary sense have been increasing. The definition of a public intellectual varies. *Collins American English Dictionary* defines a public intellectual as "an intellectual, often a noted specialist in a particular field, who has become well-known to the public for their willingness to comment on current affairs." "Public intellectuals are deeply committed to the life of the mind and to its impact on the society at large," notes Daniel W. Drezner, a political economist at Tufts University.[8] If you have written a book that has caught wide attention and interest from the public, you qualify not only as a public intellectual but also as a popullectual, regardless of your educational background or current profession.

Alan P. Lightman, a US physicist and professor of humanities at MIT, wrote in 1999 for the MIT Communication Forum an article titled, "The role of the public intellectual." In the article, he venerated public intellectuals, especially popular ones. He classified public intellectuals into three categories: level 1, level 2, and level 3.[9] According to him, the larger their audiences, the higher their level. Public intellectuals of the highest level, level 3, like Noam Chomsky (who is "arguably the most important intellectual alive today," according to a *New York Times* article of 1979), Carl Sagan, E. O. Wilson, Steven Jay Gould, Susan Sontag, John Updike, and others have been elevated to a level where they can have much larger audiences than their colleagues who are at a lower public intellectuals category, who are, in other words, less popular.[10] Lightman tries to strengthen his argument by quoting the classic notion of the intellectual of Ralph Waldo Emerson, one of the most noted US writers of the nineteenth century. As Emerson sees it in his essay, "The American Scholar," delivered to the Phi Beta Kappa society as early as 1837,[11] "intellectuals should be able to appeal to the public and should not be bound by books." Through this transformation, general intellectuals can qualify as public intellectuals. Intellectuals' most important activity is action. "Inaction is cowardice," Emerson emphasizes.

Lightman remarks that a public intellectual is often

> trained in a particular discipline, such as linguistics, biology, history, economics, literary criticism, etc., and is on the faculty of a college or university. When such a person decides to write and speak to a larger audience than their professional colleagues do, he or she becomes a public intellectual. (A. Lightman, "The role of the public intellectual," MIT Communication Forum [1999])

His observation suggests that a public intellectual is more appealing to the public than a pure academic. Lightman continues,

> For many years, it was considered a taboo, a professional stigma, for scientists ("pure" academics) to spend any time at all in writing for the public. Such an activity was considered

> a waste of precious time, a soft activity, even a feminine
> activity. (A. Lightman, "The role of the public intellectual,"
> MIT Communication Forum [1999])

Lightman, the first professor at MIT to receive a joint appointment
in the sciences and the humanities, continues that the tide that looked
down upon public intellectuals

> began to change in the 1960s, with popular books written
> by top-notch intellectuals increasing, and in the last ten
> years, we have seen an explosion of popular books written
> by world-famous public intellectuals. (A. Lightman, "The
> role of the public intellectual," MIT Communication
> Forum [1999])

The conventional concept of an intellectual in which the proper
job of an intellectual was supposed to be "penetrating the secrets of
the physical world only and anything else was considered a waste of
time and dumbing down"[12] has changed since "the public intellectual
monitors the world, communicates ideas to the world, and writes about
what moves the world."[13] This remark by the author of the international
best seller, *Einstein's Dreams* amounts to emphasizing that because of
this contribution by the public intellectual, citizens have been able to
be better educated. They are thankful to the flood of popular books
written by public intellectuals, as the ideas and insights of these intellectuals deeply touch their minds and enable them to think about a lot
of current issues freely, not bound by old, nonfunctional, or limiting
rules and practices.

British sociologist Frank Furedi not only defends but also broad-
ens the meaning of public intellectuals as he says to the effect that
regardless of academic or professional fields of expertise, the public
intellectual addresses and responds to the problems of their society
and, as such, is expected to be impartial and to "rise above the partial
preoccupation of one's own profession and engage with the global issues
of truth, judgment, and taste of the time."[14] The late Edward W. Said,

who was also active as a renowned public intellectual in US politics, remarked in 1993 that the "true" public intellectual was always an outsider, living in self-imposed exile, and on the margins of society and its institutions and actively disturbing the status quo.[15] Accordinging to the Palestinian American literary theorist and former professor of Columbia University, an intellectual's mission in life is to advance human freedom and knowledge. By this view, Edward Said, as a political activist, suggests even a more political tone to the concept of the public intellectual. Scrutinizing his thought, there is obviously a rigid dichotomy between public intellectuals and pure academics. Often, world-class public intellectuals, including Nobel Prize winners, have depreciatively been dubbed by the so-called pure intellectuals as popularizers, gadflies, journalists, or generalists.

All the arguments these pundits have made for public intellectuals naturally lead us to believe that the public badly needs level 3, or the most popular, public intellectuals. However, what they need is not only popular public intellectuals conventionally supplied mostly by the academia on a limited basis. The present-day reality that education needs increasing numbers of popular intellectuals does in no way mean that education is heading in the wrong direction. Rather, it means that contemporary education requires more effectiveness, productivity, practicability, and public appeal. A report UNESCO released about a half century ago already noted that the importance of belief in democracy, conceived of as implying each man's right to realize his own potential and to share in the building of his own future, could not be overestimated. The keystone of democracy, so conceived, is education—"not only education that is accessible to all, but education whose aims and methods have been thought out afresh."[16]

Present-day society needs more urgently than ever a much greater number of popullectuals. The public demand for popullectuals is fast rising, as this era keeps producing knowledge and skills difficult for the public to grasp. For instance, *Oxford English Dictionary* is listing on the Internet hundreds of new words monthly. This explains at least in part why celebrities like Angelina Jolie, who seems unqualified to be a professor, are joining the academic world in the capacity of a popullectual—this is expected to increase—standing in the spotlight of intellectual circles.

As mentioned in the preceding chapters, teenagers and the public at large can gain access conveniently to the knowledge they need through the Internet, but for the ordinary and well educated to keep up with ongoing developments, new terminologies, concepts, and skills related to our bread-and-butter issues in this demanding era, the knowledge has to be made available in an easy-to-follow and exciting fashion. We are no longer living simply in a knowledge-based society, but in an advanced knowledge–based society.

2. Public demand for advancing knowledge is soaring

The advanced knowledge–based society of today has become far more complicated, varied, pluralistic, and refined than the knowledge-based society of yesterday, largely thanks to rapid advances in science and technology, and the resultant changes in businesses, workplaces, demographic profiles, and so on. Irrespective of how this societal transformation affects our present and future, we need to realize anew the fact that throughout history, without up-to-date knowledge and skills, we have never flourished. This historical truth of history will hit home more strongly, as it becomes increasingly harder to keep up with evolving knowledge. Consequently, we will need as many popullectuals as possible in the years to come.

Popullectuals are quite different from level 3 public intellectuals especially in that they are required to have not only expertise in any area but also special character traits, such as a sense of humor, wit, eloquence, passion for teaching, and the ability to run through the main points of a topic in a plain and succinct manner, which enable them to approach the public easily, pleasantly, and persuasively. Their narratives for their audiences should be composed of trouble-free terminologies, enticing examples, attention-grabbing episodes, and unique personal experiences not only in specific activities but also in tiding over various hardships, sufferings, and failures. Unlike popular public intellectuals from the academia, they don't necessarily need to be outstanding scholars specializing in certain disciplines.

There has been the common criticism of intellectuals that there is a scholarly elitism among them that turns most "common" folk off. The so-called pure academics have been under fire for their insensitivity to the immediate need for knowledge for the public. This fact is well described in the following self-introduction of the nonprofit educational website PopTech.

> Yet most efforts to create positive change remain locked in "silos of excellence": public health experts talk to other public health experts; designers talk to other designers; technologists talk to other technologists, and so on. ("About PopTech," PopTech [2017], available at: https:// poptech.org/, accessed January 30, 2017. The website says, "We're a global community of innovators, working together to expand the edge of change.")

The number of popullectuals available today is so limited that they alone cannot meet the rising demand of the public for advancing knowledge and skills. The speed of their supply is too slow, while the public demand for them is rising very fast. The growing diversification of contemporary knowledge and skills is also raising the bar for public education. As a result, popullectuals need to branch out to cope with this trend. At present, the topics public intellectuals deal with are limited. On top of that, much of their discourse is still hard for the public to understand. The supply shortage of popullectuals is aggravating the widening knowledge and skill divide. For instance, already in 2002, the *Guardian* reported, "There is clear evidence of a widening digital divide" in the United Kingdom. According to the report, 44 percent of British nonusers of the Internet, whether they are refuseniks, luddites, or Internet illiterate, said they did not have an interest in using the Internet. More surprisingly, as many as 20 percent of the nonusers said that they lacked confidence or the skills to try the Internet out.[17]

The digital divide as a form of knowledge divide has hurt the public good. Let's take a simple example to show this. Assume you are not good at using mobile apps. How would you feel if one of your friends happens to say to you, "Don't you know yet? Your smartphone can help you with a lot of out-there tasks. You don't need to take a trip to an expensive hospital lab to get a detailed look at your heart health because there's a smartphone app and device for that!" Skills for using mobile apps can help ordinary citizens, say, navigate today's difficult job market or manage their digital marketing life. In other words, smartphone apps can be an important tool for them to eke out even a meager living. Using a smartphone, we can also prevent drunken driving, figure out why our 'Check Engine' light is on, save on research time as we can do a web search while riding the subway or a bus, watch over-the-air TV, and so on.

Many people have become familiar with using a variety of mobile apps these days. However, many others are struggling with comprehending even the basic outlines of, say, the emerging top ten technologies a WEF report refers to.[18] They will certainly be terrified when they realize that they will be unable to keep up even a low standard of living without the knowledge and skills required to maintain it. In fact, the digital divide has become a significant factor that contributes to economic inequality.[19]

Of the emerging top ten technologies in the WEF report, let's take just one called blockchain, for instance. Most of us would like to be well informed of this new technology, having heard that being good at using this can enable us to gain various economic benefits, such as sharply reducing the cost of transferring money; making irreversible and final transactions to merchants; not being required to open a bank account; a lot of ways to make some quick extra money with bitcoin, the first decentralized digital currency or cryptocurrency, which some argue has become a global movement. Some say that it has taken fifty years to transition from paper money to plastic card, but it may take only fifteen to twenty years for cryptocurrency to be widely accepted. The number of people curious about this technology is naturally increasing. This explains why the number of video views on websites for explanations about blockchain is rising. The downside of it is also being told as the technology is yet in the experimental stage and is not cyberrisk-free, for example. Many experts are pessimistic about the future of this technology. They are not recommending that we invest in bitcoins since its value fluctuates quite a bit, and it's very likely that we may lose money.[20] The main point is that even computer geeks, let alone laymen, may come to the realization that many emerging technologies are too difficult to understand without the aid of digital gurus. For instance, although a breakthrough technology named "AI for Everybody" is available now, even giant companies like Amazon and Google still don't have enough people who know how to use cloud AI, which will bring "AI for Everybody" to a far broader audience.[21] Such companies are setting up consultancy services. After all, most people cannot be but hungry for popullectuals who would be able to explain new technologies in easy and interesting terms so that they could feel at home in using them.

Mobile devices will continue to increase in number and complexity, while as technology advances and markets become saturated rapidly, prices will lower. There is no end in sight to the growth of faster and better digital devices, according to the research firm Gartner.[22] We are very likely to see that many new rounds of computer revolutions only in a few years. Moore's Law that computing power doubles every eighteen months while costs halve has petered out. Experts say quantum computers will be a radical game changer since they will feature extreme sophistication, plus incredible speed, performing certain calculations far faster than any silicon-based computer. The superfast computer built on the bizarre principles of quantum physics is in fact coming. Scientists and engineers have already built basic quantum computers that can perform certain calculations. When they finally get here—perhaps much sooner than expected—as the personal computer did several decades ago, they are going to change everything, according to an April 2015 *Business Insider* report.[23]

The nature of the digital divide has changed over time. Now, it is not only about our average computer literacy or our economic capacity—whether we can afford a digital device—but also about our ability and willingness to acquire up-to-the-minute knowledge and skills that our state-of-the-art-based society is constantly asking us to digest for our own survival amid constant economic and social changes. However, the education needed for this to take place has yet to come this way, although most people desire to upgrade their skills and knowledge levels and to do so with ease.

It is unclear why Nobel Prize–winning British physicist Peter Higgs (born in 1929) doesn't own a mobile phone. He didn't know he won the Nobel Prize in 2013 because he didn't use a cell phone. He found out he became a Nobel laureate when a woman on the street congratulated him. The celebrated scientist may find it unnecessary or bothersome to carry a cell phone with him, given his advanced age. Warren Buffet (born in 1930), the fourth richest person in the world (as of 2017),[24] doesn't own a mobile phone either. Let us assume the renowned philanthropist and entrepreneur, known for his unusual frugality, may prefer using his money for charity or business purposes rather than spending it on a cell phone. Let us also assume that Higgs and Buffet don't use a mobile phone because they don't know how to use iPhone apps. If this were ever the case, they would need popullectuals who could teach them how to use them. It is certain that it is more in their interest to use a smartphone when carrying out scientific studies, business management, charitable activities, and so on than not to do so. Also, since the shift from an aging society to an aged society is happening fast in many parts of the world, it is vital to bridge the digital divide between younger and older people.

In the past too, it was not easy for us to update our knowledge and skills in a timely fashion even if it was directly related to our earning a living. Nonetheless, this problem might have been ignored even up to the late twentieth century. However, since the onset of this century, we have begun to see an astonishing flood of new information and knowledge. Wikipedia alone carried over 5.5 million articles written in English only as of the end of 2017. It continues to add articles about a variety of new inventions, developments, controversies, and others. It also continues to revise and update the contents of the articles, although it has yet to be considered a reliable source for academic writing or research.[25] Many of the articles deal with a lot of new vocabularies and concepts, strange even to the experts concerned, not to speak of general readers.

The years to come will keep raising the bar even higher and faster for us, compelling us to update our knowledge and skills so that we can meet the educational demand of the times. Unless we, even when well educated in the conventional sense, get familiar with present-day knowledge, we will be at the risk of not being recognized as a truly educated personality. For example, we will have to use state-of-the-art devices and their apps very different from those that we are using today when technological breakthroughs, such as quantum computing (to be further discussed in chapter 6) or blockchain, arrive in earnest, bringing profound changes to our lives.[26]

The continuing progress in ICT, biotechnology (including genetic testing and editing), nanotechnology, health technologies, labor market–disrupting technologies (notably robotics, automation, AI and AI-based software solutions), and so on is creating new concepts, terminologies, and jargons that even many first-rate pundits will have trouble understanding them, if they are not used in the domains of their expertise. University professors and even retired university presidents are learning online what they want to learn to keep up. "Student teachers" is an expression prevalent in this advanced knowledge–based society.[27] Like Wikipedia, Webopedia—an online tech dictionary for IT professionals, educators, and students—continues to add new vocabularies almost on a daily basis, even if it says it tries to avoid the use of heavy jargon whenever possible so that the site can be better accessible to general readers.[28]

Apart from terminologies related to new technologies, it will certainly be impossible for anyone to be well versed in a significant part, let alone all, of the new vocabularies and concepts used in modern-day economics, business, education, lifestyles, arts, and so forth, whatever educational background we may have. It would also be fair to say that we don't necessarily need to be well informed of a sizable part of them either. Even so, we will have to keep updating at least the knowledge related to our occupational activities or professional specialties more aggressively and quickly in the days ahead. Since everybody must live with continuing revolutionary changes, the following advice from Ellen Bennett, founder of Hedley & Bennett, will be relevant not only to aspiring entrepreneurs but also to all of us: "The path in front of you is full of bumps, twists and turns. Embrace the bumps in the road. They are the road."[29] This prospect naturally brings up the key question of how to produce popullectuals in a number enough to meet our demand for advancing knowledge.

3. Where is the pool of popullectuals?

Although intellectuals today are more obliged to educate the public than they were yesterday, it is certainly next to impossible to produce many popullectuals in a short period as if they are manufactured goods. The supply shortage of popullectuals is bound to worsen with time due to the huge time lag between fast advances in knowledge and skills and the slow supply of popullectuals. More than ten years will be required to produce even a teen popullectual. In the academia, too, it normally takes a lot of time to produce popular public intellectuals because they are the best educated of the best educated, as Lightman suggests. The long gestation period of producing popullectuals cannot but offer grim prospects for their speedy supply.

As indicated above, the fact that areas of specialty are expanding also complicates this issue further. Some people may want to learn, say, the basics of web design, investing, and personal finance, but it is difficult for them to find proper popullectuals who might meet their educational needs. Personality features, such as the ability to use humor, are among the major factors causing their supply inelasticity. As to the value of humor, Jamie Masada, a US businessman and comedian, says, "Making someone laugh is the greatest power any human being can have!"[30] New York City–based behavioral counselor Anna Wilson advises, "Talking about your issues with humor will not only make you more pleasant to be around, but it will help you cultivate a sense of positivity when you're feeling crappiest."[31] Psychological studies offer different perspectives on whether these personality characteristics are inborn or acquired.[32] Some psychologists, such as Peter McGraw and Joel Warner, note that people think comedians are a kind of screwed-up people but that they have developed a sense of humor to cope with problems.[33] Quite a few psychologists have suggested the notion that comics have developed their humor to deal with the challenges they have faced.[34] This may mean that like comics, popullectuals are not inborn with their traits but acquire them: they develop a sense of humor over a long period of time, dealing with challenges.

Many specialists in education also suggest that self-taught celebrities are generally entitled to be popullectuals since the process of self-schooling is difficult. They point out that most successful autodidacts have the skills to teach easily and effectively the subjects that average learners and beginners find hard to study because they teach based on their own trying experiences, not based on the controversial teaching methods that many schools ask teachers to imitate.[35] In other words, the self-taught can put themselves in the learners' place and explain a problem well. For example, when they find learners do not understand something they teach, they can explain it in many different ways until they understand it. They know where the sticking points are and how to overcome them.[36]

Whether all the traits of the popullectual are innate or learned, intellectuals who have popullectual traits are always scarce. In 1936, the economist Keynes turned the formulation of Say's law that says, "Supply creates its own demand" on its head and stated instead, "Demand creates its own supply." Will the soaring demand for popullectuals create its own supply? The answer is, sadly, no, given the causes behind their supply shortage, such as a long gestation period. Nevertheless, the prospects for the future supply of popullectuals may not be so grim. Even though it seems improbable to find quick solutions to the supply shortage problem, we are likely to see an increasing pool of popullectuals in the decades to come for the following reasons.

First, the conventional conception of an intellectual is changing in the academia. The obvious derision by pure academics of even first-rate public intellectuals, let alone celebrity instructors from outside the academia, such as Angelina Jolie, finds its roots in the rigid, conventional conception of the intellectual or the role of the intellectual in public education. However, "the cult of celebrity operates within academia itself."[37] Increasing nowadays is the number of pure academics who recognize the significant role of celebrities in education. At the same time, celebrity role models who feel that they have special responsibility to show their fans how to change their life and the world are increasing and coming into the social spotlight.[38]

With traditional school education facing mounting challenges, important changes are taking place in the attitudes of pure academics toward "outsider" intellectuals, a group that comprises hands-on experience-based inventors; businessmen; entertainers; athletes; and social, political, environmental, and judicial activists. In other words, the shift in which mounting weight is being placed on popullectuals in the intellectual community is speeding up. Richard Posner, an eminent US jurist and prolific writer of nearly forty books, once suggested that the value of intellectuals can be determined in the marketplace like commodity prices that fluctuates according to how favorably the public responds to them over time, largely through communications media.[39] What the pragmatist writer and judge, who is well known for his analysis of former US president Bill Clinton's affair with Monica Lewinsky, implies is obvious: intellectuals should be able to communicate with their audiences inspiringly and captivatingly to live to tell the tale and to compete with their peers.

In fact, a lot of celebrities have been invited by renowned universities as key speakers at their commencements. From the world of comedy alone, Jim Carrey, Mindy Kaling, Andy Samberg, Ed Helms, Amy Poehler, Seth MacFarlane, Jon Stewart, Stephen Colbert, Will Ferrell, Charlie Day, and others have been invited, and all of them invariably delivered remarkably insightful, interesting commencement speeches in easy terms that have often impressed audiences far more deeply than those presented by pure academics or even level 3 public intellectuals. In other words, they are qualified as top-level popullectuals. At Harvard University alone, the commencement day speakers of this century (2001–17) were composed of five celebrities in media, four politicians, three business tycoons, two secretaries for the US federal government, one best-selling author, one jurist, and one diplomat—some of them belong to more than just one category, like author and media personality. All of them are popullectuals, although they are from outside the academia, and because they are all popular and have the great art of delivering their experience-based messages in a plain and interesting fashion, they have a big intellectual impact on their audiences.

Our traditional perception of intellectuals' characteristics and qualifications has restricted the potential pool of popullectuals. The public today is wondering more than ever if the role of customarily defined intellectuals in awakening society is expanding enough to meet public demand.[40] Such public skepticism will only be strengthened in the years ahead. For instance, many ordinary citizens question how many Nobel Prize–winning economists could predict approaching financial crises or global recessions,[41] even though they appreciate all the amazing scientific and technological advances the academia has achieved.

Second, more people are building up their self-confidence that they themselves can become popullectuals even without college degrees. Their self-assurance is being strengthened since they are witnessing such personalities increasing. At the same time, the number of people who don't take most intellectuals with advanced college degrees or university professors as special people with exceptional talent, knowledge, or skills is growing.[42] Concerned members of the public and doers have become defiant to the traditional concept of an intellectual because they think they themselves can also play a critical part in enlightening ordinary citizens, often better than academics sitting in ivory towers. As a result, the potential pool of popullectuals is expanding.

The number of people who can be recognized as popullectuals for their remarkable specialty and forward-looking capacity is growing fast nowadays. With this trend, celebrities with special talents and unusual experiences, including artists, media personalities, generalists, pop musicians, app developers, engineers, and so on have been able to join the ranks of popullectuals. At the same time, cooks, barbers, adventurers, farmers, soldiers of various ranks, carpenters, hotel service personnel, and many others engaged in ordinary occupations are potentially eligible to become popullectuals like celebrities. It is true that such potential popullectuals by and large prefer the status quo and don't even dream of climbing the social ladder to become real popullectuals. However, if they change their traditional conception of the intellectual and are determined enough to break the existing state of affairs, many of them can join the ranks of popullectuals.

Jamie Oliver nicknamed "Naked Chef," a US chef and food activist, appeared in a TED talk in February 2010 and excited the audience.[43] He has made himself a famous media celebrity and a popullectual as a result. During the talk, he emphasized the importance of people's lifestyles and the usual dietary pattern to stay healthy based on his hands-on experience and independent study. We are also seeing an increasing number of experienced workers and professionals from nonacademic occupations becoming popular professors of vocational colleges and institutions—that is, popullectuals, who often appear in mass media and inform their audiences of practical expert skills in a fascinating manner.

Third, the diversifying digital media is contributing to increasing popullectuals. In the past, popular public intellectuals were mostly popular authors for print media, as Lightman notes. However, present-day popullectuals do not necessarily need to be popular writers. The number of people who turn into overnight social media celebrities is rising.[44] The celebrities who social media not only discover but also produce are increasing in number, and they are becoming popullectuals.[45] Also, some intellectuals who are not necessarily good at writing can also deliver illuminating ideas and comments on various issues to the public through a variety of media, and they too can become popullectuals. This reminds us of the well-known equation—"The medium is the message"—coined by Marshall McLuhan.[46] The Canadian public intellectual's observation here means a communication medium embeds itself in the message, creating a synergetic relationship by which the medium influences how the message is understood.

The educational media is also increasing rapidly and enables many people in many parts of the world to share one popullectual online anytime they want. MIT Video (containing more than twelve thousand videos), YouTube EDU, TED, PopTech, WGBH-TV, and a long list of other educational websites and nonprofit television stations are available to many people. Depending upon our educational level and field of interest, we can choose for free a considerable number of popullectuals we need and help keep our knowledge and skills up to date. These media can stimulate us to become a popullectual ourselves, depending upon our propensity to talk about our specialty for the public.

TED alone has provided since its foundation in 1984 more than twenty-six hundred exciting and thought-provoking talks (as of the end of 2017) in more than one hundred languages, which cover a wide range of topics. Although all the talks have not always been delivered by popullectuals, by early 2013, TED talks had already been watched over one billion times worldwide. One of the most important features of TED talks seems to be that the talks are mostly delivered in brief (about twenty minutes or so at most) in a relatively easy-to-understand and pleasing fashion, even though many of them are delivered by the world's leading thinkers and doers whose talks have often been expected to be lengthy, difficult to understand, and boring.

Also, with the changing educational setting, the competition in the intellectual market between educational institutions looking for popullectuals will become increasingly intense. With this development, popullectuals will be placed higher in the hierarchy of the educational world, as they will enjoy more honor, prestige, and material reward than general experts. Business schools, for example, are becoming increasingly interested in finding instructors who can deliver experience-based, attention-grabbing lectures for their students, such as popular rags-to-riches business people, who are, as popullectuals, able to appeal to their audiences more powerfully than pure academics without practical business experience. In fact, the number of such personalities invited by business schools for special lectures has been rising over the last ten years or so.[47]

Fourth, witnessing this trend, intellectuals will certainly make extra efforts to train or transform themselves into popullectuals. Also, the current tenure systems adopted by many universities and colleges in the United States, Canada, and other countries are likely to radically change. Tenure means a contractual right of a teacher or professor to enjoy permanent employment. At present, tenure at many universities depends mainly on a professor's research publications and research grants. Poor performance in these two criteria result in a professor's failure to earn tenure at such universities. Looking ahead, how well-received or popular a professor's lectures have been not only in the classroom but also outside the campus will be one of the major criteria that heavily count toward the eligibility for tenure.

In fact, quite a few professors and teachers have been making efforts for a long time to become popullectuals. Justin J. Lehmiller, a self-taught professor of psychological sciences at Purdue University, has received teaching awards and consistently achieved high evaluations of his teaching from students. He has learned how to teach students in a captivating manner through his own experiences, which he says have been full of difficulties and pains. One of his secrets for good teaching has been to collect as much feedback as possible from students about his teaching. This can also be interpreted as reflecting his strenuous effort to put himself in his students' shoes[48]—that is, to become a popullectual. Jennifer Roig-Francolí, a faculty member at the University of Cincinnati College–Conservatory of Music, has been making similar efforts over a long period of time to be a popular teacher. The passion of the internationally recognized musician and professor is to inspire and teach musicians how to free themselves from pain, tension, and anxiety, so they can enjoy what they want to pursue with ease and interest. She is doing her best nowadays to be the best teacher and emphasizes that teachers need to assume complete responsibility for themselves by mustering up the courage, desire, and self-discipline to be a good and popular instructor.[49]

However, educational institutions should be careful of the trap of making teachers popular in the short run by forcing them to take courses in so-called teaching methods, as mentioned previously. For example, the Seoul National University (SNU), the most competitive school in South Korea, announced in September 2016 that it had made it mandatory that SNU professors who would receive poor evaluations of their classroom lectures from their students would be obliged to take a few lectures on teaching methods. Critics reacted saying that the idea of professors compulsorily attending such lectures was bureaucratic and myopic. It won't help howsoever since good teaching never does come from learning in a short time or by imitating any imported teaching method but from teachers' voluntary and long-term efforts that match the individual teacher's character, inspiration, and aspiration. Such efforts also require a teacher's enduring practice and learning through trial and error. A professor at SNU fumed over the school policy, saying that one could never be a good pianist by only reading a book on how to become a good pianist. In fact, schools have introduced a variety of teaching techniques developed outside and coerced their instructors to learn them by attending a couple of lectures on teaching methods, which, however, have proved futile, even counterproductive.[50] Latest surveys show that replacing their existing teaching methods with imported ones has failed to achieve the intended goal to improve students' academic performances.[51] The key reason for this failure can be explained as follows: if one were a popullectual, he or she would be an instructor who had already mastered all kinds of efficient teaching skills and schemes, not as a theorist but as a doer.

Finally, a growing number of schools are likely to offer courses about how to become a popullectual outright. Most importantly perhaps, K–12 schools should offer such courses, as it is most productive to educate and train future popullectuals while students are young; they usually learn many skills faster than adults. In addition, private academies and institutes specializing in training prospective popullectuals are likely to flourish in the years to come.

Theoretically, the nonprofit Public Broadcasting Service (PBS) in the United States whose service has more than 350-member television stations—many owned by educational institutions—may also help alleviate the lack of supply on a long-term basis if it ever starts to provide for programs to train potential popullectuals at early ages. Regarding this prospect, an article titled "What really makes a good teacher?" seems relevant. The article reported in the *Telegraph* in January 2015 highlights that a good teacher should be capable of "acting" in the classroom, as the acting ability helps teaching greatly.[52] For the present, educational institutions should be more aggressive in recruiting popullectuals and unearthing hidden popullectuals. Fortunately, world-famous institutions like LSE that are interested in recruiting popullectuals are increasing.

Educational institutions, formal or informal, that aim to produce popullectuals will have to get over other problems and dilemmas that come in the way of achieving their goals, though. One of the key dilemmas is that, ideally, the teachers themselves of such institutions should be able to deliver lessons that should be easily communicated to and be able to fascinate their students. For example, teachers of humor may teach what humor is, what social functions it serves, what would be considered humorous, and so on, but most of them may not be good humorists. Considering this, a growing number of educational institutions are likely to emerge to produce "popullectual" teachers. Considering that education is the key to national development,[53] as Borge Brende, former minister of foreign affairs of Norway, emphasizes, forward-looking governments of the world are likely to develop long-term planning to ensure enough supply of popullectuals.

Some may wonder if advances in robotics and AI could put an end to the problem of the popullectuals' supply inelasticity someday in the future. The prospect of robots replacing professionals has already been suggested in chapter 3. In fact, artificially intelligent robot teachers or teaching assistants are being used at some schools, although they are yet at a primitive stage.[54] Even if they continue to develop and continue to be used as aiding tools for teaching, it will probably take an unknown amount of time or might be impossible forever for robots to come close to being a match for human popullectuals. Popullectuals differ from robots since they appeal to humans by portraying a variety of human traits, such as emotion, passion, feeling, courage, humor, and so on, that robots as machines fundamentally lack.[55] Even if robots could read a human mind someday,[56] they would never be able to replace humans at emotional and spiritual dimensions. In sum, the possibility that robots could work like human popullectuals cannot be totally ruled out, but it remains very slight. Also, this century full of "dangerous" technologies[57] requires more intensive moral education to produce virtuous human leaders of society. Our reasonable expectation should be that evolving technologies will never ever be able to give the answers to all these concerns.[58]

So far, some possible ways of securing an expanded supply of popullectuals and the hurdles that go with them have been suggested. The central point here is that we can realistically expect the supply of popullectuals to fall short of the demand for an unknown period still to come. To recap, it is simply too demanding and time consuming to produce a popullectual. For the moment, we may only conclude that this innovative century is taking us in an inevitable direction in which we cannot but make every possible effort to alleviate the popullectual supply scarcity. The following simple remark by Rita F. Pierson, a US professional educator, has important implications for the future of education: "Kids don't learn from people they don't like."[59]

4. The future of "pure" academics

Given the rising importance of popullectuals for public education, what future is ahead for pure academics? In a word, the role of pure academics in education and social progress will remain intact as far as they can continue to open new frontiers in the sciences and humanities. We have no reason whatsoever to dismiss or downgrade pure intellectuals who cannot but communicate mostly with their peers in the academia in professional terminologies and jargons that ordinary folks can hardly understand. Top-notch experts don't necessarily need to make extra efforts to be popular among the public either.

It is needless to say that rocket scientists are playing crucial roles in making societal progress. It is recognized that pure academics opening new frontiers of knowledge have the right and even duty to transmit information relating to their specialties and research findings to their colleagues who are also experts. For example, however closely genome mapping or the human cell atlas project to map all thirty-five trillion cells in our bodies may be related to our life and whatever efforts a specialist in genetics may make to try to explain this relationship to laypeople, there will always be huge obstacles standing in the way of their comprehension of, say, even a graphic representation of the locations of genes.

The claim that today's society faces an increasing demand for popullectuals is one thing, and the argument that pure academics are supposed to perform their business as usual is quite another. Also, we need to recall that many Level 3 public intellectuals were originally trained as pure academics in schools, research organizations, and so on, before they became popular. In that capacity, they are performing the dual role of public intellectuals and pure academics, contributing to building up scientific knowledge on one hand and to enlightening the public on the other. Those intellectuals, whether they are performing the single role as pure academics or the dual role as public intellectuals, will continue to command respect from the public, as they will keep making advances in science and technology.

It is also noteworthy that quite a few public intellectuals have defended pure academics, contending that the reason they hold fast to the stubborn pedantry or detachment from the public is at least in part because of their innately limited ability to access the public. Samuel P. Huntington, the late renowned political scientist at Harvard University and author of the well-known book, *The Clash of Civilizations and the Remaking of World Order*, was an outstanding pundit but a slow, dull speaker. In the preface of another seminal book he wrote, *American Politics: The Promise of Disharmony*, he confided that he almost failed in oral defense of his PhD thesis.[60] It is simply silly to expect all intellectuals to be popullectuals. Not only intellectuals but also all human beings have their own unique innate character.

An article titled "Scientists talk privately about creating a synthetic human genome" appeared in the *New York Times* in May 2016.[61] The scientists are said to be "contemplating the fabrication of a human genome," meaning they would use chemicals to manufacture all the DNA contained in human chromosomes.[62] Many general readers will find it hard to understand even the ABCs of the project initially called Human Genome Synthesis Project 2 (HGP2), with HGP referring to the Human Genome Project. George Church, professor of genetics at Harvard Medical School and professor of health sciences and technology at both Harvard and MIT, is an organizer of the proposed project. Professor Church talked about DNA in a TED talk in 2010, but it is questionable how many viewers would have understood his explanation of DNA properly.

Church's TED talk about DNA collected about 7,000 views, compared with 42,386,905 views of the talk delivered by Sir Robinson—who is absolutely a fantastic popullectual—as of December 2016. The number of the views of Robinson's talk was about six thousand times more than that of Church's. It would be of course nonsense if anybody ever thought that the vast difference in the number of views had something to do with the importance of the topic. Any attempt to draw a dichotomy between public intellectuals and pure academics according to the level of their popularity would not be well advised.

For now, we may just say that whatever hurdles there may be in the way of the swelling demand for popullectuals and however serious the imbalance between their supply and demand will get in the future, an undisputed fact is that we will not only need more popullectuals but also should be able to increase their number in the years ahead.

Chapter 6

Hutechciety

1. From science fiction to science fact

Whichever way one chooses to characterize contemporary society, we are living in hutechciety—a compound I've coined with three words—"human," "technology," and "society"—to explain how a changing human-technology relationship is impacting humans as a society at national and global levels. The continuous emergence of cutting-edge technologies and their applications, including AI-based machines, is transforming human-machine interaction at a dazzling pace. As human-technology divide is narrowing, tension between technology and its creator, humanity, is mounting. Humans are now ambivalent about technology. They are enjoying the benefits of advancing technologies on one hand but are at a loss about what to do with their negative impacts on their lives on the other.

Take the 2018 PyeongChang Winter Olympics held in South Korea, for example. The Olympic Games highlighted another set of new innovative ICT systems to support their successful hosting. The games offered, for instance, an AI technology–based automatic translation app called Genie Talk in real time between Korean and other languages, including English, Chinese, Japanese, German, French, Spanish, Russian, and Arabic, for the convenience of athletes and visitors to the games.[1] However, university students who are specializing in translating foreign languages are deeply worrying that a jobless future is waiting for them. In fact, the "Babel-Fish Earbuds" technology is already available. A US$159 (as of early 2018) pair of earbuds called Pixel Buds developed by Google work with its Pixel smartphones and the Google Translate app to produce practically real-time translation.[2] Many terrified students are opting to change their majors and comforting themselves with the saying, "It's never too late to learn." But even then, they despair, finding that technology is adversely affecting other job-related disciplines.

Various machines, such as computers and smartphones, have become an essential component in fulfilling everyday tasks in our professional and personal lives. However, people nowadays seem to think more of the negative impacts of advances in technology and overlook their advantages. They think of the negative effects largely in two broad categories. One involves criminal acts, such as online banking fraud and the spread of misinformation. The other is legal but makes people feel powerless, even useless—for example, job loss due to automation.

To better understand human-technology linkage and the positive and negative impacts of this linkage, it is necessary to first look at how technology has evolved. Let us look back at some milestone events demonstrating advances in technology and their impacts on conventional human life. AlphaGo—the first computer Go program developed by Google DeepMind in London to play the board game Go—recorded a milestone in AI evolution. AlphaGo beat and terrified the world's best human Go players in 2016 and 2017 and retired shortly thereafter. We have a history of the computer beating human players or getting beaten in chess. Go is by far the most complicated mental sport, far more complex than chess. Go was thus regarded as a hard problem in machine learning that was expected to be out of reach for the technology of the time. Nonetheless, the victory of AlphaGo surprised the world. AlphaGo used AI exhibited by highly technical and specialized machines or software capable of intelligent behavior like humans.

The AlphaGo's win over human intelligence needs to be examined in the larger context of the changing relationship between humans and technology. After the overwhelming victory of AlphaGo's AI over human intelligence, AlphaGos played against each other as if they were human players, demonstrating the marvelous skills required to win at this game. Now, the world's top-notch players are trying to achieve the skill level the AlphaGos exhibited, which are way beyond imagination. Humans created AlphaGo, but the creature defeated its creator. This tends to give further credence to the idea that evolving technologies can and will overwhelm their creators in positive and negative ways. Naturally, we would wish to know what technologies are emerging that can do this. Such technologies are simply too many to mention but illustrate a few of them will help us understand their power and impact on our life.

Every year since 2001 the *MIT Technology Review* (MTR) has picked what it calls "10 breakthrough technologies" reshaping our lives. The ten it picked in 2018 were (1) 3D metal printing, (2) artificial embryos, (3) sensing city, (4) AI for everybody, (5) dueling neural networks, (6) Babel-Fish Earbuds, (7) zero-carbon natural gas, (8) perfect online privacy, (9) genetic fortune telling, and (10) materials' quantum leap.[3] The ten breakthrough technologies selected by MTR in 2017 were (1) reversing paralysis, (2) self-driving trucks, (3) paying with your face, (4) practical quantum computers, (5) The 360-degree selfie, (6) hot solar cells, (7) gene therapy 2.0, (8) cell atlas, (9) botnets of things, and (10) reinforcement learning.[4] In 2019, Bill Gates curated MTR's "10 breakthrough technologies."

Likewise, in September 2018, the WEF selected top 10 emerging technologies. They were (1) augmented reality, (2) personalized medicine, (3) AI-led molecular design, (4) more capable digital helpers, (5) implantable drug-making cells, (6) gene drive, (7) algorithms for quantum computers, (8) plasmonic materials, (9) lab-grown meat, and (10) electroceuticals.[5] In June 2017 the WEF in collaboration with *Scientific American* published a report that listed top ten emerging technologies. They were (1) liquid biopsies, (2) harvesting clean water from air, (3) deep learning for visual tasks, (4) liquid fuels from sunshine, (5) human cell atlas, (6) precision farming, (7) affordable catalysts for green vehicles, (8) genomic vaccines, (9) sustainable design of communities, and (10) quantum computing.[6] The WEF's top ten in 2016 were (1) nanosensors and the Internet of nanothings, (2) next-generation batteries, (3) block-chain supporting bitcoin, (4) 2D materials, (5) autonomous vehicles, (6) organs-on-chips, (7) perovskite solar cells, (8) open AI ecosystem, (9) optogenetics, and (10) systems metabolic engineering.[7] A fast glance at these uncanny breakthroughs alone will help us understand how fast new technologies are emerging. Some, if not all, of the technologies MTR and the WEF selected are briefly touched upon here and other chapters.

Breakthrough technologies will continue to be predicted year after year beyond 2020. To general readers, the emerging technologies will look curious and important. But they cannot and need not be familiar with all of them. They can, however, understand with ease at least five major aspects of these enigmatic technologies. First, these new technologies will continue to change our lives. Second, many of these technologies are being built on their preceding cohorts and are inter-related. Third, evolving technologies are quickly putting to shame past technologies, such as AlphaGo's AI, which were considered amazing only a couple of years ago. Fourth, most so-called fictional technolo-gies are no longer fictional; they already exist. For example, artificial embryos are available now. This technology could enable mammals to be born without an egg at all.[8] Finally and most importantly perhaps, all the technologies are getting more closely connected with human life for better or for worse, as members of the WEF, *Scientific American*, and MTR note. The integration of technology into humans has been gaining striking momentum, especially in the last few decades.

Let's look at some interesting events that have happened in the process of this integration. On March 23, 1983, then US president Ronald Reagan announced the Strategic Defense Initiative (SDI), which is a defense system of lasers and missiles meant to intercept incoming intercontinental ballistic missiles. The SDI plan was quickly labeled "Star Wars," implying that it was science fiction and linked to Reagan's acting career. According to Frances FitzGerald, a US journalist and historian, this annoyed Reagan, but then assistant secretary of Defense Richard Perle told colleagues that he thought the name was not so bad. "Why not? It's a good movie. Besides, the good guys won," he added.[9] The ideas of President Reagan finally emerged as a reality.

In the movie world, science fiction (SF) films have been flourishing. For example, the first of the Star Wars sequel trilogy—*The Force Awakens*—that was released in December 2015, broke the opening weekend box office records in North America with US$248 million and totals of US$529 million worldwide, the largest opening ever. Whatever has happened in the film world, events like those the SF film series show are no longer fictitious. Many of the technologies portrayed by Star Wars have become real-life technologies. A major difference between modern military robotics and that of the Star Wars universe is that different robots are built and designed for different purposes, whether they are used for ground, maritime, aerial, or space warfare. However, they use analogous concepts. Soldiers and robots fight hand in hand against their enemies.

Just take, for example, the well-known Star Wars–like episode that took place on May 2, 2011. Shortly after 1:00 a.m. (Pakistan Standard Time), the United States Navy SEALs carried out a CIA-led maneuver code-named Operation Neptune Spear, and killed Osama bin Laden, the founder and head of the Islamist militant group al-Qaeda. The unmanned aerial vehicle (UAV) called RQ-170 drone contributed decisively to the success of the operation, although the Star Wars' weapon of choice, the lightsaber—the super-powered high frequency laser beam sword commonly recognized in pop culture—was not used in the operation. Although the Star Wars drones we see today are much more ingenious than the one the Navy SEALs used in 2011, they are still at a primitive stage. A solar-powered autonomous plane called "a flying saucer" and "a mechanical bird of prey" were just some of the drones of the first generation that went on show at an event held in May 2015 in Atlanta, Georgia. They showed what might be next for this mind-blowing industry. Although many of them have military purposes, they indicate how new technologies will help novel vehicles take to the sky for many other purposes.

Military UAVs are already being widely used to spy or launch missiles, while making rapid progress. Drones can also be used as research tools, delivery robots, high-tech toys, and so forth. Maybe you've seen one flying at your local park or caught some viral video footage of a drone swooping through a firework display.

> By 2030, UAVs could be in common use to monitor intrastate and interstate conflicts, enforce no-fly zones, or survey national borders. Low-cost UAVs with cameras and other types of sensors could support wide-area geo-prospecting, support precision farming, or inspect remote power lines. (*Global Trends 2030: Alternative Worlds*, National Intelligence Council [NIC] [2012], 92, available at: https://www.dni.gov/, accessed May 15, 2014)

The point is that rapidly changing human-technology interactions are relentlessly reshaping our society.

Humans have created and used technology to enhance their welfare for at least two hundred thousand years. Technology has served our safety, comfort, health, efficiency, entertainment, and many other necessities. Before long, an ordinary office worker named Tom will depend on his digital device to wake him up early in the morning before an app turns on the coffee pot in the kitchen for a caffeine fix that can be enjoyed in the comfort of a home kept at an ideal temperature by an Internet-connected thermostat designed to learn the occupant's preferences. Within the next few years, he will be able to unlock his doors with high-tech watches after being chauffeured home in robotic cars. Looking ahead to the next thirty years or so, sweeping changes will certainly happen in our life thanks to a wide breadth of astonishing state-of-the-art technologies, some of them emerging sooner than expected.

The history of technology has centered largely on the upside of it—that is, the benefits that the invention of tools and techniques has brought to humanity. However, whenever a new technology emerges in the days ahead, it will bring positives and negatives to our lives, reminding us, for example, that military technologies have been used to remove mischief-makers destructive to world peace, but at enormous human and property costs in many cases. The fact that technology is changing from being fictional to being factual is unsettling the conventional human-technology relationship—a reality that deserves a prime concern in any analysis of the impact of advances in technology on humans as a society.

2. Hutechciety is a double-edged sword

Technology is supposed to serve humanity, not the other way around. In other words, humans advocate for advanced technologies with the assumption that they will work as their faithful and efficient servants. However, the ongoing change in human-technology connection has created a dilemma for humans. For example, digital connectedness is prompting people to be less connected to each other. A trend like this will become more conspicuous in the years to come. People nowadays seem to be more concerned about the negatives of technology. On March 18, 2018, an uber self-driving car hit a pedestrian, who later died of her injuries, sending shock waves across the United States. The afore-mentioned dueling neural networks or generative adversarial networks may improve the safety of self-driving cars, but this technology has its own problems. As time passes, any discussion of technology will con-sider its upside and downside. Stephen Hawking spoke of AI. "There's a thin line between the technology helping and hindering us," he said at a technology conference in Lisbon in November 2017. He continued,

> Success in creating effective A.I. could be the biggest event in the history of our civilization, or the worst. We just don't know. We cannot know if we will be infinitely helped by A.I. or ignored by it and sidelined or conceivably destroyed by it. (P. Leskin, "A.I. could be the 'worst thing ever to happen to humanity,' Stephen Hawking says," Inverse [2017], available at: https://www.inverse.com/, accessed November 7, 2017)

Different research organizations use different classification systems for evolving technologies. However, the technologies they have paid special attention to for the last few years are generally the same. In the years 2012–13, the Alternative Energies and Atomic Energy Commission (CEA), a well-known French government–funded technological research organization, classified them into six categories: ICT, health care and biotechnologies, energies, materials, supercomputing, and system software.[10] The NIC categorized them in December 2012 into four arenas: ICT, automation/manufacturing technologies, resource technologies, and health technologies.[11] The similarity between such classifications have so far lasted, although the research focuses for evolving technologies have been more itemized over time. The NIC's 2017 report, for example, introduces synthetic biology, genome editing, AI, robotics and automation, ICT, and other technologies the agency mentioned previously.

The classification systems inform us of the major technologies we should scrutinize to understand in detail their positive and negative aspects. Computers, when linked together with billions of other electronic devices and household appliances through the Internet of things (IoT), will incredibly increase the complexity of the systems and raise the risks of massive breakdowns, either through an inadvertent glitch or a malicious attack.[12] Along with the IoT, studies and workshops about the Internet of everything, web of things, and web of everything have been increasing as they seek to understand how these technologies will negatively as well as positively impact our lives.[13]

"Advances at Google, Intel, and several research groups indicate that computers with previously unimaginable power are finally within reach,"[14] according to Russ Juskalian, a contributor to MTR. If practical quantum computers are available in a few years as experts predict, the double-edged character of hutechciety will become more salient. Computers are performing legal discoveries; winning game shows; deciding which products to stock on shelves; providing car-to-car communication, which is a simple wireless technology that promises to make driving safer, to make medical diagnoses; you name it.[15] However, quantum computers can pose a much more serious threat to the security of our data. It has been quite some time since experts began asking, "So what can be done to keep it safe?"[16] A new technology called Magic Leap joined the list of the recent breakthroughs in 2015. Magic Leap is a US startup company working on a head-mounted virtual retinal display that superimposes 3D computer-generated imagery over real-world objects, by projecting a digital light field into the user's eye. All these advancing computing technologies come down to the broad arena called ICT[17] and are vulnerable to cyberattacks.

Advances in robotics and AI are posing a serious threat to ordinary workers' basic needs of life. About 38 percent of jobs in the United States are at high risk of being replaced by robots and AI over the next fifteen years, according to a 2017 PwC report.[18] Such dangers are increasing in many other economies. In the United Kingdom, 30 percent of jobs are at the same risk. The same problem applies to 21 percent of the jobs in Japan. The US and UK labor markets are more vulnerable to such risks than the Japanese market, as they are dominated by service jobs, and roughly the same share of workers is employed in key sectors, including finance, transportation, education, manufacturing and food services, which can more easily substituted by AI and robots.[19] A WEF report, "The future of jobs," says that in the next five years, fifteen developed and emerging economies—Australia, Brazil, China, France, Germany, India, Italy, Japan, Mexico, South Africa, Turkey, the United Kingdom, the United States, the Association of Southeast Asian Nations, and the Gulf Cooperation Council—will see a net loss of over five million jobs, thanks to emerging technologies.[20] "In terms of overall impact, the nature of change over the next five years is such that as many as 7.1 million jobs could be lost."[21]

While smart cities seek to improve the efficiency and sustainability of urban spaces while reducing costs and resource consumption by implementing ICT technologies, the high level of big data collection and analytics in smart cities enable governments to maximize effective surveillance of their citizens (we will talk more about this in this and the next chapter). Citizens living in smart cities today, including Santa Cruz (a county seat in California), Barcelona, Amsterdam, and Stockholm, can be located at any time without their knowledge—thus affording the law enforcement an omnipresent position.

Many consider cloud computing as one of the most important technologies in decades, which emerged in a process called "democratization of information technology."[22] To put it simply, cloud computing is a method employed to allow services used in everyday practice to be moved onto the Internet rather than be stored on a local computer. Some experts caution, though, that the new digital frontier means that we're coming to the end of our current digital paradigm and on the brink of a new digital paradigm in which the capabilities of technology will outstrip our own.

We have entered the big data era, although it is expected that it will take a few years more before ordinary people keenly feel its real impact on their day-to-day life. Although none of the following measurements is strict, data come in three sizes—small, medium, and big. Big data are measurements of data that have grown so large that normal databases are unable to contain and work with them. Big data need special machines, much larger and more complex than those used for ordinary databases. Mammoth organizations, such as governments, defense and intelligence agencies, and scientific establishments, usually use these types of data, but some very large websites also contain such large amounts of information.[23] A database that we are conventionally familiar with can handle medium-sized data at most. No database, no matter how large it is, can work with big data. Big data is often linked or compared to cloud computing. The two are "proving to be the ideal combination," according to analysts, "to provide a cost effective and scalable infrastructure to support big data and business analytics."[24] In the big data era, process power and data storage are becoming almost free; networks and the cloud will provide global access and pervasive services.

"From healthcare, to sports, to the way one elects a president, big data will make big changes to the way we live our lives," the US-based Channel Company says.[25] Our ability to manage and analyze the massive amounts of data spawned by new data sources like social media is sparking an "extraordinary knowledge revolution," according to Rick Smolan, the US-based coauthor of *The Human Face of Big Data* best known as the creator of A Day in the Life book series.[26] Big data also applies to all major arenas of innovative technologies.

However, we should realize that despite the various advantages of big data, we cannot afford to welcome it absent-mindedly. Societies are enjoying the increasing benefits of new ICT technologies, but at the same time they must boost their efforts to protect themselves from the threats to security the technologies keep posing. As a result, escalating new ICT technologies accompany growing cybersecurity markets. The increasing problems of cybersecurity in the big data era will make our lives more uncomfortable. As the cybersecurity business grows, more specialists, not only benevolent but also malignant, join the ranks, and more cyberthreats surface.

Numerous resources are being deployed to counter cyberattacks. As of April 2015, the estimated annual cost for cybercrime committed globally added up to US$100 billion, according to Andra Zaharia, MARCOM Manager of Heimdal, a Copenhagen-based cybersecurity firm.[27] Another study says the estimated cost reaches US$160 billion per year,[28] and cybercrime costs are jumping rapidly.[29] The Federal Bureau of Investigation (FBI) has kept updating its most wanted list of cyber-criminals.[30] Each of these top thirty or so individuals are responsible for consumer losses ranging from US$350,000 to more than US$100 million. They are from all over the world, including Russia, China, and Ukraine, and are living affluently like business tycoons. The FBI has offered huge rewards for their capture.[31] The criminals' targets are not only corporations, banks, or wealthy celebrities but also ordinary Internet users.[32] Those in the FBI's most wanted list have been known to have been involved in conspiracy to participate in racketeering activity, bank fraud, wire fraud, money laundering, conspiracy to violate the Computer Fraud and Abuse Act, conspiracy to violate the Identity Theft and Assumption Deterrence Act, and aggravated identity theft.[33]

In 2016, FBI's most wanted cybercriminal was Evgeniy Mikhailovich Bogachev,[34] who was not included in FBI's top ten most wanted in early 2018. The FBI indicted Bogachev in 2012 for a variety of cybercrimes. One event related to his charges that the FBI began investigating in September 2011 was a modified, more effective version of the Zeus Trojan known as GameOver Zeus (GOZ). Zeus that runs on versions of Microsoft Windows is a type of malicious software designed to block access to a computer system until a sum of money is paid. The ransomware is used to capture bank account numbers, passwords, personal identification numbers, and other confidential information necessary to log into online banking accounts. It is believed GOZ was responsible for more than one million computer infections, resulting in financial losses of more than US$100 million.[35] The United States Department of State's Transnational Organized Crime Rewards Program offered a reward of up to US$3 million for information leading to the arrest or conviction of Bogachev.[36]

Ordinary people's fear of cybercrimes is mounting since the crimes are spreading fast across the world, and cybersecurity is falling behind the criminal techniques. The advent of public blockchain systems enabling transactions through digital currencies, such as bitcoin, and their use by criminals has further complicated the battle against cybercrimes and drawn the attention of financial regulators, legislative bodies, the media, and law enforcement agencies. It is also widely known that your most dependable allies—that is, your governments—are often working as your enemies in cyberspace. This will prove even truer as the big data era advances. Everyone has the right to encryption to ensure their cybersecurity. Encryption is the process of encoding messages or information in such a way that only authorized parties can read it. However, governments try to restrict or use backdoor means to break encryption[37] often in the name of transparency and protection against cybercriminals and terrorists. Governments all over the world are trying to limit every individual's right to encrypt confidential information. This is the reason that cyber policies can often do more damage than good.[38]

Many governments are creating malware and using them as digital weapons or in espionage programs. In the past five years, more than a handful of government malware have been discovered, but their origins have yet to receive full attribution.[39] To add insult to injury, government malware can encourage cybercriminals who are, say, on FBI's most wanted list, as it can accelerate the evolution of criminal malware. Some key cybercriminals, such as Bogachev and members of the JABBER-ZEUS subjects, who were also on FBI's most wanted list in 2016, often announce they are "retiring," but experts warn their "retirement" is a ruse and expect their return with new tricks. Cybercriminals can do a lot of reverse engineering on government malware and use its tactics and technical approach to create new, more advanced malware of their own and attack not only big public agencies, corporations, financial institutions, and so on but also general citizens.[40] Reuters reported in December 2014 that the FBI warned US businesses that hackers had used malicious software to launch a destructive cyberattack in the United States, following a devastating breach at Sony Pictures Entertainment in late November 2014.[41]

Governments have also fortified zero-day vulnerability black markets. A zero-day vulnerability or exploit is one that takes advantage of a software security vulnerability on the same day that the vulnerability has not yet been detected by the dealer.

> Zero Day vulnerabilities auctions have become common, but governments are buying the intelligence related to these vulnerabilities and weaponizing them, instead of disclosing them responsibly, as is the norm in the cybersecurity industry, although zero-day attacks are a severe threat to everybody. In fact, there is a long list of other things that allow our governments to make us more vulnerable. (A. Zaharia, "10 alarming cyber security facts that threaten your data," Heimdal [2016], available at: https://heimdalsecurity.com/, accessed May 12, 2016)

These few examples of both positive and negative impacts of technology as discussed above can help us understand how hutechciety is akin to a double-edged sword.[42] The NIC predicts that new technologies "will continue to empower individuals, small groups, corporations, and states, as well as accelerate the pace of change and spawn new complex challenges, discontinuities, and tensions."[43] It warns that "the achievements of the industrial and information ages are shaping a world to come that is both more dangerous and richer with opportunity than ever before."[44] Advances in technologies will disrupt the labor market, transform economic development, magnifying values differences across societies, or norms in these areas.[45] The intelligence agency raises the most fundamental question of "what it means to be human,"[46] which suggests the traditional socioeconomic status of human beings is crumbling in hutechciety.

3. Evolving technologies are sharpening the double-edged sword

The speed of shift from traditional society to hutechciety will gather speed with increasing availability of risk capital, advancing rules of law to protect intellectual property rights in developing markets, and growing desire of companies in those markets to get more competitive globally based on innovative technologies. To better understand the promises and the challenges from double-edged hutechciety, it is necessary to further examine the ongoing impacts on our lives of other emerging technologies in addition to those we have examined above.

This time, let us look at the progress of automation, robotics, 3D printing, and other technologies. Robotic systems used in a range of civil and military applications perform physical manipulations like us. Such manipulations are programmable and can be carried out autonomously or by teleoperation. Automation and robotics are different, but they are often confused. One of the main differences is that automation can only follow one set of operations, and it cannot be changed once programmed, but robots are made to perform several jobs at once, and the sequence of operations can be switched around to make the processes more efficient. The timing of the operations also can be changed in robotics, when necessary. The difference becomes clearer when we understand that "a robot that is used to defuse bombs, yet is entirely controlled by a remote human operator, is not entirely automated."[47] That is to say, robots may operate robots, but the ultimate operators of robots are humans.

Robots are not products of this century. The first robot resembling a human in its shape debuted in 1939. In that year, Westinghouse built the smoking robot Electro and introduced it at New York World's Fair. It was seven feet tall and could speak seven hundred words.[48] In July 1981, a robot killed a human for the first time. Kenji Urada, a Japanese engineer, was working on a broken robot. Urada failed to turn it off completely, resulting in the robot pushing him into a grinding machine with its hydraulic arm. As a result, the first robot homicide happened in Japan. As of 2016, Japan was the world's no. 1 in using operational robots with 310,508 robots, followed by the United States (168,623) and Germany (161,988). "In the last 10 years, the number of global industrial robots has grown 72%," according to Bank of America Merrill Lynch.[49] Robots are becoming increasingly sophisticated thanks to advances in AI. To put it another way, robots of today are more AI-based, and this trend will keep growing. In fact, robots running on AI technology have already become ubiquitous in our lives. For centuries, experts have predicted that robots would make workers obsolete.

A cyborg is a person whose body contains mechanical or electrical devices and whose abilities are greater than the abilities of normal humans. A cyborg is often regarded as a fictional or hypothetical person, but Kevin Warwick is the world's first human cyborg.[50] Warwick, a British engineer, and deputy vice chancellor at Coventry University in the United Kingdom, is known for his studies on direct interfaces between computer systems and the human nervous system and has also done research in the field of robotics. Warwick uses chips in his arm to remotely operate doors, an artificial arm, and an electronic wheelchair. He has very outspoken views on the future, particularly with respect to AI and its impact on humans. He argues that humanity will need to use technology to enhance itself to avoid being overtaken by machines. The cyborg specialist points out that many human limitations can be overcome with machines and is on record as saying that he wants to gain these abilities. What he emphasizes amounts to predicting that we will be living in a dumbfounding hutechciety. "There is no way I want to stay a mere human," he remarks. He also observes, "I feel that we are all philosophers, and that those who describe themselves as a 'philosopher' simply do not have a day job to go to."[51] With this view, Warwick symbolizes how members of hutechciety will live in the decades ahead. Hans Moravec, founder of Carnegie Mellon University's Robotics Institute, also offers a dramatic prediction that robots will emerge on their own as their own species by 2040.[52] His prediction indicates that the final operators of robots may not be humans. These robots will certainly disrupt the human workplace on an unknown scale in the next few decades, but humans have yet to be ready for it.[53] Such robots will further sharpen the double-edged sword.

Additive manufacturing (AM), commonly called 3D printing, is one of the revolutionary manufacturing technologies developing fast. AM is of course different from traditional paper printing, where a two-dimensional image is formed by ink on paper. 3D printing is a group of technologies that can literally take a three dimensional "real world" object and create (print) it out of plastic or metal. It allows a machine to build an object based strictly on the concept as it exists in the creator's mind. AM constructs objects by building matter up, rather than removing it, as its process involves production of parts through successive additions of layers, unlike traditional manufacturing in which parts and pieces are removed during the creation of a product. "Additive" thus represents the key concept that makes 3D printing different from conventional "subtractive" manufacturing techniques. In other words, the object is made layer by layer as a person adds one layer of material at a time until the complete object is formed.[54] Paired with computer-aided design software, this technique affords the creation of new types of objects with unique material properties. Printing objects with anything other than plastics—in particular, metal—has been expensive and painfully slow, but 3D metal printing is cheap, easy, practical, and is available today.

Initial versions of AM equipment and materials were developed in the 1980s. The global market for AM products and services has been growing rapidly since 2009, when key 3D printing patents for fuse deposition modeling (FDM) expired. FDM technology is commonly used for modeling, prototyping, and production applications. The expiration of the patents for FDM paved the way for today's thriving open-source—a development model that promotes universal access via a free license to a product's design or blueprint—3D printing movement and the initial rise of MakerBot Replicator 2, a simple at-home desktop 3D printer. Also known as Replicator 2 Desktop 3D Printer, the MakerBot Replicator 2 was introduced by MakerBot Industries, a New York City–based company founded in 2009 to engineer and produce 3D printers.[55] Another major shift came in 2014 as key patents targeting laser sintering additive technology, the lowest-cost 3D printing technology, expired. Patents for other key 3D printing technologies expired at the end of 2017. The series of patent expirations have been bringing remarkable changes to the world of 3D printing, lowering costs for those methods and widening the range of capabilities available to users.

Even more fabulously, 3D printers can do bioprinting, which means the production of human organs for transplant, as MyLikes, a social media advertising platform, notes. They "can create replacement tissues and organs. The parts are made from the organ recipient's own genetic matter. This allows the new organ or tissue to precisely match the patient's own body and needs."[56] Likewise, this technology can be used to save the lives of animals. For example, a hapless penguin at the Warsaw Zoo lost his lower beak, and many worried that the bird might starve to death because the damage left him unable to eat. Omni3D, a Polish 3D printer firm, came to the rescue and reconstructed the bird's beak using 3D technology.[57] It was the first time in Europe (and only the second time in the world) that a bird's beak had been recreated.

Recently, 3D printing itself made a major breakthrough—namely, the aforementioned 3D metal printing, which is much cheaper and faster than conventional 3D printing. Its key feature is that it can print objects with any material, including plastics, particularly, metal.[58] We may be inclined to think that 3D printing will be an incredible blessing for humankind. However, we should realize that it has frightening negatives as well. For instance, Defense Distributed—a Texas-based online open-source organization that designs firearms that can be downloaded from the Internet and then be created with a 3D printer—made it public in 2013 that it had created the world's first 3D-printed handgun.[59] The news sent shock waves throughout the United States and the rest of the world. In mid-2018, it had already become easy to produce a firearm with the proper 3D files and desktop printer. As a result, US officials and lawmakers were grappling with a new reality—the ability for citizens to print firearms at home.[60] Terrorists and the mentally ill can use gun-printing machines, whatever laws may be enacted to make it illegal to produce a 3D printed gun. Much of the public has realized by now the technology can have horrible consequences.

Furthermore, many technologies have their own inherent drawbacks that can have negative impacts on our lives, increasing the diversity of the double-edged sword. Resource technologies for food and water supply have focused on genetically modified (GM) crops, water management, and precision agriculture or farming (mentioned above)—a set of technologies that have helped propel agriculture into the computerized information-based world. They have helped farmers get greater control over the management of farm operations. Resource technologies for sustainable energy supply have centered on bioenergy, hydroelectricity, solar energy, wind energy, wave power, geothermal energy, tidal power, and so on. We are hoping that these technologies will be able to accommodate the increasing demand for resources for the growing global population. However, scientists note that significant hurdles should be overcome before these technologies can become indispensable agencies for human life. The environmental and human safety concerns arising from GM foods have yet to be resolved. Thus far, in about two decades of their existence, GM crops have not yet been verified to be of much benefit. Most scientists agree that they require continuous modifications in terms of not only productivity but also human safety. This means advancing food technologies may be harmful rather than beneficial to humans. The issue of adaptation also gets in the way of developing GM foods since GM crops do not fit in with any place. They need to be tailored for specific environments and regions with different weeds and pests.

Precision farming, also known as satellite farming or site specific crop management (SSCM), seems to have many benefits, but many issues involved necessitate serious consideration before adopting the technology. As for the advantages, the technology uses the global positioning system allowing fields to be surveyed with ease. This technology enables yield and soil characteristics to be mapped. The technology also allows nonuniform fields to be subdivided into smaller plots according to their specific requirements. As the technology advances, it will bring other benefits to farming. It has become a cornerstone of sustainable agriculture. However, the technology requires extremely arduous work particularly collecting and then analyzing the data. It is also important to take specialist advice before making expensive decisions. Initial capital costs involving the technology are quite high, necessitating that it be a long-term investment, especially in developing countries. According to the aforementioned top ten emerging technologies of 2017 selected by the WEF, a streamlined, low-cost monitoring system that relies on solar power and cell phones is being used as a precision farming technology in Indonesia. However, it remains uncertain as to when we might have enough data to fully implement the system.

Bio-based energy is a part of the bio-based economy or bioeconomy derived from scientific and research activity focused on biotechnology. Its advantages include, for instance, reduced greenhouse gas emissions and giving assistance to future development of crop residues such as straw, stalks, and other by-products as a primary fuel source. However, its most serious intrinsic disadvantages include food security and huge investment costs. Biofuel technology will operate differently in engines designed for petroleum-based fuel. In the United States, after many years and billions of dollars in government and industry supports, there still are no commercially viable biofuel plants online. Most seriously, biofuel production using food crops such as corn and soybeans has the potential to alter drastically the world's access to affordable food and can pose a threat to some regions' food security. In addition, biofuel production could lead to a perfect monoculture, which refers to the practice of growing one heavily concentrated crop. In sum, tension is likely to increase between humans and biofuel technology.

It is generally said that solar energy could disrupt the global energy environment, but we still should consider the pros and cons of this energy. Solar energy has a lot of advantages; it is renewable, abundant, sustainable, environment friendly, and available all over the world. We have every reason to expect that it will be able to increase countries' energy security through reliance on an indigenous, inexhaustible, and import-independent resource; enhance sustainability; reduce pollution; lower the costs of mitigating global warming; and keep fossil fuel prices lower than otherwise. These advantages seem global.

However, quite a few analysts have offered negative views, arguing that it is expensive as compared with other energy sources; intermittent as access to sunlight is limited at certain times, such as morning and night; and requires expensive energy storage systems, such as batteries, which need improvements to store heat less expensively. The good news in this regard is that a new solar device called hot solar cells MIT scientists are developing is the first one that could continuously create cheaper and more power than conventional photovoltaics. They say that "the approach could dramatically increase efficiency" and the device will be available in ten to fifteen years.[61] Nonetheless, other scientists still worry that some production processes of solar energy are associated with greenhouse gas emissions,[62] contending that there is nothing that's completely risk-free in the energy world. As a result, ongoing research focuses on dealing with negative environmental consequences of the technology.

Health technologies consist largely of two fields—disease management and human enhancement (sometimes referred to as "Human 2.0"). Technologies for disease management, which refers to the effective control and treatment of communicable and noncommunicable illnesses, have the potential to transform medicine. Successful disease management through new technologies will make obsolete the current bitter, time-consuming efforts of physicians to differentiate between many illnesses with similar symptoms. For example, the shortcoming of today's genetic profiling—the analysis of DNA from samples of body tissues or fluids, such as saliva, semen, and urine—is that the number of known disease-related genes is insufficient to provide mass screening.[63] New technologies will overcome such drawbacks. Diagnostic and pathogen-detection techniques are among the key technologies being improved for future disease management. However, these new technologies are not infallible. New genetic profiling technologies can give incorrect results due to errors such as cross-contamination of samples.[64] Also, cost will be a major barrier preventing molecular diagnostic technologies from becoming routinely available in a physician's surgeries for an unknown period to come.[65]

Regenerative medicine—a branch of research in tissue engineering and molecular biology, which deals with the "process of replacing, engineering, or regenerating human cells, tissues or organs to restore or establish normal function,"[66] will also continue to evolve and make it possible to develop replacement organs, such as hearts, kidneys, livers, and lungs, by the year 2040. About twenty thousand Americans each year receive life-saving transplants from people.[67] However, the supply of human organs remains seriously limited. To meet the demand, scientists and biotechnology companies have been working on a technology called xenotransplantation that uses organs from animals. This biotechnology seems fictional, but some researchers believe they are on the verge of making xenotransplantation of all organs work.[68] However, there are pros and cons of this technology, indicating that the double-edged sword is getting sharper. Pros include life-saving benefits, opening new areas of research, satisfying the supply and demand of organs, and so on, while cons comprise the risk of disease transmission, risking shorter life-spans of animal organs, moral and religious issues, and so on.[69]

A dramatic example of human enhancement technologies in progress is brain-machine or brain-computer interfaces in the form of brain-implants that can provide superhuman abilities, augmenting, say, strength and speed. A lot of scientists don't rule out the possibility that this futuristic technology could one day make commercially available products to allow anyone to boost their memory. In fact, the memory chips have already been successfully tested in rats.[70] Advances in genomics and AI will be combined to result in dramatic human enhancement to the extent that all current limitations of the human body in terms of intelligence, athletic ability, psychological health, and so on will be overcome. Quite a few scientists also anticipate the days are not so far off when artificial human beings can be created through DNA synthesis (as in the HGP2 project briefly mentioned in chapter 5).[71]

Health technologies are certainly making astounding progress. They seem to be heralding the days when they will be able to bless all humans on the globe. However, a lot of hurdles have yet to be overcome. Human augmentation technologies are very costly for average citizens even in most advanced countries to afford, and it will probably be available even in some twenty years only to the wealthiest.[72] For the poor living in poor countries that do not have even basic health coverage for all, dramatic health technologies will certainly be out of reach and look like dramas for an unknown time to come. We need to recall how miserable the realities of poor nations are. According to the 2014 estimates of the infant mortality rate by the CIA, for instance, 50 to 120 babies born in the forty poorest countries of the world die under one year per one thousand live births, as compared with less than five in the forty richest countries.[73] This situation will inevitably result in an extremely polarized society, both nationally and globally. We are already living in such a divided world. Deepening inequality among human beings is a major source of global instability.

Quite a few health technologies, such as DNA synthesizing, have also given rise to ethical controversies,[74] as xenotransplantation has. Moreover, a more fundamental question is raised. If advances in health technologies could extend the life-span of every human on Earth indefinitely within a couple of decades, as some thinkers predict,[75] what would happen on this planet? Overpopulation and overconsumption are very likely to result in mass extinction.[76] Advances in health technologies may be considered a boon to humanity, but they are further sharpening the double-edged sword.

4. Technology will remain at the service of humankind

As hutechciety advances, new technologies that even the best science fiction writers could not imagine will continue to emerge. Technologies have the propensity to keep creating new ones like a car with broken brakes running downhill. They have come a long way indeed. Robert Liston was a famous pioneering Scottish surgeon of the nineteenth century. When he died, a meeting was held of his friends and admirers, who "unanimously resolved to establish some public and lasting testimonial to the memory of this distinguished surgeon."[77] He was known as, above all, as the fastest surgeon of the nineteenth century. Prior to anesthesia, speed was essential to minimizing pain and improving the odds of survival. This means that, by the standard of the day, the surgeon had a remarkable medical technology of his own.

He is also known for the Liston's most dishonorable case, though. While amputating a patient's leg at the hip, he accidentally sliced through the fingers of one of his assistants. That would have been bad enough, but it proved disastrous when the patient's stump became affected with gangrene—death and decay of body tissue. The saw must have been contaminated because the assistant became ill and infected too. Within a few days, both the patient and the assistant died. However, this single surgery took a victim even earlier. The procedure was being observed by an elderly doctor in a dress coat with long tails. In the confusion, Liston cut through the man's coat. He wasn't cut, but because blood was spurting around, the old gentleman didn't know that. Feeling the tug and seeing himself covered in blood, the man collapsed on the floor, had a heart attack, and died. That was the only operation in history with a mortality rate of 300 percent. Despite the three deaths, by far the most unsuccessful of his career, Liston remained a distinguished surgeon. "After his death, his peers erected a marble statue in his honor and created an award for students of distinction in his name."[78] Liston's case must sound like a nymph tale, compared with today's health technology.

Although the gap between technology and humans has continued to be bridged since the dawn of humanity, an academic discipline studying this relationship started in earnest in the 1970s, when Elting E. Morison, a US historian of technology, founded the science, technology, and society (STS) program at MIT, which served as a model for similar programs that have followed. STS bridges humanities, social sciences, science, technology, and medicine.[79] Nowadays an increasing number of institutions, including Harvard University, University of Pennsylvania, King's College London, and National University of Singapore, are offering courses and programs on human-technology interaction.[80] The *Boston Globe*, reporting on professor Morison's death at age eighty-five in 1995, called him "an educator and industrial historian who believed that technology could only be harnessed to serve human beings when scientists and poets could meet with mutual understanding."[81] Given the fact that positive and negative aspects of technologies are increasing, the efforts to investigate how the human-technology relationship is changing will continue to rise.

Most global thinkers today are apparently concerned more than ever about what Albert Einstein predicted: "I fear the day technology will surpass our human interaction. The world will have a generation of idiots." His prediction seems to have been proved correct now. The *Times* reported in October 2014,

> The average Briton spends the equivalent of almost an entire day each week glued to their smartphone screen and uses it 221 times in every 24 hours for social networking, emailing, texting and other tasks. An animalistic thirst for socializing has made us a nation addicted to our smartphones, often wandering blindly into Facebook without quite knowing why. (J. Dean, "Smartphone users are busy 221 times a day," *Times* [2014], available at: https://www.thetimes.co.uk/, accessed January 28, 2015)[82]

For an average of three and a quarter hours a day, their eyes are glued to their phones, blind to the world around them, degrading themselves to the level of "idiots."[83] Dave Barry, a Pulitzer Prize–winning US author and humorist, remarks, "The population of earth has reached 7 billion people, every single one of whom send you irritating emails to join something called LinkedIn."[84] The *New York Times* reported in 2012 a set of rules that then First Lady Michelle Obama had mentioned over the years that her two children—Malia and Sasha—had to follow during their time in the White House, as well as in general. The rules included that Malia may use her cell phone only on weekends, and she and her sister could not watch television or use a computer for anything but homework during the week.[85] These stories raise the need for us to look at the double-edged sword in additional dimensions.

Based on what we have discussed so far, hutechciety can be characterized by the following three features at least. First, technologies will continue to transform our everyday lives. Second, technologies have already penetrated deeply into human beings not only as their essential apparatuses but also as their physical parts or substitutes. Third, it hardly seems possible at present for even the scientists and engineers developing new technologies to say for sure where technologies will lead us: to a sustainable world or a catastrophe. The following quote gives us both hope and caution: "Whether promise or peril prevails will turn on the choices of humankind."[86] This advice seem to be an all-embracing warning to double-edged hutechciety.

Whatever may come, we have every reason to be optimistic about hutechciety, though. With all the conveniences and problems technologies are bringing to us, the global community at large has made unrelenting progress, rewarding our intelligence, creative talent, hard work, ability to cooperate, love, and faith. A robot may accidentally kill the very person who made it. Nonetheless, human beings will remain the last species that could be subjugated to or fatally hurt by any technology they create. A 3D printer can create handguns that may fall into the wrong hands. However, already available is the "Genetic Fortune-Telling" technology (mentioned above) that could enable babies to get DNA report cards at birth, which would offer predictions about their chances not only of suffering a heart attack or cancer but also of getting hooked on tobacco, of being smarter than average, and of getting mentally ill. This technology could prevent, say, a mass shooting like that which transpired at a Florida high school in February in 2018.

Some also worry that human society may see, for instance, a jobless future thanks to advances in technology.[87] However, if we believe humans can make machines that only prune away our jobs and not create them, we must be a disbeliever in the extraordinary capability inherent in humanity to make continuing progress.

> Study of census results in England and Wales since 1871 finds rise of machines has been a job creator rather than making human workers obsolete. Machines will take on more repetitive and laborious tasks, but seem no closer to eliminating the need for human labor than at any time in the last 150 years. (K. Allen, "'Technology has created more jobs than it has destroyed,' says 140 years of data," *Guardian* [2015], available at: https://www.theguardian.com/, accessed August 18, 2015)[88]

Machines will not just be replacing human jobs but also creating new opportunities to replace the ones that are too mundane for humans to do.[89] For instance, foreign language translation, which is considered an intellectual job today, may soon be categorized as a mundane job. Humans can collectively use technology to the good of everyone. Hard, dangerous, and dull jobs have declined with advances in technology. Humankind will never lose this intrinsic, collective ability in hutechciety. Contrary to Einstein's satirical quip about "a generation of idiots," humankind in general will be able to continue to be intelligent enough to stand out over stupidity. The written history of human-technology relationship has so far that shown humans have typically been smart enough to take forward steps backward, using technology constructively, not destructively, after all.

Today's world is more creative, pioneering, productive, respectful of entrepreneurship, valuing of education, committed to resolving global issues confronting humankind through cooperative endeavors, and aware of the values of mutual love and trust than ever before. There is no definite sign in sight that this progress could backtrack in the future. Humans have the innate capability to tell positives from negatives and to turn disadvantages to advantages.

Looking ahead, humans will continue to be in control of all up-to-the-minute technologies they will create and use. To recap, machines are the works of humans' own hands. Human life and work are not simple machine tasks.[90] For one thing, they are full of twists and turns that should be dealt with emotionally and spiritually rather than mechanically. In short, humans want to remain human. Although AlphaGo overwhelmed human Go players with brilliant mechanical skills, humans prefer to watch humans, not machines, play against each other in Go games. However sophisticated machines may become, they will never be able to perform the entire range of human activities. Accessing quick answers and jumping to conclusions through complex calculations will certainly become easier, thanks to advances in technology. Nonetheless, such conveniences are "basically mental placebos that might make us feel better, but they don't make a problem go away."[91] Humans will forever triumph over technology, no matter what new technologies come.[92] Technology will remain at the service of humanity, and never vice versa.

CHAPTER 7

Publivacy

1. Our personal life keeps being laid bare

Another new word for this chapter, "publivacy," combines the two incompatible words, "public" and "privacy." The compound suggests we are losing a great deal of personal privacy largely because an increasing number of organizations and individuals are invading our privacy for national security, corporate interests, malicious intent, nasty self-satisfaction, you name it. Advances in technologies are mostly responsible for privacy invasion. Intelligence organizations are invading our privacy in the name of public safety. We are also voluntarily allowing our privacy to go public for our personal benefits. Richard van Hooijdonk, a guest lecturer at Nyenrode and Erasmus Universities, observes, "Nothing that you thought only you could see is safe anymore."[1]

In the last in the WGBH-produced series of twelve video lectures delivered by Michael Sandel, professor of philosophy at Harvard University,[2] a female student named Hannah challenged the view on the same-sex marriage that a student named Mark suggested. Hannah reacted to Mark: "I hate to be uncouth and rude, but have you engaged in masturbation?" Her question made the audience burst out in laughter, and suddenly she looked like something of a pop entertainer. Shortly before Hannah asked this question, Mark defined the purpose of marriage as procreation and union of a man and a woman. Professor

Sandel, obviously a little embarrassed at that moment, interrupted the exchanges between the two students, saying, "All right, Mark, you don't have to answer the (Hannah's) question."

Masturbation is a private thing that most people want to hide, but Hannah publicly asked about one aspect of Mark's privacy. Let's think of the following hypothetical scenario in the context of the importance of privacy protection. What if a professor engaged in masturbation and a malicious intruder photographed the scene of this act secretly with a digital device, and the footage went viral on social media? What would happen to the professor's future as an educator, even if his or her private act did no harm to anybody and was socially acceptable?

It seems easy to answer the questions, but they reawaken us to the importance of privacy. The word, "privacy" consisting of the adjective "private" and the suffix "-cy," is generally defined as the state of being free from being observed or disturbed by other people. The idea that citizens of a democracy have a right to privacy dates to at least Aristotle, who, more than two thousand years ago, drew a distinction between politics and private life. Although the definition of privacy has changed a little bit over time, it has remained roughly the same until modern times. In the early fifteenth century, it meant "a secret, secret deed or solitude." In the late sixteenth century, it meant "a private matter or a secret." Then around the early seventeenth century, it meant "seclusion." Since the early nineteenth century, the word has been used to mainly mean a "state of freedom from intrusion."[3]

Most of us must be wondering today how many of us still believe that the American birthright guaranteed by the Founding Fathers in the Fourth Amendment remains intact. "The right of the people to be secure in their persons, houses, papers, and effects, against unreasonable searches and seizures, shall not be violated." Already in 1980, Terry Fox, a heroic Canadian athlete, humanitarian, and cancer research activist, said, "Our privacy is starting to be invaded and we can't get anything done."[4] US actress and activist Olivia Wilde offers a similar view, "At one point, I thought changing my name might help with privacy, but that was before the Internet." She emphasizes, "Everyone needs evenings of their own."[5]

Various organizations and individuals are invading our privacy on an unknown scale using a variety of technologies. The problem-ridden world allows intelligence agencies to justify their privacy attack against not only criminal suspects but also general citizens. They claim one of the major functions of the government is to protect citizens from various threats, such as acts of terrorism and mass gun shootings as well as cybercrimes. The problem, however, is that no government can perfectly know, say, who are the real or potential criminals and how international terrorists and domestic villains are operating. Governments' privacy invasion cannot resolve all the troubles, but it helps. Nonetheless, even this incomplete help would be impossible without a blanket surveillance of all people in any country. Technologies for intelligence gathering are evolving, but no society in the world can be completely free from the mounting threats from a variety of malignant elements who themselves keep updating their strategies to attack innocent people. Under the circumstances, privacy invasion cannot but continue to grow.

Nowadays, most of us already think that somebody may be reading somewhere the e-mail we are writing right at this moment. John W. Whitehead, a constitutional lawyer, and founder and president of the Rutherford Institute, a prominent US civil liberties and human rights organization, remarks on the perils privacy has faced in the United States and the rest of the world,

> You did not imagine that machines in distant places ever would analyze your intimate behaviors. You thought that only in fiction might government be spying on you, an innocent person suspected of nothing. Privacy was not a setting on Facebook. Privacy meant your permission mattered. It enhanced your well-being. (For John W. Whitehead's remarks, see, for instance, G. Miller, "Is privacy dying?" [2013], available at: https://www.rutherford.org/, accessed July 27, 2013)

In the wake of Edward Snowden's revelations about the National Security Agency (NSA), in July 2013, the *Providence Journal* nicknamed

ProJo carried a story that recalled that privacy that used to be our healthy and powerful ally has gone away now. The four-time Pulitzer Prize–winning daily reported to the effect that we used to be the king of our own house as what we were doing in our own room was pretty much our own business anybody could hardly creep into. It was undreamed of that some outsider on the other side of the world could closely be looking at our home on a digital device and that when we stepped outside, our whereabouts could be tracked and recorded.[6] According to a Pew survey on the condition of privacy in the United States in 2013, 81.1 percent of Americans think privacy is "dead" or "on life support," and 11.6 percent of them believe it is "ailing." Only 7.2 percent responded it is "alive and well."[7]

Despite such studies, most ordinary citizens nowadays seem to be less and less sensitive to the fact that privacy invasion has become commonplace. They seem to accept the trend of diminishing privacy as unavoidable. They seem to be concerned about privacy related to their economic life only, such as banking activities. Their desertion of the right to privacy means they are living in a democracy that has failed to allow them to enjoy basic human rights. Nonetheless, people nowadays give up their privacy according to their own preferences. "Privacy may be voluntarily sacrificed, normally in exchange for perceived benefits and very often with specific dangers and losses."[8]

We have agreed to provide intimate details of our lives to entrepreneurs and others who govern the digital world. "Digital technology has not debilitated our privacy on its own. Many of us have been complicit. We have bought the machines and subscribed to the services."[9] "In return, we have received connection and gratification, 10 percent off our next purchase, etc. It has been so seductive. The siren called, and we opened our arms."[10] To the extent that we are getting more comfortable with technology and are thus allowing it to become more involved with our work lives, it is becoming increasingly integrated with and intrusive to our personal lives. "Certainly, in the last few years, when we've gone to smaller devices, more mobile devices, we've agreed that the excitement, the interest and the convenience is worth the surrendering of various bits of privacy,"[11] says Robert Beck, professor and chairman of the Department of Computing Sciences at Villanova University. "A lot of this we've done to ourselves."[12]

With the advent of the cybersuperpower called Google and other digital powers, the word, "cyberimperialism," has begun to be used. By far, Google is the strongest cyberimperial power in the world, and its digital imperialism is continuing to grow, threatening to subjugate the whole cyberworld under its domination. In terms of its search engine alone, across the world, Google is the most popular. Google's global market share of search engine stood at 92.06 percent from November 2016 to November 2017.[13] However, Google has long been attacked for its lack of privacy in the United States as well as abroad. Despite Google's slogan, "Your privacy matters," it has been investigated, sued, or threatened with legal action on privacy issues by government entities in many countries including in the European Union. As widely reported, it paid large fines, including US$22.5 million ordered in 2012 by the US Federal Trade Commission (FTC), the largest civil penalty the FTC ever levied.[14]

The tragic consequences privacy invasion has brought are too many to illustrate here. Take an old story for example. On September 22, 2010, Tyler Clementi, an eighteen-year-old student at Rutgers University in Piscataway, New Jersey, jumped to his death from the George Washington Bridge. Clementi committed suicide shortly after he learned what had happened. His death brought national and international attention to the problem of privacy invasion. On September 19 that year, Dharun Ravi, a first-year student at Rutgers University in New Brunswick, New Jersey, and a fellow hall mate, Molly Wei, used a webcam on Ravi's computer and a computer in Wei's dorm room to view, without Clementi's knowledge, Clementi kissing another man. Two days later, Ravi urged friends and Twitter followers to watch via his webcam a second tryst between Clementi and his friend though the viewing never occurred.

On March 16, 2012, a jury found Dharun Ravi guilty of invasion of privacy, hate crime, and tampering with evidence. Though Ravi was not charged with manslaughter, Clementi's suicide hung heavy in the proceedings. Under federal law, the penalty for video voyeurism is just one year in prison or a fine. In New Jersey, the penalty for invasion of privacy is a maximum penalty of five years. But because of the hate crime charge and the jury's finding that Clementi might have felt intimidated because of his sexual orientation, Ravi faced up to ten years in prison as well as deportation to India, where he was born but hasn't lived since he was two years old. On May 21, 2012, Ravi was sentenced to thirty days in jail, three years of probation, three hundred hours of community service, and a US$10,000 fine, but both the prosecutors and Ravi filed separate appeals. Whatever the legal punishment, nobody could bring Clementi back to life.

Webcams can invade our privacy on a much larger scale. Even educational authorities, which should normally be the last to invade students' privacy in view of the ideal and purpose of education, often commit privacy invasion on an institutional scale. On Feb 18, 2010, a well-heeled Philadelphia school district gave out laptops to students and then its administrators activated remotely the built-in webcams to covertly spy on them at school and at home. This privacy invasion led to a federal class-action lawsuit, brought on behalf of all the students and their parents. The case, *Blake J. Robbins v. Lower Merion School District*,[15] was filed after one of the school's vice principals disciplined Robbins' son for "improper behavior in his home," using a photo secretly taken of the fifteen-year-old high school sophomore Robbins in his bedroom as evidence. The webcam-attached laptops were issued to eighteen hundred students at three high schools in the district. The students and their parents were seeking damages for invasion of privacy, theft of private information, and unlawful interception and access of electronic information in what was dubbed the WebcamGate scandal. In October 2010, the school district agreed to pay US$610,000 to settle the Robbins and parallel Hasan lawsuits against it.[16] These incidents amount to the tip of the iceberg.

Although experts share the view of Whitehead that speedy advances in technology are the main culprit of this crime, many of them also admit that the complex and threat-ridden world of today has made it necessary for government intelligence bodies, law enforcement, ethical hackers, and so on to use state-of-the-art technologies to invade the privacy of their citizens. They say,

> Mainframe computers gave way to smaller, more powerful machines. The internet matured. Broadband replaced dial-up. Cell phones became smart phones with biometric authentication system. Email and texting abounded. Social media proliferated. Clandestine data-stealing programs known as spyware and malware multiplied. Cameras sprouted everywhere and drones took to the civilian skies. (G. Miller, "eWave: Is privacy dying? Technology is pervasive and invasive," *Providence Journal* [2013], available at: http://www.providencejournal.com/, accessed July 27, 2013)

"The technology is so pervasive and invasive, and driving the show," emphasizes Whitehead.[17]

Nowadays our devices know more about our personal lives than our close friends. Although older adults face more barriers and challenges when it comes to adopting new technologies, as of 2013, 86 percent of all US adults went online, according to a Pew research released in April 2014.[18] Today, almost all Americans have at least one of the three digital devices—smartphone or cell phone, tablet, or laptop, according to studies conducted by leading research organizations, including Pew.[19] Right at this moment, personal information about individuals is constantly being gathered not only by government intelligence services but also by giant business conglomerates; telecommunications companies that provide text messages and data services for phones, tablets, and computers; software businesses; various types of social media; and so forth. They are by and large ignoring the laws prohibiting privacy invasion. Countries and corporations also have different laws and regulations about privacy invasion.

One of the best-known cases worldwide of Internet privacy invasion is the censorship by Baidu, a Chinese web services company, which is the Chinese version of Google. Baidu has a long history of being the most proactive and restrictive online censor in the search arena. Documents leaked in April 2009 from an employee in Baidu's internal monitoring and censorship department show numerous blocked websites and censored topics on Baidu search.[20] In May 2011, pro-democracy activists sued Baidu for violating the US constitution by the censorship it conducts in accord with the demand of the Chinese government.[21] Whatever the laws and regulations about privacy incursion in effect, we've gotten into the habit of storing personal information on various state-of-the-art digital machines. This personal information can include anything from our e-mail addresses and passwords and social security numbers to our bank account and credit card numbers and mobile payment options, but most of us do not feel uncomfortable with privacy-invasive technologies.

2. Privacy invasion in the workplace

Even when we feel uncomfortable with privacy-invasive technologies, we cannot but swallow them especially in the workplace. Employee monitoring software (EMS) is just one example of employee monitoring, the act of monitoring employee activity and tracking employee performance. This allows company administrators to monitor and supervise all their employee computers from a central location. If employees use company computers for their work, companies often utilize EMS to monitor and track everything their employees do on their computers. It keeps an eye on what e-mails were received, what applications were used, and what keys were pressed.

Employers argue they have every reason to conduct this surveillance, even though they know well this practice hurts employee privacy and satisfaction. Employers say they want to make sure company resources are not misused. They believe it is legitimate to check whether employees are wasting time on recreational websites or sending unprofessional e-mails. Employee monitoring thus collects data not only about work-related activities but also about an employee's personal information that is unrelated to work. Employees refute that it is illegal for employers to monitor all their private e-mail exchanges and other types of communication that consume only a little time, like a few minutes, which do not cause meaningful detriment to their normal business in workplaces and sometimes even provide information beneficial to their employers.

Companies, in response to such complaints, claim that they maintain ethical monitoring policies to avoid indiscriminate monitoring of employees' activities. They say monitoring does not mean there are no limits to what should be collected. Nonetheless, the tension between the two sides continues because the key problem with employers, however, is that employers always value their interests over employees' and third parties' privacy. Employee surveillance may also lead to an executive's decision on whether to promote or demote an employee, and in some cases, it may cause employees to get fired. In case employers take the stance of "take it or leave it" toward employees who disagree with their surveillance, most employees cannot but "take it," as they must earn a living. Switching jobs is usually not easy, and job changes do not guarantee a monitoring-free work environment either.

Besides the EMS supervising employee computers, a variety of other means are available for employee monitoring. The introduction of security cameras to provide traffic safety and crime control has been expanded to include surveillance of employees at their desks, in washrooms, and throughout the factory or the store. In fact, video surveillance is one of the most effective forms of employee monitoring. Video feeds of employee activities are fed back to a central location where they are either recorded or monitored live by another person. Hotels, stores, restaurants, and so on favor this method because they need to monitor housekeeping staff's misconducts, internal theft, staff etiquette and manners, hospitality, and so on. By doing so, video surveillance ensures near perpetual activity monitoring, or maximum exploitation. Video surveillance has become more convenient and prevalent as camera sizes are shrinking, thus making it easier to conceal the equipment. Video surveillance cameras can be so small that they can be hidden almost anywhere in the workplace and even worn on clothing. Looking ahead, just think of a device that is much smaller than a "yellow Babel fish" in the cult sci-fi classic *The Hitchhiker's Guide to the Galaxy* that slides into your ear.[22] Such little gadgets can zoom in on the smallest of details and can pan and tilt. The continuing development of nanotechnology and AI will make the digital tools much tinier or invisible.

Some cases of abuse of this technology as reported by the Yale-New Haven Teachers Institute, which maintains an educational partnership between Yale University and the New Haven Public Schools, show in detail how seriously video surveillance is invading our privacy as well as a gob of loopholes in laws and regulations concerned.[23]

Case 1: In Florida, the general manager of the *Apalachicola Times* extended a legitimate system to include a hidden video camera in his employees' bathroom. It was found that the camera was not against the law.

Case 2: Employees of the Dunkin' Donuts chain used its video surveillance technology to listen in on customers. The company was forced to remove the cameras.

Case 3: The management at Boston's Sheraton Hotel was recording workers as they changed clothes in a locker room on the pretext that it was investigating suspected drug use by its workers.

Case 4: In Concord, California, a JC Penney employee discovered that a guard was showing a videotape in which he had zoomed in on her breasts. He made the tape with the store's ceiling cameras.

Case 5: In England, which is the most videotaped society in the world because of Irish Republican Army terrorism, B-grade filmmakers have raided footage from public video cameras to make movies of sexual impropriety, often featuring unsuspecting couples.

Many employers defend video surveillance of their employees, arguing that there is a benefit because the technology it provides is an unbiased method of performance evaluation and prevents the interference of a manager's feelings and biased views in an employee's review. They add that management can review the performance of an employee by checking the surveillance and detecting problems before they become too costly. The corporate arguments in favor of such employee monitoring also include crime prevention and protection of staff. However, few employers are concerned about employee privacy relating to the monitoring. Employers hardly like to put themselves in their employees' shoes.

The extensive use of corporate security systems requiring all workers to wear an employee badge containing an implanted computer microchip has also become commonplace. As employees enter their office, the computer records the exact time and will quietly monitor every move they make throughout the day. Sensors placed at strategic locations throughout the building record the location and duration of every movement by the badge wearer. Such systems have given companies the ability to monitor the location and activity of every worker. Delivery and transportation industries widely use location monitoring. In these industries employees do not work in static locations, and their supervisors like to track their locations. Even though location monitoring can be incidental in some of these cases when the location is tracked for other purposes, such as determining the amount of time before a parcel will be delivered or which taxi is closest, the outcome may be the same, as it can still invade employee privacy, whatever its pronounced objectives may be.

The sophisticated office phone system also allows our boss to secretly monitor any private phone calls we make. Computerized office phone systems contain a record of all possible legitimate business phone numbers. If an employee makes a personal call to a friend, the office phone system will record the unauthorized number and produce a report of the private call and its duration as ammunition for his supervisor at the next evaluation interview. Employees' phone call details as well as actual conversations can be recorded during monitoring. The exact number of calls and duration of each call, and the idle time between calls can go into an automatic log for analysis.

Against this backdrop, the International Labor Organization conducted a research in Geneva in 2013 and warned, "Workers in industrialized countries are losing privacy in the workplace as technological advances allow employers to monitor nearly every facet of time on the job."[24] Their study claimed that the United States was the worst offender. The American Civil Liberties Union backed up the results of this research. The union went out of its way to declare, "Criminals have more privacy rights than employees. Police should get a court order, whereas in the workplace, surveillance can be conducted without safeguards."[25] Such warnings have yielded little effects and employee privacy invasion is only expanding.

Intelligence agencies and law enforcement hardly find any reason to care about the kind of privacy invasion against employees by corporate employers either. The intelligence community in the United States, for example, "maintains relationships with private corporations to help meet national security goals."[26] Intelligence agencies have their own systems for employee surveillance. The personnel structures of intelligence services are strictly hierarchical like military ranks. Public employers or bosses of such organizations ensure absolute obedience from their subordinates. Their surveillance of not only their employees but also the public at large has been getting increasingly indiscriminate. They claim that such wholesale supervision of all sorts of people has become unavoidable nowadays because without it they cannot fully protect citizens from imminent and present dangers.

When it comes to the matter of privacy, it is no exaggeration to say that citizens of democratic countries are living today in a totalitarian society like the former Soviet Union, which thoroughly monitored the population in concert with "thought police." In no time, this societal situation will associate us with the Big Brother authority figure who ruthlessly keeps watch on the public—the despotic character described by George Orwell in his fear-provoking fiction *Nineteen Eighty-Four* published some seventy years ago (in 1949). Orwell's imaginary tale depicts a society under strict observation by technologies of oppression that look a lot like the ubiquitous telescreen, for example, which keeps monitoring the private and public lives of the populace. Going a step further, constant advances in surveillance technologies make us suspect that George Orwell's imagination of Big Brother was too naïve or optimistic. Vytautas Butrimas, chief adviser for cybersecurity at the Ministry of National Defense of Lithuania, notes that we are at a crossroads where we are at a loss for words, seeing the technological change, ever-growing monetization of digital encounters, and shifting relationship of citizens and their governments, all of which are depriving the public of personal privacy.[27]

3. Our privacy is being lost with our own consent

Since Snowden leaked classified information from the NSA in June 2013, debates have been fueled over mass surveillance, government secrecy, and the need for a balance between national security and personal privacy. Snowden has been variously called a hero, a whistleblower, a dissident, a patriot, a defector, and a traitor. For those who challenge the constitutionality of the NSA's bulk collection of telephone metadata, the former CIA agent is considered a hero, a whistleblower, a dissident, or a patriot. For those who defend NSA's invasion of privacy in the name of national security and public safety, he is regarded as a traitor. On November 16, 2015, then CIA director John Brennan, speaking about the ISIS terrorist attack that occurred in Paris three days before, remarked that "unauthorized disclosures" such as the Snowden's had made it "much more difficult" to track down terrorists.[28]

Snowden said earlier,

> I don't want to live in a society that does these sort of things (invasion of citizens' privacy by the government) ... I do not want to live in a world where everything I do and say is recorded ... My sole motive is to inform the public as to that which is done in their name and that which is done against them. (See, for instance, G. Greenwald, E. MacAskill, and L. Poitras, "Edward Snowden: The whistleblower behind the NSA surveillance revelations," *Guardian* [2013], available at: https://www.theguardian.com/, accessed June 11, 2013)

He declared later in an interview: "For me, in terms of personal satisfaction, the mission is already accomplished. I already won." Snowden's most surprising statements included: "I, sitting at my desk, certainly had the authorities to wiretap anyone, from you or your accountant, to a federal judge or even the president, if I had a personal email."[29]

The NSA is one of the sixteen spy agencies comprising the US intelligence community. The spy agency was shown to be "secretly" tapping into Google and Yahoo data centers to collect information from "hundreds of millions" of account holders worldwide by tapping undersea cables.[30] The NSA was said to be tracking the online sexual activity of people to discredit them. It was accused of going "beyond its core mission of national security and public safety" when articles were published showing the NSA's intelligence-gathering operations had targeted Brazil's largest oil company, Petrobras.[31] The NSA was also shown to be tailing charities including the United Nations Children's Fund and Médecins du Monde as well as allies, such as the EU chief and the Israeli prime minister.[32]

By October 2013, Snowden's disclosures had created tensions between the United States and some of its close allies, as they revealed that the United States had spied on many countries and their leaders, including Brazil, France, Mexico, Britain, Germany, Spain, and China, and thirty-five world leaders, most notably German chancellor Angela Merkel. Chancellor Merkel said, "spying among friends" was "unacceptable" and compared the NSA with the Stasi, which used to be the official state security service of former East Germany. Leaked documents published by *Der Spiegel* in 2014 appeared to show that the NSA had targeted 122 "high ranking" national leaders in the world.[33]

The *New York Times* reported in July 2013 that Snowden was employed as an analyst by NSA contractor Booz Allen Hamilton and had been a model employee, taking a course to join the elite ranks of "certified ethical hackers."[34] In the wake of the Snowden's "ethical" revelations, a lot of intelligence-gathering personnel from the US government, Congress, and military circles as well as journalists and academics began to discuss the so-called right balance between national security, public safety, and personal privacy. Despite the numerous debates they have had and the various ideas they have suggested as to the "right balance," the Wisdom of Solomon about it has yet to come. The "right balance" is easier said than done. By all accounts, those who have been involved in the debates would have looked more candid and clearer if they had flatly defined this situation as a catch-22 or drawn a conclusion to the effect that "you can't have your cake and eat it too."

They must have chosen to use the word "right balance" as a whack-a-mole tactic to sooth down the raging controversy. When we cannot clearly define the meaning of an expression like "right balance" as used in this context, it is practically impossible for us to get to the goal such an expression intends to accomplish. To put it another way, if the concept of an expression is hard to clearly define or remains ambiguous, it is difficult to solve any problem related to it. This situation may well be compared to putting the cart before the horse. In the final analysis, we cannot but accept the ugly truth of our privacy being encroached upon for two reasons: first, we should survive the present and impending dangers, notably terrors; second, we should stay online for our own needs in an Internet society.

Of course, the unthinkable tragedy that happened on September 11, 2001, when terrorists attacked the World Trade Center in New York, killing nearly three thousand innocent people, should be the last thing we ever see on this planet. The barbarian attack led then US president George W. Bush to set the country up for a war against terrorism, and the terrified US public at large obviously applauded the president's decision. The NSA was thus empowered more than ever before to monitor domestic communications of suspected terrorists without obtaining a warrant. Congress also passed in no time the Patriot Act in October 2001, almost unanimously. As a result, the US government has since been able to wield exceptional new powers of surveillance. Since 9/11, it has repeatedly amended the Foreign Intelligence Surveillance Act (FISA), which was enacted in 1978 and originally prescribed procedures for the physical and electronic surveillance and collection of "foreign intelligence information" between "foreign powers" and "agents of foreign powers" suspected of espionage or terrorism.[35]

Barack Obama, who succeeded Bush as US president did not prove to be any different when it comes to the Patriot Act, one of the four major amendments of FISA, even though in a memo he signed on January 21, 2009, the day after he was inaugurated president, he declared

"My administration is committed to creating an unprecedented level of openness in government." In the memo, he also said, "We will work together to ensure the public trust and establish a system of transparency, public participation, and collaboration." Nonetheless, the US chief executive signed in a 2011 congressional legislation the Patriot Sunsets Extension Act of 2011, which was a four-year extension of three key provisions in the Patriot Act: roving wiretaps, searches of business records, and conducting surveillance of "lone wolves"—individuals suspected of terrorist-related activities not linked to terrorist groups. As a result, the NSA, the FBI, and other intelligence agencies have been further empowered to perform almost all types of surveillance on anybody for security reasons.

Although the Foreign Intelligence Surveillance Court (FISC), in its capacity of a federal court established and authorized under the FISA, oversees requests for surveillance warrants against suspected foreign intelligence agents inside the United States by federal law enforcement agencies, the court has been accused of being a "kangaroo court with a rubber stamp."[36] In the wake of the public controversy about privacy invasion sparked by Snowden's NSA disclosures, then President Obama joined some congressional leaders and NSA and FBI officials in seeking to convince the public that the government had struck "the right balance" between privacy and security.

However, the series of security-related incidents that have subsequently ensued in the United States and the rest of the world have led most global thinkers and experts to rethink the present and impending dangers from nonstate extremist militant groups and the mentally ill with devastating impulses and the role of intelligence services in combating against them. After all, they have generally recognized the uncomfortable reality that makes it inevitable for citizens to sacrifice their privacy to an unknown extent for their own safety and other benefits that the intelligence agencies are bringing to the public. Any reasonable citizen would not refute the efforts of intelligence organizations to thwart terrorist plots aimed at civilian and military targets. In fact, they have foiled many plots for terror attacks by Islamist extremists in the post-9/11 United States. The repetitive amendments of the FISA have also authorized the NSA's phone surveillance program, which is "almost Orwellian" and unconstitutional.[37]

Privacy invasion has become an inevitable aspect of our present-day life. All intelligence services and law enforcement agencies in most countries and territories of the world are using privacy-invading technologies to protect citizens from dangers. Any troublemaker endangering public safety is not entitled to personal privacy. Blind and wholesale criticisms of intelligence-gathering organizations and privacy-invasive technologies are not sensible. Their role in protecting the public good deserves appreciation. In fact, terror attacks are showing no signs of slowing down. Thousands of terrorist incidents have been taking place across the world for the past few years. For example, for less than ten months of 2018 – January 1 to mid-October – 1,031 such incidents happened.[38] Also, we are also worrying about a wider range of advanced devices being used for acts of terrorism that can bring about catastrophic results. Terrorists can use weapons with precision-strike capabilities, digital instruments for massive-scale cyberattacks, and so on. The possibility cannot be excluded either that even nuclear, biological, and chemical weapons can fall into the hands of nonstate terrorist actors.

In these circumstances, the bulk of the public, while they are concerned about their privacy and the realistic impossibility of the so-called right balance, is inclined to believe that their governments and intelligences services are trying their best to ensure national security and public safety. An odd reality of this century is that we are moving forward in a direction in which we are consenting to encroachments on own privacy.

4. Emerging privacy-invasive technologies and the future of privacy

Whatever justification for constraining privacy may be made and whatever changes may be taking place in our attitudes toward the issue of privacy, it is undisputed that humans still have the natural, instinctive disposition to protect privacy. Evolving privacy-invasive technologies and the organizations and individuals using them will become more ubiquitous and powerful. Remote surveillance technologies can track even uncontacted indigenous societies like the Amazon Basin, where computers, the Internet, and other digital devices are mostly unavailable yet, even though terrorists see little reason to set up their strongholds in such areas.

In-built drawbacks in emerging privacy-related technologies are also aggravating the privacy problem. For example, biometrics—the measurement and analysis of unique physical or behavioral characteristics, such as our face, fingerprint, signature, the way we touch the keyboard, or voice patterns, as a means of verifying our personal identity—presents more serious threats to our privacy since the unique characteristics are permanent and cannot be replaced like stolen credit cards or bank account numbers. The FBI is currently reinforcing its Next Generation Identification database, which contains fingerprints, palm prints, iris scans, voice data, and photographs of faces. Your cell phone can also be secured by information that resides in a distant biometric database like the FBI's.[39] The United States and many other countries have biometric databases. Currently, India has the largest biometric database of the world called Aadhaar, a national ID program.

The exponential growth of digitized information that has occurred over the past few decades, combined with the skyrocketing popularity of mobile networks, has led to a huge surge in the sheer volume of digital content. The flood of information about digital progress has all but neglected effective measures to protect individual privacy. Furthermore, a variety of forthcoming information and communications technologies will put in the shade the current technological threats to privacy. As indicated above, when the NSA manages to build a quantum computer to break most of the encryption standards on the Internet, individual privacy will become far more helpless. To elaborate, quantum computers will be able to crack complex encryption technologies much more easily or in a few minutes or seconds. This technology can be used for invading in no time the privacy of millions upon millions of citizens across the world, although it can be harnessed to solve many globally relevant problems like curing health problems, predicting weather patterns, and so on. The incredible privacy-invading capability of quantum computers may be best explained by the fact that we haven't yet figured out what we might do with their inconceivable powers.[40]

The eye-tracking technology is making rapid advances. "Once the technology for eye-tracking is in place in earnest, it will glean information conveying not only what we read online, but also how we read it," writes electrical engineering professor John Villasenor of the University of California, Los Angeles (UCLA). He adds, "In the future, we will be served online ads based not only on what we've shopped for, but also on the thoughts reflected in our eye movements."[41] In fact, many experts fear that mind invasion technology may soon emerge, perhaps before 2030, with acceleration of AI innovation, posing another grave threat to privacy.

The remark that US actor James Woods, an MIT dropout with an IQ of 184, made for Futurescape during an interview in 2014 does no longer sound dramatic.

> I personally most fear the technology that allows invasion of our thoughts, our feelings, our aspirations, our intellectual achievements. The notion of some ill-equipped bureaucratic bozo getting into my inner thoughts and feelings fills me with dread and I think is probably the greatest challenge for the future of mankind. (Big Think Editors, "Future technology: Mind invasion?" Big Think [2015], available at: http://bigthink.com/, accessed December 20, 2015)

Such incredible privacy-invading technologies are evolving heartlessly, whatever may critics be telling about them.

Going a step further, the days are not far away when a mosquito-sized drone or an even smaller, invisible, miniscule robot will monitor every move we make in our home, car, or bedroom. It has already been some ten years since a life-size robotic fly, weighing only sixty milligrams with a wingspan of three centimeters, took flight at Harvard University.[42] Many small flying machines are expected to come along any minute now, and the US military is working now on a version that's three times smaller.

Such a miniature flying machine for reconnaissance will be able to watch any of our activities. An estimated US$6.4 billion is being spent developing drone technology each year around the world, and that number is expected to nearly double in coming years, bringing the total amount spent on drones for both military and commercial applications to US$11.5 billion annually by 2024, according to a report published in July 2014 by the Teal Group Corporation, an aerospace and defense market research firm headquartered in Fairfax, Virginia.[43] As nanosensors, nanorobots, the IoT, Internet of nanothings, and so on continue to develop, drones of all sizes are going to take their place among such state-of-the-art devices feeding back torrents of data for analysis, an occurrence that would make even the word "privacy" obsolete.

However, as the use of all other privacy-invasive technologies can be justified when they work to, say, attack terror suspects, a realistic scenario as follows can help us take a positive view of these drone technologies. About five years have already passed since it was reported that insect-sized micro drones could land on anybody and then use its needle to take a DNA sample.[44] This technology, too, has been making unremitting progress and could be used soon to remove or capture various troublemakers, such as terrorists, underground gangsters, cybercriminals, drug traffickers, human traders, dictators of rogue states, and so on. Theoretically, once DNA is collected by physically invisible drones from such people, undetectable, tiny drones loaded with the genetic information about every such mischief-maker and lethal elements could then be deployed in their residences, private rooms, or the whole areas of their activities to eliminate them.

As mentioned in chapter 6, advances in technology are resulting in trade-offs—that is, advantages and disadvantages—for all of us as a hutechciety. Some may argue that the advent of the perfect online privacy technology (mentioned in chapter 6) or zero-knowledge-proof technology, Internet privacy could finally become possible, as the technology could protect us from risking our privacy when we need to disclose personal information to get something done online. However, it may only limit and not totally remove the risk of a privacy breach or identity theft.[45] It would be reasonable to expect that any privacy protection technology will remain vulnerable forever, as evolving technologies will continue to increase the capacity not only to protect but also to break any encryption. Also, the intelligence agencies of democratic governments have every reason to try to access the personal information of terror and other criminal suspects.

All told, new technologies will cost us more of our privacy, but we will have to live with a permanent dilemma between the need to protect our privacy on one hand and to secure national security, public safety, and personal benefits on the other. We cannot have it both ways. Also, the so-called Google generation place far less weight on their privacy than previous generations. Some analysts even argue in support of the Google generation that "(young) people often behave better when they have the sense that their actions are being watched."[46]

Recently, about 66 percent of Swiss voters have given a strong approval to a new law on far-reaching surveillance powers for the intelligence agencies, uncharacteristic of the Swiss who have historically valued civil liberties. The result of the Swiss referendum held on September 26, 2016, is to allow the Swiss intelligence and security services to put suspects under electronic surveillance using wiretaps, Internet-based software, and hidden devices such as cameras and microphones, as reported.[47] This event means that the Swiss are much more concerned about possible terrorist attacks in their homeland than about their privacy. It should be made clear, however, that the Swiss voted for public safety, never for cybercrimes or attacks by nation-states as well as nonstate actors and individual criminals.[48]

Although personal privacy is expected to continue to shrink in the days ahead, we must not forget that all privacy-invasive intelligence agencies, business corporations, and technologies are products of human beings. This means that humans may still have some control over the destiny of their privacy. If we could demonstrate untapped human genius, wisdom, and united efforts, privacy as the time-honored basic human right might not completely die yet. Some experts argue, unlike Thomas Friedman's suggestion in the *New York Times* that "privacy is over,"[49] that "incrementally, the Internet has been transformed from a place of anarchic freedom to an environment of total tracking and total control."[50] For example, the perfect online privacy technology is a move in this direction. In sum, human beings produce privacy-invasive technologies but, at the same time, have the potential to use them wisely enough to minimize privacy invasion.

CHAPTER 8

Widening Life-Expectancy Divide

1. The widening gap in life expectancy between the rich and the poor

Apple cofounder Steve Jobs once said, "No one wants to die. Even people who want to go to heaven don't want to die to get there."[1] Unfortunately, the charismatic inventor and entrepreneur died relatively young at the age of fifty-six, but his remark reminds us that everybody wants to live long. Our standard of living and the quality of health care we receive have a great deal to do with our life expectancy defined as the average amount of time we can expect to live.

Of course, it also matters to our longevity how we manage our own health through our own efforts, such as refraining from smoking and heavy drinking, avoiding foolhardy acts like drunken driving, developing healthy eating habits, keeping a consistent workout schedule, and so on. The following is not so much humor as a piece of good advice to anyone who wants to live long.

A woman walked up to a little old man rocking in a chair on his porch. "I couldn't help noticing how happy you look," she said. "What's your secret for a long happy life?"

"I smoke three packs of cigarettes a day and I also drink a case of whiskey a week, eat fatty foods, and never exercise," he said.

"That's amazing," the woman responded and asked, "How old are you?"

"Twenty-six!" he replied.

("Happy old man," ArcaMax [2017], available at: https://www.arcamax.com/, accessed June 5, 2017)

Life expectancy has increased across the world by five years since 2000, the fastest rise in life-span since the 1960s, the *Guardian* reported in May 2016 based on a survey by the World Health Organization (WHO).[2] Improving economic standards of living; better access to resources and education; remarkable advances in health sciences, such as liquid biopsies marking a step forward in the fight against cancer; and so on have enabled people to live longer and healthier globally. The number of people who believe they can be a centenarian or a supercentenarian is increasing nowadays. A centenarian is a person who lives up to or beyond the age of 100 years. A supercentenarian is a person who has lived up to the age of 110 or more, something only achieved by about one in a thousand centenarians. Even rarer is a person who has lived to the age of 115. There are only forty-three people in recorded history who have indisputably reached the age of 115 years. Among them, eleven reached the age of 116, and five people are still living.[3] There has only been one known case of a person of 120 years of age or older. French woman Jeanne Calment lived to the age of 122 years, 164 days, outliving both her daughter and grandson by several decades.[4]

In 2012, the UN estimated that there were 316,600 living centenarians worldwide. In 2015, the estimated figure increased to 451,000 and Japan was at the top in the number of centenarians per one hundred thousand people with 48. The country had a total of sixty-one thousand centenarians at the end of 2015, according to a Pew report.[5] The other four countries among the top five were Portugal (38.9 in 2015), Spain (35.44 in 2016), France (32.1 in 2016), and Italy (31.41 in 2016), but the world's average stood at only 6.2 (2015). The surveys of centenarians were conducted in forty countries by several world-famous organizations, including the United Nations Population Fund (UNFPA) and Pew Research Center.[6] The factors contributing to the longevity in centenarians, according to John W. Santrock, professor at University of Texas at Dallas, include education; personality; lifestyle; heredity; family story; health involving weight, diet, smoking, exercise; and so on.[7] These factors, however, are topics for debate mostly in advanced countries that are already enjoying high life-expectancy levels.

The population of centenarians will rise rapidly in affluent countries. About one-third of all babies born in such countries in 2012 are expected to live to be one hundred years old.[8] For example, the Office for National Statistics (ONS) of the United Kingdom says one-third of the babies born in 2012 in the United Kingdom are expected to live to be one hundred years old.[9] This projection indicates that we can expect to see some 274,000 centenarians in 2113 in that country alone. This means that we will frequently come across centenarians anywhere in the nation in less than a century from now. The United Kingdom had 13,780 centenarians in all and 21.49 centenarians per one hundred thousand people in 2013.

Population aging, defined as a phenomenon that occurs when the median age of a country or region rises due to increasing life expectancy, is most evident in wealthy developed nations. As of 2016, life expectancy of the United Kingdom was estimated to be 80.7 years and ranked thirty-fourth and the United States was ranked forty-third with 79.8 years among the 223 countries and territories the CIA surveyed.[10] The top ten countries with the highest life expectancy studied up to 2016 by the CIA, the WHO, and other research institutions are enjoying the rewards of a prosperous economy with no exception.[11]

However, their studies have shown the dark side of the world's life expectancy overall. The gap in life expectancy between rich and poor countries and individuals has been widening. The WHO has noted for decades that "poverty is the major contributor" to the widening gap.[12] The UN agency concerned with international public health has underscored that the expanding gap "should stir the conscience of the world," but the life-expectancy picture in poorest countries "is getting worse."[13]

A survey of 183 countries the WHO released in 2016 also showed a wide gap of 33.6 years in average life expectancy between the first (Japan with 83.7 years) and the last country (Sierra Leone with 50.1 years).[14] The data released in 2012 by the WHO showed that the gap between the first and the last country was about 27 years,[15] validating the UN agency's consistent claim that the life-expectancy landscape is worsening in the poorest countries. Another report the WHO released in 2015 showed that globally, a boy born in 2012 in high-income countries can expect to live to the age of around 76 on an average—16 years longer than a boy born in low-income countries. For girls, the difference is a little wider—a gap of 19 years separates life expectancy in high-income (82 years) and low-income countries (63 years).[16] The gender gap in life expectancy is being closed in advanced countries, as more women smoke and are obese today,[17] but this narrowing gender difference is not a significant factor that affects the average longevity of the world population.

The variations in survey results from different organizations are insignificant. The top ten countries in the CIA study in order of highest to lowest were Monaco, Singapore, Japan, Macau, San Marino, Iceland, Hong Kong, Andorra, Switzerland, and Guernsey. The life expectancy of these ten countries ranged from 89.5 to 82.4 years, with the average of the top ten standing at 84 years.[18] The average nominal per capita GDP of the top ten countries was estimated to be US$65,652 in 2016.[19] The governments of these rich countries have been able to invest heavily in life expectancy–related areas, especially in public health care. Also, in the wealthy countries, most of the population is engaged in office-based work rather than heavy industry and labor. On the other hand, the average life expectancy of the bottom ten countries, all in sub-Saharan Africa—Republic of the Congo, Liberia, Gambia, Niger, Mozambique, Madagascar, Central African Republic, Burundi, Malawi, and South Sudan—was 59 years in the same year.[20] The gap in life expectancy between the top ten and the bottom ten was thus 25 years on average in 2016. Especially, the gap between the fist (Monaco's 89.5 years) and the last (Chad's 50.2 years) was almost 40 years.[21] The average nominal per capita GDP of the bottom countries was estimated to be only US$385.[22] In the poorest countries, not only food but also vaccination, clean water, sanitation, curative drugs, and other medical treatments were inaccessible to most people. The main point is that the CIA, the WHO, and other studies show similar findings to validate that the gap in life expectancy between rich and poor countries is constantly broadening.

The vast gap is also noted between poor countries and advanced and fast-growing economies combined. Inequality Watch—a European observatory of inequality—offers a global picture of the worsening gap in life expectancy. A report it released in 2012 said that there was now a gap of some twenty-one years in life expectancy between the poorest regions (fifty-six years) and developed and fast-developing regions (seventy-seven years) combined.[23] The key concern is that the gap cannot but be further widening, considering the limited capacity of the poorest countries for improving their standards of living through robust economic growth. "In parts of sub-Saharan Africa adult mortality rates are now higher than they were 30 years ago."[24]

The close link between living conditions and life expectancy is not a modern-day fact. The *Telegraph*, reported in February 2015:

> Britons, on average, lived for around two years longer following the fall of the Roman Empire. Robin Fleming, professor of history from Boston College in the US, said that once Britons were no longer forced to pay taxes, they were able to eat more nutritious food which increased longevity. (S. Knapton, "The best thing the Romans did for Britain was leave, historian claims," *Telegraph* [2015], available at: https://www.telegraph.co.uk/, accessed February 16, 2015)

Romans also brought superb sanitation and medicine to Britain.

> The Roman Empire was excellent when it came to sewage,
> sanitary plumbing and medicine. Romans had medics who
> were in use for any complications. (See, for example, K.
> Vyas, "19 Greatest Inventions of the Roman Empire That
> Helped Shape the Modern World," Interesting Engineering
> (2018), available at: https://interestingengineering.com/,
> accessed March 6, 2018)

In the United States, for instance, the average life-span increased by more than thirty years during the twentieth century, of which twenty-five years can be attributed to advances in public health, according to the *Morbidity and Mortality Weekly Report*—a US weekly digest specializing in health and disease issues—published in 2015 by the Centers for Disease Control and Prevention.[25]

Along with public health–related factors, the economic standard of living matters most to our longevity. A lot of failing economies of the poorest countries have lost the potential to catch up with not only advanced but also emerging, dynamic economies, including E7—BRICs, Indonesia, Mexico, and Turkey.[26] In fact, the rise in global life expectancy in the last several decades has been possible due in a great part to the remarkable improvement in the material standards of living of two fast-growing economies, China and India. The two giant economies have seen a seven-year jump in average life expectancy since 1990.[27] The outstanding leap in longevity of the two most populous countries in the world, the combined population of which account for some 2.7 billion or 36.4 percent of the world population as of 2016, has been largely responsible for extending global life expectancy to seventy-two years (as of 2015),[28] compared with forty-seven years in the early 1950s. This is indeed an astounding feat of twenty-five years achieved within about sixty years.

However, the life expectancy level remains highly uneven across countries. Sierra Leone, one of the world's poorest countries, has continuously suffered from epidemic outbreaks of diseases, including yellow fever, cholera, and malaria as well as poor economic performance. The country had the fifth highest maternal mortality rate in the world in 2017.[29] In 2014, there was an outbreak of the Ebola virus in the country and other West African countries. The WHO warned in early 2016 that more flare-ups of the virus in these countries were expected.[30] In Sierra Leone and many other countries in Africa, people's access to safe drinking water is seriously limited. The economic and social conditions in the poorest countries in other regions of the world remain roughly the same.

Wealth and income disparity between the rich and poor within a developed or rapidly growing economy also heavily affects the life expectancy of the population. The *Wall Street Journal* reported in April 2014 a study conducted by economist Barry Bosworth at the Brookings Institution that showed that the life expectancy of the wealthy is growing much faster than that of the poor within one of the richest countries in the world, the United States.[31] "And it's a gap (in life expectancy between the rich and the poor) that is widening (within the U.S.)."[32] The study shows that there is about a ten-year gap between the richest and the poorest among men in the United States. If one were born in 1940 and were in the richest 10 percent, he or she could expect at age 55 to live an additional 34.9 years, but if one were born in the same year and were in the poorest 10 percent, he or she could expect at the same age to only live an additional 24.2 years. Women live longer than men in the United States, but the gap between wealthy and poor females is about the same, according to the study.

A subsequent 2016 study by Brookings shows once again that the gap is widening in the United States. The study provides data about the disparity in life expectancy between the rich and the poor according to different earnings deciles. As *CNN* notes based on the study, "on average, a rich man born in the U.S. in 1920 could expect to live about six years longer than a poor man born in the same year. By 1940, this gap had more than doubled."[33] Another Brookings study that followed later in 2016 observed that low-income citizens in the United States remained outside the overall national progress in life expectancy. It said, "Low-income workers have experienced stagnating or even falling life expectancy over the past 30 years." It continued, "These trends demand that we continue to focus our attention on investing in the health and well-being of all Americans."[34]

The gap is widening within the United Kingdom too.[35] The disparity in life expectancy between the poor and the rich is expected to be more conspicuous in the United Kingdom by 2030, according to studies conducted in 2015 by the Imperial College of London and the ONS.[36] Australia is another notable example that clearly shows a huge life expectancy gap between the rich and the poor within a country. The life expectancy of indigenous poor Australians is about twenty years less than that of white rich Aussies, due to the higher rates of all economic factors that shorten life. The aboriginals cannot afford the very best in nutrition and medical care.[37]

The widening life-expectancy divide between the rich and the poor in both wealthy and poor countries only supports the conventional knowledge that even if we can consider a variety of factors affecting life expectancy, the most important and immediate global concern must be how to elevate the level of income and wealth for low-income people, especially of the poorest countries, through robust and sustained economic growth. "Economic growth is the most powerful instrument for reducing poverty and improving the quality of life in developing countries,"[38] the OECD has consistently emphasized.

However, the reality betrays this requirement. For instance, according to an IMF report on Regional Economic Outlook, economic activity in sub-Saharan Africa has weakened markedly. Economic growth for the region as a whole fell to 3.5 percent in 2015, the lowest level in some fifteen years and, from bad to worse, sharply decelerated to 1.3 percent in 2016,[39] although it recovered somewhat in 2017. All ten of the world's poorest countries are in sub-Saharan Africa.[40] Also, the severe income inequality has remained unchanged in most sub-Saharan countries at least for the last fifteen years, according to an IMF Working Paper.[41] Analysts have long recognized a more egalitarian income distribution would lift average life expectancy.[42] Inequality in income and other socioeconomic entitlements in the African region is among the highest in the world.[43]

According to World Bank data, among the top ten worst income inequality countries, seven countries whose world rankings range from no.1 to no. 9 (1. South Africa, 3. Namibia, 4. Botswana, 6. Central African Republic, 7. Comoros, 8. Zambia, 9. Lesotho) are sub-Saharan,[44] and the region consisting of forty-nine countries has the highest average income inequality in the world.[45] Globally, African and Latin American countries are the worst in income inequality.[46] Income inequality in the poorest and developing countries has generally been known to be more serious than in developed nations. A 2014 UNDP report notes that more than 75 percent of the world population is living in underdeveloped economies, and income inequality increased by 11 percent in these economies between 1990 and 2010, while advanced economies were generally seeing declining income inequality[47] although income inequality in some advanced and dynamic economies, including the United States, China, Brazil, Singapore, and Hong Kong, remained as serious as underdeveloped economies.[48] The UNDP and CIA reports thus support the prospects that the gulf in life expectancy between rich and poor countries and individuals will widen further in the years to come.

2. Global life-expectancy divide will continue to widen

Most of the poorest countries and regions have been deemed hotbeds to cultivate not only national but also global problems, such as militant extremism, international refugees, pandemics, threats to cybersecurity, organized crimes, piracy, global warming, and so on. All these are hazardous to global security and progress. For instance, many terrorist groups found their local networks in poor countries, such as Afghanistan, Syria, Pakistan, State of Palestine, Somalia, and so on and then expand their operations into other countries, notably advanced societies in North America and Europe. Poverty alone cannot be to blame for terrorism, but it is a major contributing factor.[49] Young people living in these poverty-stricken countries seem to have lost all kinds of "patience as the art of hoping."[50] In these circumstances, the global community, especially the developed world, for its own benefits, needs to do its best to maximize collaborative efforts to help the poorest countries promote economic growth and reduce economic inequality.

On humanitarian grounds, too, global efforts to defeat poverty, to save the lives of those who are starving to death, to improve human dignity and security, and to achieve social justice have become more urgent than ever. Many international, regional, national, and local organizations, both governmental and nongovernmental, have joined the efforts. For instance, of the seventeen goals the UN is pursuing for sustainable development, goal no. 1 calls for ending poverty in all its forms everywhere. The UN highlights that one in five people in developing regions lives below the poverty threshold or extreme poverty of US$1.25 a day,[51] and millions more make just a little more than this daily amount, with many risking slipping back into poverty.[52] According to World Bank projections, about 10 percent of the global population is living under extreme poverty of US$1.90.[53] The World Bank's mandate is to promote long-term economic development to reduce poverty.[54] Besides, there are many notable organizations committed to the fight against extreme poverty, hunger, preventable diseases, improving the livelihoods of the poor living in the poorest countries and regions, including Africa, Asia, and Latin America. Such organizations include ONE, Oxfam, Hunger Project, Hunger Site, CARE, to name a few.

Despite their laudable movements worldwide to end poverty and hunger and to achieve a world of hope, tolerance, social justice, and compassionate conscience, the poorest countries have remained largely unchanged. This means that compared with the amount of the effort required to significantly improve the miserable situation faced by the huge number of people groaning under poverty, the actual global efforts to improve the situation have fallen far short of the entire demand. On no account is it considered an easy task to end global poverty. The Borgen Project (BP), which the *Huffington Post* hailed as "an incredible nonprofit organization that is addressing poverty and hunger and working towards ending them,"[55] suggests six methods that it says euphemistically are "simple" to end global poverty. They are (1) Install a well, (2) Teach poor farmers how to grow more food, (3) Provide shelter, (4) Build schools, (5) Provide vaccines against diseases, and (6) Build small medical clinics. Of course, these are easier said than done.

Humanitarian organizations have been admitting that it is too demanding to solve the problem of poverty at its roots. They agree that it takes an unknown time period and a huge amount of resources to resolve the problem. Even so, all the six methods the Seattle-based humanitarian organization suggests sound reasonable and do not seem too costly for powerful countries in the world to put into practice if they are willing to and cooperate. The *Borgen Magazine* reported "the cost to end global poverty would be approximately $58 billion" as of 2014.[56] In 2015, the world's military expenditure totaled US$1,676 billion,[57] of which that of the top fifteen most powerful countries accounted for US$1,350 billion or 81 percent of the total. Of the top fifteen, eleven are wealthy, advanced countries, and four are BRICs. The expenditure of the United States alone stood at US$596 billion. Theoretically, it costs only 3 percent of the world's military expenditure to end global poverty. In short, the world lacks a global leadership committed to ending global poverty. The BP underlines that "leaders of the most powerful nation (the United States) on earth should be doing more to address global poverty."[58]

If such leadership is realistically impossible, poor countries will have to stand on their own feet, taking South Korea, Hong Kong, Singapore, Taiwan,[59] and so on, which have gone from poor to rich, as their role models. However, the realities of poor countries generally offer grim prospects for the efforts to improve their own miserable socioeconomic conditions. Lots of internal problems that complicate possible solutions have been too deep-rooted for them to alleviate their poverty on their own.

In 2000, Samuel Huntington compared economic data of Ghana and South Korea in the early 1960s and found these two countries were roughly comparable in terms of per capita GNP, structure of production, and foreign aid.

> Thirty years later, South Korea had become an economic giant as the 14th largest economy in the world. Moreover,

> it was on its way to the consolidation of democratic institutions. No such changes had happened in Ghana, whose per capita GNP was now about one fifteenth of South Korea's. (S. Huntington, "Cultures Count," in *Culture Matters: How Values Shape Human Progress.* 1st ed., eds. L. Harrison and S. Huntington [New York: Basic Books, 2000], xiii)

Huntington argued that "undoubtedly, many factors played a role, but it seemed to me that culture had to be a large part of the explanation" about the huge difference between the two states. "South Koreans valued thrift, investment, hard work, education, organization and discipline. Ghanaians had different values. In short, cultures count."[60]

The World Bank's 2017 data show that the gap between the two countries in terms of per capita nominal GDP has further widened: that of Ghana was US$1,642, about one-eighteenth of South Korea's US$ 29,743.[61] South Koreans are now enjoying political rights and the civil liberties democracy presents, but Ghanaians are under authoritarian rule.[62] Some may challenge Huntington's view on the role of culture in economic development and strengthening democratic institutions.[63] However, it is undisputed that poorest countries[64] are trapped in deep-seated cultural problems, such as a lack of quality education, discrimination against women in education and employment, citizens' lack of motivation for hard work and merit-based competition due to, among others, governmental improprieties, including power elites' corruption and monopoly of resources.[65] The sociopolitical culture of many poor countries works as some toxic substance in the soil that makes it impossible for economic development to take root there.[66]

Africa has suffered from not only horrible socioeconomic problems but also political problems. Africa, the world's second-largest and second-most populous continent, has the largest number of the poorest countries of the world, and most of the continent has been plagued by long-lasting dictatorships lacking the commitment to eradicate poverty.[67] Most African countries are among the most corrupt, according to CPI 2017 released by Transparency International.[68] Numerous studies have found that the foreign aid flows to Africa has mainly been misused since they are used for, say, supporting bloated bureaucracies and fueling graft.[69] Foreign aid to most African countries is not being used for the needs of their people but for the interests of political leaders, their families, and power elites.[70] Foreign aid is worsening, rather than alleviating, the miserable conditions of the poor since it serves to beef up and perpetuate the corrupt rule of wrong political leaders in Africa. In most African countries, it is the rule that "by seizing the seat of power, the victor gains virtually unfettered access to the package of aid that comes with it."[71] As authoritarian power elites, their families, associates, major business owners and executives, and so on have taken the bulk of the wealth in the poorest countries, the number of ordinary people in poverty is bound to increase, and acute income inequality cannot but persist, contributing to widening the gap in global life expectancy.

The top five worst political leaders in Africa have been known to be the president of Equatorial Guinea Teodoro Obiang Nguema Mbasogo, the president of Angola José Eduardo dos Santos, former president of Zimbabwe Robert Mugabe (who stepped down as president on November 21, 2017, after thirty-seven years in power, as parliament began impeachment proceedings against him), the king of Swaziland King Mswati III, and the president of Sudan Omar Al-Bashir.[72] African political leaders prefer Chinese aid because of Beijing's policy of noninterference in the internal affairs and recognition of the autonomy of recipient governments to manage their own development policies.[73]

The poorest countries in Africa also dominate the list of ongoing civil wars that have aggravated people's livelihood.[74] Civil wars in West Africa have brought many economies to near collapse. Contrary to the prevalent belief that Africa's civil wars are due to its ethnic and religious diversity, recent studies have found that the causes are largely economic. At the root of the conflicts in African countries lie economic dependence on natural resources in particular as well as failed political institutions.[75] Contending power elites of poor African countries mobilize their constituents to vie with other groups for scarce state-controlled resources, contributing to factional disputes and the emergence of conflicts.[76]

Conflicts in African countries, including Angola, the Democratic Republic of the Congo, and Sierra Leone, which have an abundance of natural resources, such as diamonds, oil, copper, and gold, are the typical examples that show most civil wars and domestic disputes in Africa have been fueled for economic gains.[77] In short, the struggle for economic gains lies at the root of most civil conflicts in Africa.[78]

Raging civil conflicts make it impossible for members of society to cooperate for their own betterment. Perhaps no study could better show the importance of cooperation among community members for their own progress than the one Edward Banfield, the late professor of political science at Harvard University, published in 1958.[79] The seminal study has important implications for the dire circumstances in African and other poor countries. Banfield noted that the backwardness of a society could be explained "largely but not entirely" by "the inability of the villagers to act together for their common good.[80] He observed that the "Mafia" or families in Southern Italy cared only for its own "members" at the expense of their fellow citizens and societal unity. He concluded that the town's plight was rooted in the incapacity of inhabitants for mutual support to get out the age-old predicament.[81] Although he conducted the field research in a town called Chiaromonte in the Southern Italy of the 1950s, not in a poor country or region, in the Africa of today, his study has had important implications for the need for cooperation among the poor themselves to fight against hunger and poverty. For the poorest countries in the world, such cooperation remains a remote possibility since they lack the kind of political leadership that would encourage such cooperation.

According to the historical mortality levels shown by the *Encyclopedia of Population* published in 2003, average life expectancy for prehistoric humans was estimated at just twenty to thirty-five years.[82] Despite the striking disparities in life expectancy between countries and individuals, the general trend that the world population is living longer is showing no signs of abating. The facts and projections available today strongly indicate that the increase in global life expectancy is expected to accelerate in the years to come. "The global life expectancy has increased from 64 years in 1990 to 70 years in 2011. That's dramatic. That's an average increase in life expectancy of 8 hours a day over the last 20 years," Colin Mathers, coordinator for mortality and burden of disease at the WHO, said in 2013.[83] In addition to sustained global economic growth; continuing scientific, technological, medical breakthroughs in hygiene, nursing care, disease treatments using new antibiotics, vaccines, and so on; and cultural innovations will be among the major factors that keep humans living longer.

Nevertheless, the poor are unable to access most of these advances. The living standards of poor people in rich countries cannot be compared with the poor in poor countries with various factors affecting life expectancy. However, poor people anywhere in the world are suffering far more disadvantages affecting their life expectancy than the rich. Life expectancy has even decreased in some of the poorest countries. Ordinary people living in sub-Saharan African countries, for example, are among the least blessed in the innovations that extend life expectancy. People in these countries have often seen rises and falls in life expectancy in recent years. In sub-Saharan Africa, life expectancy went up from 37.8 years in the 1950s to 51.5 years in 2010, according to a 2014 Inequality Watch report.[84] This increase has, however, slowed down significantly from the 1980s onward. It was estimated at 48.3 years in 1980 and has gained only 3 years so far. The emergence of AIDS explains this small change, although many international initiatives have been launched in various parts of this region to prevent this infection from spreading that has significantly reduced the number of AIDS-related deaths. Southern Africa has suffered most severely. At the beginning of the 1950s, its population had a life expectancy of 44.7 years, roughly corresponding to the world average of 46.6 years. Half a century later, life expectancy in the region increased by only 4 years, showing a gap of 16 years toward the world average (51.6 against 67.6 years). Since the beginning of the 1990s, life expectancy in the region has decreased by 10 years up to now, the Inequality Watch report said.[85]

In sum, if one is among the poorest people living in a poor country, the funeral bell may already be ready to toll for him or her. Could the world ever find humanitarian ways and means to redress the sad situation of the poor anytime soon? No such possibility is in sight. At this point, we may only reemphasize that the broadening gap in life expectancy will have a negative impact on the global community. A world where this disparity is expanding will most likely increase the number of the people who believe this planet is designed not to embrace them but to alienate them. John Donne, an English poet and cleric of the seventeenth century, gave humankind words of wisdom hundreds of years ago: "Because we are all part of mankind, any person's death is a loss to all of us. Any man's death diminishes me, because I am involved in mankind; and therefore, never send to know for whom the bell tolls; it tolls for thee."[86]

We may have by now realized more keenly that our knowledge about how long we will be able to live should go beyond the common impressionable understanding that global economic growth and all the beautiful achievements in health technologies will bring healthier and longer lives to all humans living on this planet. For the moment, we may only take some comfort in the fact that the number of organizations and individuals that are devoted to improving the miserable socioeconomic conditions of the poorest people in the poorest countries is increasing and convince those in despair that humanitarian wisdom is still alive and on their side.

3. The super race will be able to live in an ageless society

"We are on the cusp of being able to extend human life-span significantly, because we've got most of the technologies we need to do it," says Shripad Tuljapurkar of Stanford University.[87] Medical biotechnology, including antiaging technologies, is making fast progress toward the repair and reversal of the known root causes of aging. The sooner these treatments arrive, the more lives will be saved, according to the well-known biologist.[88]

Given this prospect, an interesting question may be raised as to exactly how long we could extend our lives or to what age. Advancing genetic and medical treatments have yet to increase average life-span, say, over a hundred years. The "Fountain of Youth," a mythical spring that supposedly restores the youth of anyone who drinks or bathes in its waters, which a lot of scientists have attempted to discover, aims at increasing the average life expectancy over a hundred years. To achieve this goal, the Institute for Regenerative Medicine in Pittsburgh, for instance, conducted a research on fast-aging elderly mice with a usual life-span of approximately twenty-one days.[89] They were injected with stem cells from younger mice. They were given the injection approximately four days before they were expected to die, and the results were astounding. Mice that were injected not only lived but also lived three times their normal life-span, surviving for an additional seventy-one days. In human terms, that would be the equivalent of an eighty-year-old living to be a way over two hundred years old.[90]

Specifically, the researchers injected the so-called muscle-derived stem/progenitor cells (MDSPCs) into fast-aging mice. MDSPCs are multipotent murine cells that display a capacity for long-term proliferation. Stem cells and progenitor cells are different from each other. The most important difference is that the former can replicate indefinitely, whereas the latter can divide only a limited number of times. With controversy about the exact definition remaining and the concept still evolving, the two kinds of cells are sometimes equated. Since age-related degenerative changes are universal in the musculoskeletal system, the impact on the musculoskeletal system by murine MDSPCs became the primary focus of their experiments. The results of their experiments suggest that it is reasonable to conclude that MDSPCs may have therapeutic value of delaying age-related functional decline in human aging. "This is a huge breakthrough for medicine because it will not only extend the life of humans in the future, but will also delay symptoms correlated with aging," their study says.[91] The results of this research were first reported in *Nature Communications* in 2012 and later in *Dartmouth Undergraduate Journal of Science* in 2013. This means the initial research was already completed five years ago.

We have heard stem cells are prized by scientists as miracle cures "because they can replicate and morph into any cell in the body—be it heart, liver or nerve cells."[92] Stem cells are special cells that can specialize into various types. They fall generally into two key categories—

adult stem cells and pluripotent stem cells. Adult stem cells, also known as somatic stem cells, are found inside people of all ages. Their task is to replace cells that wear out. Although adult stem cells can develop into many different types of cells, they cannot become every type. Pluripotent stem cells are omnipotent and can become any type of cell. Traditionally, these cells have been taken from human embryos. For this reason, researchers refer to them as embryonic stem cells.[93]

All the cells in an embryo, during the very earliest phase of growing life, are pluripotent stem cells. To obtain embryonic stem cells, the early embryo should be destroyed. This means destroying a potential human life. That is why human embryonic stem cell research has been ethically controversial.[94] Many critics have been concerned that research on embryonic stem cell may stray into the realm of cloning, and various communities oppose cloning of human beings for a range of reasons.[95] Many governments have focused on creating clear and understandable legislation about stem cell research in the hopes of harnessing their immense potential without causing controversy."[96] Recent advances in cell biology have led to yet a third type of surprising stem cell. These are called artificial or induced pluripotent stem cells also known as iPSCs. They behave like embryonic stem cells but can be made from any cell.[97] To elaborate, this biotechnology enables scientists to make embryo-like structures from stem cells alone without using eggs or sperm cells. The selection of artificial embryos as one of the ten breakthrough technologies of 2018 confirms that rapid progress in stem cell research is being made.[98]

Scientists at the Stanford University School of Medicine announced in January 2015 that they have found that telomere extension turns back the aging clock in cultured human cells. Telomere is a compound structure at the end of a chromosome, which is a threadlike structure of nucleic acids and protein found in the nucleus of most living cells, carrying genetic information in the form of genes. To put it another way, what they have found about the issue of aging largely amounts to the genetic information of the central and most important part of living cells called nucleus. The Stanford scientists delivered a modified ribonucleic acid (RNA), which is a nucleic acid present in all living cells, to cultured human cells. The RNA can encode a telomere-extending protein. This successful delivery has caused cell proliferation capacity to dramatically increase, yielding large numbers of cells for study or drug development for antiaging and other purposes.

It has yet to be known how great and realistic success these scientists will ultimately achieve in lengthening human lives. Nevertheless, advances in researches on adult stem cells, pluripotent stem cells, iP, muscle-derived stem cells, and all other types of stem cells are likely to result in a dramatic reality to extend human lives well beyond the age of 120 soon or even indefinitely in the near future.[99] Already in 2009, Ian Goldin, professor of globalization and development at the University of Oxford, who served as director of the university's think tank-cum-research center called the 21st Century School, talked about stem cells being developed at Oxford. He remarked that we can develop any part of the body and over time, this would be possible from our own skin. We will be "able to replicate parts of the body," meaning we're on the verge of turning our fantastic potential for regenerative medicine into a reality. "I don't think there will be a Special Olympics long after 2030 because of this capacity to regenerate parts of the body," said the former vice president of the World Bank.[100] All stem cell–related researches are not immune from ethical controversy. With that said, yet another critical question is raised as to the issue of life-expectancy divide. Even if longevity-related medical research continues to make miracles, could such achievements could be a universal boon to everybody on this planet? Professor Goldin asks, "Who will be able to afford it?" He continues, "But will this only be available for the superrich? Will only those that can afford it be able to be this super race of the future?"[101]

We already have this super race. At the end of 2016, there were just over thirteen million high net-worth individuals (HNWIs) in the world.[102] The *Guardian* reported in 2013,

> HNWIs or the global super-rich are defined as those with investable finance (financial assets, excluding their primary residence, art collection, vintage sports cars, etc.) of more

than US$1 million in constant 2006 dollars and are on the rise. (H. Stewart, "A million more people join the ranks of the global super-rich," *Guardian* [2013], available at: https://www.theguardian.com/, accessed June 18, 2013)[103]

HNWIs account for only 0.19 percent of the world population. The United States had the highest number of HNWIs (4.4 million or 31 percent of the world's total) of any country at the end of 2016.[104] There are also ultrahigh net-worth individuals (UHNWIs) defined as having a net worth of over US$30 million in constant 2012 dollars (after accounting for shares in public and private companies, residential, and passion investments such as art, planes, and real estate). There were 226,450 UHNWIs in the world with a total combined net worth of US$27 trillion as of 2017.[105] The New York metropolitan area alone had 8,350 UHNWIs. Most of UHNWIs are concentrated in North America and Europe.[106] E7 economies had 16,934 UHNWIs or 13 percent of the world's total as of 2014,[107] according to Statista Inc., one of the leading Germany-based statistics companies on the Internet. The number of UHNWIs is steadily rising.[108]

Oxfam—an international confederation headquartered in Oxford, United Kingdom, of seventeen charity organizations working in approximately ninety-four countries worldwide to find solutions to poverty and what it considers injustice around the world—said in 2016 that the richest 1 percent in the world owned more than the other 99 percent put together.[109] Significantly, the wealth gap is widening faster than anyone anticipated, with the 1 percent overtaking the rest a year earlier than Oxfam had predicted previously. The 2016 report of the antipoverty charity also said that just sixty-two people, fifty-three of them men, own US$1.76 trillion, which equals the total wealth of the poorest half (3.8 billion) of the entire world population.[110] In 2010, it took 388 super-rich individuals to equal the wealth of the poorest half of the world's population. While this number has fallen to only sixty-two individuals in six years, the amount of "wealth" held by the poorest half had shrunk by US$1 trillion in the same period, the charity noted.[111] Oxfam also said a year earlier that only 5 percent of global wealth belonged to the poorest 80 percent of the world, with billions of people around the globe living on less than US$2 a day.[112]

World leaders have faced "an increasingly divided world, with the poor falling further behind the super-rich, and political fissures in the United States, Europe and the Middle East running deeper than at any time in decades," *CNBC* reported in January 2016, based on the Oxfam calculations.[113] In early 2017, Oxfam released an even more surprising updated report that said that "Just eight individuals, all men, own as much wealth as the poorest half of the world's population." The charity called for action once again to curtail rewards for those at the top.[114] In November 2017, *CNBC*, based on the 2017 Credit Suisse report, said that the wealthiest 1 percent of the world's population now owns more than half of the world's wealth or 50.1 percent of the world's wealth, up from 45.5 percent in 2001, indicating the wealth gap between the rich and the poor is widening.[115]

Such a huge widening gap is also found in terms of income as opposed to wealth. The Global Issues—a website dealing with social, political, economic, and environmental issues of global concern—says,

> At least 80 percent of humanity lives on less than $10 a day. More than 80 percent of the world's population lives in countries where income differentials are widening. The poorest 40 percent of the world's population accounts for 5 percent of global income. (A. Shah, "Poverty facts and stats," Statista [2013], available at: https://www.statista.com/, accessed January 7, 2013)

Also, leading global organizations concerned, including WHO, released updated statistics that showed that the per capita GDP of more than half of the countries in the world remained below US$5,000. They added that "almost half the world's population is at risk of malaria."[116] All analysts agree that even if global economy is expected to continue to grow, the dismal economic, social, and political realities these poor countries face are not expected to significantly improve anytime soon.

All told, whatever advances in medical technologies and health care polices may occur, they will be able to extend the life expectancy of the richest mostly in advanced and dynamic economies. For an unknown period to come, the funeral bell will continue to toll much earlier for the bulk of the world population who are poor and cannot afford even a meager standard of living. Many poverty-stricken children under a year old in many countries of the world will also continue to perish. Meanwhile, the super race or superhumans will certainly continue to live in a special sanctuary that may be termed an "ageless society," which is likely to emerge as a reality within the next few decades or sooner. This severe imbalance is in no way good news for any of us, including superhumans, as we will be living in a global community that will have lost balance and stability and become restless and dangerous, especially to the super race who will continue to be diminished.[117]

CHAPTER 9

The Aging Workforce

1. The aging workforce in an aging society

Digital-age jokes belittling the aged seem to be increasing. Since more seniors are texting and tweeting nowadays, there seems to be a glossary of STCs (senior texting codes) that include BTW ("bring the wheelchair" instead of "by the way"), FYI ("found your insulin" instead of "for your information"), IMHO ("Is my hearing-aid on?" instead of "in my humble opinion"), BYOT (bring your own teeth instead of "bring your own technology or device"), and so on. However, STCs are likely to be short lived, as a growing number of the aged will not only remain in the workplace but also work as competently as or even better than younger workers.

The demographic profile of the workforce is changing fast across the world, except for the poorest parts of the world in Africa, Asia, and Latin America. Increasing human life-span in developed and dynamic economies is a major factor contributing to this change. Population is also aging quickly in poor but dynamic economies like Vietnam and Nigeria. The PPP-based per capita GDP of Vietnam was estimated to be US$6,876 in 2017 and ranked 125th out of 187 countries studied.[1] Nigeria, the largest economy in Africa, was ranked 129th with a per capita GDP of US$5,927.[2] Nigeria is called "a demographic powerhouse" since the population of the country is one of the ten largest in the world, and the African country is expected to "have no shortage of working-age citizens in coming decades."[3] Africa is expected to account for more than half of the world's population growth between 2015 and 2050.[4]

Overall, global demographic change toward an older workforce will become more striking as time goes on. Most noteworthy perhaps is that China, the world's most populous country, is getting old. "In fact, they are getting older faster than anywhere else in the world."[5] However, the employment demographic change will be most noticeable in high-income countries with the lowest birth rates. The declining birth rate that affects the availability of a young workforce in developed countries has been a global issue for a long time.[6] A *World Atlas* survey shows that among the top twenty-five countries with the lowest birth rates in 2017,[7] twenty-three countries had PPP-based per capita GDP exceeding US$22,000. For example, the workforce of Germany, one of the top five countries with lowest birth rates,[8] "will shrink by six million over the next 15 years, declining even faster than Japan's."[9]

In the United States, the nation's population aged sixty-five and older is projected to reach 83.7 million in the year 2050, nearly doubling the from 2012 at 43.1 million.[10] By 2022, 27 percent of men and 20 percent of women ages sixty-five and older are projected to be in the labor force, compared with 23 percent of men and about 15 percent of women in 2014.[11] The aging of the working population will be placed ever higher among major socioeconomic priority issues in the years ahead in North America, Europe, and other fast-growing economies. Although the United States has been preparing for an aging society for over fifty years, the nation has yet to be well prepared to meet the economic, social, and health care needs of the aged.[12] The US government will have to continue to develop well-advised public policies especially for an aging workforce.

Joseph Coleman, a journalist and professor at Indiana University, published in 2015 a book titled, *Unfinished Work: The Struggle to Build an Aging American Workforce.*[13] The *Wall Street Journal* reported in May

2015, to the effect that if one was curious about what awaits him or her, and the country, start reading his book.

> What he found is both troubling and inspiring: companies and bureaucracies that all but ignore older adults and their abilities, and people and programs that are fighting stereotypes and age bias. ("The aging American workforce," A book review article, *Wall Street Journal* [2015], available at: https://www.wsj.com/, accessed May 31, 2015)

Ray Williams Associates (RWA)—a Canadian firm providing executive coaching services—offers a twofold advice for both the aging population and its employment. It emphasizes that all countries, especially those in the advanced world, should keep working harder to prepare for their aging world population and their employment.[14]

Japan, the world's no. 2 in the lowest birth rate,[15] and no. 1 in life expectancy[16] may perhaps face more challenges from the aging workforce than any other country. The country has the highest proportion of elderly citizens in the world.[17] Those aged sixty-five or over accounted for more than 25 percent of the overall population as of 2015, and this figure is projected to reach 40 percent in 2060.[18] "In Japan, over one million people ages 90 to 100 will be working by 2030," according to the RWA.[19]

On September 19, 2015, the Japanese observed Respect for the Aged day. The *Yomiuri Shimbun*, one of the largest newspapers in Japan, subsequently carried a story that has important implications for the impact of an aging workforce as well as for extending life expectancy in the country. *Yomiuri* reported that with Japan's society aging faster, such problems as relative shrinkage in the young workforce and swelling expenses for social security programs have arisen.[20] *Yomiuri* continued,

> It is important to increase opportunities in which the elderly who want to work can exhibit their ability so they can actively support society. The creation of such a society

in which people vigorously contribute through their whole lives will hold the key for Japan to overcome the ultra-aging of its society. ("Increase opportunities for elderly to remain active in aging society" [an editorial reported on September 22, 2015], *Yomiuri Shimbun* [2015], available at: http://www.yomiuri.co.jp/, accessed October 31, 2015)

The Japanese daily added that "The average Japanese life expectancy stood at 80.5 years for men and 86.83 years for women and both are projected to rise even more in the future. This will herald the era of 90-year life spans."[21] In 2016, the rising cost of supporting the aging population—almost thirty-two thousand people were eligible to receive a silver cup from the prime minister, up 4.5 percent from the preceding year—prompted the Japanese government to present silver-plated cups rather than sterling silver cups, downgrading the gift traditionally awarded to citizens in their one hundredth year.[22] In sum, the Japanese might have rejoiced in the fact that Japan has become one of the world's foremost countries in longevity, but a longer life-span may not be a perfect blessing for the country, depending upon how effective Japan's policies for the aging workforce will prove.

Well known is the global prospect that the growth of the older population will continue to outpace that of younger population over the next thirty-five years.[23] For aging countries, the key question is how to create a society in which the elderly would be able to contribute to the development of their society. Worldwide, the number of people aged sixty-five or older is projected to grow from an estimated 524 million in 2010 to nearly 1.5 billion in 2050, according to a report released in 2011 by the WHO.[24] A number of international organizations, universities, academics, public and private research bodies, independently or in groups, have offered their research findings on how to cope with the problems arising from an aging population. However, most companies have yet to take their study results seriously. Their studies note that "despite a rising number of over-65s choosing to stay in work, only a small minority of businesses are taking the issue of an aging workforce seriously."[25] As the aging of society is accelerating across the world, "it makes sense from a business point of view that companies are using the skills and expertise that all ages bring to their workforce," says Christopher Brooks, policy adviser on employment and skills at Age UK.[26] Supporting Brooks' view is the fact that elders have typically been thought of having some special knowledge, skills, experience, and wisdom that young people don't.

Nonetheless, the younger generation believes they can easily acquire the kind of knowledge and skills the elderly have since they are better at using the Internet and many other emerging technologies. They think old people's knowledge and skills are becoming less and less valued or obsolete. They also believe that old persons have outdated views and values. In fact, a report the US Bureau of Labor Statistics (BLS) released in 2011 show that older information technology (IT) workers have higher rates of unemployment than both younger IT workers and older workers in other professions.[27] The so-called digital ageism has become one of the prime concerns the aging society needs to address.[28]

It seems, therefore, legitimate to claim that well-educated youths should make up the mainstream workforce of a state-of-the-art society in all corners of the globe, and the elders should be pushed to retire or become youthful enough to demonstrate physical and cognitive functions to use new skills and keep up, if they compete with youths. It is true that many aged are being moved to retirement communities, as their health and cognitive function decline and they become unable to keep up with the times in using new technologies in the workplace. As a result, there is an increasing lack of their influence on modern life;[29] this warning from the American Psychological Association implies that even if the elderly in general cannot play dominant roles in societal progress, we should somehow find ways to give them the opportunities to play some influential roles based on their experiences, expertise, and maturity that can contribute to the economy and society. However, such positive perspective on the aged may only remind younger workers of the conventional understanding that the more aged one is, the more limited the scope of their productive action.

2. The positives and negatives of the aging workforce

The changing demographic profile in the workplace is good news for the elderly. In many respects, the realities of the aging society strongly challenge the traditional perception that the more aged one is, the less useful one is in the workplace. In the United States, projections show that the demand for labor needed now is not being fulfilled by the young workforce only; the gap between young labor needed and young labor available will continue to expand in the future. The difference in terms of population size between baby boomers and their younger generations is to blame for negative growth in the working age population. The baby boomer generation started to turn sixty-five in 2011. About ten thousand baby boomers in the United States will turn sixty-five every day until about 2030, according to the US Census Bureau. Some years, this daily average will exceed thirteen thousand.[30]

The BLS gives more details. It says that the overall labor force participation rate in the United States—meaning the ratio between the labor force and the overall national population of the same age range—is projected to fall to 62.5 percent in 2020, compared with 62.8 percent in 2014. The declining labor participation rate will lead to a shortage of workers in the United States. In this declining trend, it is projected that by the year 2020, 25.2 percent of the workforce or the labor pool in employment in the United States will be composed of older adults who are aged fifty-five and over.[31] The labor force participation rates of old adults were 13.1 percent in 2000 and 19.5 percent in 2010, a remarkable growth by 6.4 percent in a decade. A complementary trend that follows this has been the increasing median age of the US workforce. By 2026, the workforce is expected to have a median age of 42.3, an increase from 40.8 in 2006 and 42.0 in 2016.[32] With the young labor force participation rate projected to continue to decline in the years to come, the trend of the increasing number of older adults remaining in the workforce will be inevitable. Even more outstanding in the BLS projection is that the agency estimates that by 2022, 31.9 percent of those aged sixty-five to seventy-four will still be working compared with 20.4 percent in 2002 and 26.8 percent in 2012.[33]

In Europe, there will be just two working age people per one elderly person by 2050.[34] Across the world, that number will shrink to less than four people for each elderly person by 2050.[35] Perhaps most significant in present-day workplaces is the fact that many older adults remaining in the workforce are more valued than they were in the past. Many Americans are worrying about the impending repercussions of "the silver tsunami" (also known as "the grey tsunami" or "rising tide"), which means a rise in the median age of the US workforce to levels unseen since the passage of the Social Security Act of 1935.[36] This metaphorical expression has been controversial due to its ageist connotations.[37]

Forbes reported in 2015,

> One of the biggest megatrends impacting the world today is population aging. By 2020, for the first time in history, the number of older people will outnumber the number of children younger than 5 years of age. In the next 25 years, the number of people older than 65 will double. (R. Das, "A silver tsunami invades the health of nations," *Forbes* [2015], available at: https://www.forbes.com/, accessed August 11, 2015)

Given this prospect, advanced societies and dynamic economies, in general, should develop policies for the "Rising Tide" as fast as they can. Japan and Germany are already termed superaged nations officially, where more than 20 percent of the population is over sixty-five. France, Sweden, and the Netherlands are expected to join the superaged category in 2020, and Canada, Finland, Spain, and Greece will also move into this category by 2025. The United States, the United Kingdom, Australia, Singapore, Brazil, South Korea, and China are projected to join the superaged group by 2030.[38] *Huffington Post* reported in 2015, "For the first time in history, there will be four generations of employees in the American workforce by 2020."[39] According to the Global Age Watch Index, which measures the social and economic welfare of those over sixty, 21 percent of the world population will be over sixty by

2050, and some 40 countries in the index will have populations where 30 percent are aged sixty. Norway is the best place to grow old among the ninety-six countries it studied.[40] The citizens of Norway with a small population of some 5.3 million "benefit from decades-old policies designed to provide financial security in old age, plus an efficient public transport system, a strong sense of security and a high level of employment among senior citizens."[41] Norway, however, is unique, and only four other countries (Sweden, the United States, the Netherlands, Japan) are more or less close to the Nordic country in this respect.[42]

The aging workforce has led analysts to intensify their investigations of the economic, social, and other impacts a labor force with an increasing median age will have in fast-aging countries. Many studies have found that increasing older workers alleviate skilled labor shortage. For example, an analysis of the Wharton School of the University of Pennsylvania says older workers "bring a lifetime of skills to their jobs and can be highly motivated and productive members of the workplace."[43] Older workers who are normally supposed to enter retirement can help fill the void of skilled labor shortage, if they delay retirement and continue working. Ray Williams, president of RWA, values the aging labor force.

> The recent recession has placed a myopic emphasis on the need to deal with the millions of baby boomers. In fact, we will need those aging workers. And we need to revise our view of aging, which for the most part, is portrayed in a negative way. (R. Williams, "The silver tsunami—the workplace needs aging workers," *Financial Post* [2011], available at: http://business.financialpost.com/, accessed July 19, 2011)

Most analysts agree that for potential aged retirees, their capacity to choose not to retire can be a boon not only for themselves but also for their economy. They emphasize that aging societies should double their efforts to handle the phenomenon of the "Grey Tsunami" to their own advantage.[44]

The dearth of funds for a range of welfare programs, such as social security and Medicare, has greatly contributed to increasing the number of older adults opting to remain in the workforce. The average social security benefits for an individual retiree are expected to continue to shrink in the years ahead as the old age dependency ratio (people aged sixty-five or above divided by people aged from fifteen to sixty-four) will rise sharply in many countries over the next forty years, according to the European Commission.[45] In the United States, for example, old age dependency ratio stood at 18.4 percent in 2005, but it rose to 23 percent in 2017.[46]

According to Alicia Munnell, head of the Center for Retirement Research at Boston College, Americans' stark retirement futures give older employees only three realistic options: (1) be poor, (2) save more money, and be a little less poor, (3) keep working.[47] Increasingly, many older Americans are choosing the financial equivalent of door no. 3. In other words, earning a living after retirement is the most important factor that prevents older workers from retirement. *U.S. News & World Report* reported in June 2015 that the Employee Benefit Research Institute–sponsored 2013 Retirement Confidence Survey of 1,254 individuals that included 251 retirees found only 24 percent of workers at least fifty-five years old had set aside more than US$250,000 for retirement (excluding the value of their primary residence and any traditional pensions). More surprisingly, 36 percent of this group had saved less than US$10,000.[48]

For many employers, on their own part, a growing challenge is to find enough new workers. They know new entrants into the workforce will steadily be outnumbered by baby boomers heading for the exits. It must thus be good news for many employers that the number of baby boomers extending their careers is increasing. The reality of the rising number of older workers choosing to remain in the workforce has obviously become a solution where everyone benefits—that is, both employees and employers. However, it takes much effort to achieve a work environment in which workers, young and old, and employers benefit together. Many hurdles have to be overcome. For example, governments must deal with the problem of rising health-care spending for the elderly as a smaller pool of taxpayers must fund the rising costs of the growing numbers of seniors.[49] For businesses, "Succession planning is becoming increasingly important,"[50] since many employers will find it difficult to get someone out of school who possesses the knowledge they need.

The benefits businesses get from the elderly staying in the workforce may greatly decrease when employers must wrestle with a host of higher costs that many older employees incur—from higher pay levels to more expensive charges for health and disability insurance and other benefits.[51] Older workers tend to exhibit losses in eyesight, hearing, and physical strength more than their younger counterparts. Occupational safety also matters for older workers.[52] Despite more experience in workplaces, older workers are usually at greater risk of occupational injury than their younger counterparts due to physical declines associated with aging. Studies show that older workers have low overall injury rates compared to all other age groups,[53] but are more likely to suffer from fatal and more severe occupational injuries. Old workers need special health care through geriatrics that aims to promote health by preventing and treating diseases and disabilities in older adults.[54]

As a result, how to help older workers deal with geriatric and chronic diseases is becoming one of the key issues in the societies where the number of aging workers is increasing while the number of young workers is decreasing. As economic, social, and human issues created by the aging workforce grows, a range of notions about how to cope with the problems are being offered for business employers. Besides economic costs, "employers will need to confront many other challenges to accommodate more older employees,"[55] such as training and flexible work schedules. "Employers who successfully attract, retain, train and motivate older employees may enjoy a competitive edge, but it will be a big adjustment from the youth-centric culture of many workplaces."[56]

Despite all the problems associated with older workers, seasoned employers, who have compared the advantages and disadvantages of the aging workforce, tend to think the positives outdo negatives for a number of reasons nowadays. Among other reasons, under current labor market constraints, it is impossible to recruit a sufficient number of dependable young workers over the short term. Also, since a longer life expectancy reflects the success of human efforts to improve human health, the elderly today can work longer and more productively than their predecessors. In fact, if we look closely at the body movements of the aged from the 1950s, which documentary films show, and compare them with those of their counterparts living today, we will see clear differences.[57] The body posture of the elderly today is much straighter, their steps are much livelier and faster, and their speech is much more clearer, according to a 2015 report released by the National Institute of Aging (NIA)—one of the eleven operating divisions of the US Department of Health & Human Services.[58] In accordance with improving physical health, most of the present-day elderly enjoy more cognitive strength. Many of the elderly in their seventies and eighties today are found equal to or even better in cognitive ability than younger adults of the past.[59] As they age, more adults today improve in many cognitive areas, such as vocabulary and other forms of knowledge.[60]

New medical and psychological findings challenge the common view that as we age, our brain functions slow down.[61] Dr. Joanna Brooks of the University of Adelaide in Australia found in 2014 that there are areas of the brain that remain as effective in old age as they are in youth.[62] The elderly who are healthy not only physically but also cognitively will be able to remain productive in the workforce after all. In conclusion, educated employers know older people can contribute on a macro level to their organizations. They take note of the fact that older workers not only have a wealth of skills and knowledge but also have lived through situations young workers cannot even imagine.[63] All things considered, the healthy elderly brings tremendous potential for economic and social development as well as for personal fulfillment.[64]

3. The tide is turning for elderly workers

Obviously, aged workers are accessing job-related advantages more than before, including advances in medicine for the aged. Nicholas Pimlott, a renowned physician and scientific editor of the *Canadian*

Family Physician, says that in all countries of the world the global future of medicine will be mostly about the aged.[65] The prospect as suggested by Pimlott poses enormous medical challenges, as many countries must prepare for and deal with medical problems associated with an aging society. In fact, research and development of geriatric medicine is making rapid progress. For example, the NIA has recognized remarkable advances in medicine for the aged. The US national institute has been making a wide range of efforts to deal with heart disease, memory problems, inappropriate behavioral response, cancer, diabetes, dementia, and other issues associated with aging. The institute's efforts have led to steady breakthroughs in discovering the causes and treatments of major health problems of the aged.[66] The kind of progress the NIA and other medical research organizations are making has also led to significant changes in the concept of aging and physical capability.[67]

Against this background, criticisms of age bias and ideas on how to beat ageism in the workplace are increasing. However, as for digital ageism in particular, it is conceded that the special characteristics of the IT industry—highly competitive, fast paced, short skill-update cycle—do not generally favor older workers, according to Jing Quan, a professor at Salisbury University in the United States.[68] In just one year from 2009 to 2010, the overall unemployment rate for people fifty-five and over engaged in computer and mathematical occupations jumped from 6 to 8.4 percent, compared to the total unemployment rate of 7 percent of this age group in the same period, according to a study done by the Employee Benefit Research Institute, a Washington-based nonprofit research institute.[69]

Also, even though unemployment rates for older workers outside the IT industry are generally lower than in the IT industry, older laborers working outside the IT industry remain more vulnerable than younger workers due to IT's rapid incorporation into every sector of the economy. For example, elderly administrative staff members who haven't learned how to use the latest office productivity software in a timely fashion or even senior journalists and teachers who have impressive educational backgrounds but are not good at using multimedia are more vulnerable as far as their job security is concerned. Constantly emerging technologies are getting more pervasive in all kinds of jobs, creating the pressure for a wider swath of the population to adapt to and to keep up with the pace of this change. Otherwise, their chances for being kicked out of the workplace will increase.

Nevertheless, the future of elderly workers is not that bleak even in the innovative technology-related workplace. The number of aging workers who are trying to keep their skills up to date is increasing, elevating their chances for remaining in or joining the workforce. As the number of such senior people is rising, an increasing number of companies are trying to avoid the trap of stereotyping against the elderly with regard to advances in technologies. Rather, the number of firms that tend to believe that if one is willing to attend training to update skills, then he or she is young is increasing. This trend reflects their recognition of the reality, which compels them to take proactive steps earlier than their competitors to keep older workers in their workplaces.

The companies that are trying to avoid a talent gap in management being created by retiring baby boomers are looking for older workers who come ready with skills they need. Nowadays companies seem more willing to hire older executives and managers than they were five to ten years ago, as businesses need someone who can hit the ground running.[70] "There's less interest in giving a honeymoon period to a newcomer, less time for training than there was in the past."[71] More employers nowadays believe "there is value in the maturity and experience typical of many older workers."[72] Stable and responsible workers can also mentor younger staffers, and mentoring is "the best kind of training," as Lynnette Fallon, a US expert in human resources development, points out.[73] In fact, experts have frequently spotted the weaknesses of young workers. *Forbes* reported in 2014 that with global business changes at such a stunning pace, entry-level employees barely have time to acclimatize themselves to a new company, a new competitive environment, or new operational requirements.[74] "The challenges faced by young workers include lack of experience, a complex corporate world, and business education that is too theoretical and uncoordinated with companies' day-to-day needs."[75]

The future competitiveness of companies will largely depend on their ability to ensure a right balance between younger and older workers. Also encouraging for older workers who tend to struggle with new technologies is that they will be able to access evolving technologies much more easily. In the 1980s, it was hard even for the well-educated, let alone the modestly educated, to be good at using a computer since the machine was not user friendly. "Computer fear" was a buzzword then. However, the speed of change in computer technology in terms of user-friendliness has been so astounding that it has enabled modestly educated workers, not to speak of the well-educated, to easily access a range of new technologies for their routine work in the workplace. It has already been some time since businesses started to make and sell desktops and tablets designed specifically for seniors who have little to no computer experience.[76] Simultaneously, the studies, ideas, and recommendations about how to make evolving mobile technologies friendly for the elderly are increasing.[77]

Besides, a variety of educational facilities that teach new technologies for senior adults is mushrooming. Senior centers, retirement communities, and advocacy groups are offering free courses for older adults.[78] The Senior Planet Exploration Center (SPEC) in Manhattan, New York, teaches older adults how to become more comfortable being online. At the SPEC, a woman named Marian Goldberg, aged seventy, has learned to use Pinterest, send messages on Facebook, and embed emoji in her emails. She has a part-time beaded jewelry business. Goldberg said she mastered enough tools to reframe herself as a digital entrepreneur.[79] Terry Bradwell, chief enterprise strategy and information officer at AARP Inc., a US advocacy group headquartered in Washington, DC, notes that the digital divide is still relevant but closing. "The tide is starting to turn," he says. It has been quite some time in advanced societies since societal and governmental efforts to help elderly people learn new technology began. As a result, "a robust digital toolbox can help seniors even jump-start new careers as in Ms. Goldberg's case."[80]

In place of "computer fear," "the new old age"[81] or "the old age as the new normal"[82] has become the buzzword today. Advances in technologies are making the world more complex, but there has never been a better time for older workers to use various software packages with ease, and this trend will gain momentum in the years ahead.[83] As long as elderly workers can expend a little effort to keep up with technology, the software packages they use to do their jobs will put them in control. In sum, the number of the companies that are competing to create easy-to-use digital devices for the elderly and institutions for technological education for the elderly is rising.[84] In parallel with this trend, a variety of assistive technology devices for seniors are also being developed fast.[85] The evolving innovative technology for older workers constantly changes the way one ages in the workplace.[86]

Businesses are also finding that their workers, young or old, are expecting their work technology to be easy to understand and use. Consequently, employers are looking to business technologies that combine flexibility and high-level functionality with software and hardware that their employees can use in the workplace without difficulty. This business demand goes well with the goal of state-of-the-art product manufacturers—the goal of expanding their market shares and profits by producing easy-to-use goods and services for all users across the board.

An article of the *Telegraph* titled "Older workers healthier and more reliable" introduced in May 2015 the findings of a research conducted by the insurance company RIAS, an England-based specialist provider of insurance products for those over fifty years of age. According to the RIAS research, younger people are more likely to fake being ill and take more sick days. More than 50 percent of those aged between twenty and twenty-nine took time off sick in 2014, compared to just a quarter of those over fifty. Compared to just 12 percent of those over fifty, 44 percent of younger people were found to have faked being ill to avoid coming into work, and almost a third of twenty- to thirty-nine-year-olds also see a sick leave as an "additional holiday" that they deserve and are entitled to, according to the study.[87] The *Telegraph* also reported a little earlier in March 2015 the findings of another study commissioned by the Department for Work and Pensions (DWP) of the United Kingdom. The study has discovered, among others, that older workers do not steal jobs from young people, as those over fifty add value to the economy, which creates jobs for younger people. "Older and younger workers are not readily substituted for each other and there are not a fixed number of jobs in the economy. The more spending power in the economy, the more jobs can be created," adds the DWP-commissioned research.[88]

As the WHO suggests, the population aging is a success story for public health researches and policies for socioeconomic advancement developed and implemented mostly in advanced societies, although it still challenges the societies to adapt to maximize the health and functional capacities of older people as well as their social participation and security. The WHO identifies six major determinants of active aging (i.e., healthy, successful, productive, competent, and vital aging). They are (1) behavioral styles; (2) personal, biological, and psychological conditions; (3) health and social services; (4) physical environment; (5) social factors involving education, profession, status, and so forth; and (6) economic factors. An increasing number of countries are making extra efforts to make improvements on these determinants.[89] It is undisputed that active aging has become a global goal and reality as well today, says *Current Gerontology and Geriatrics Research*, an authoritative medical journal published in the United States.[90]

Despite the notions the world leading organizations and experts are offering to demonstrate that the population aging is a success story for socioeconomic progress and active aging will be a great factor contributing to economic development, the issue of age discrimination should be resolved so that an economy can fully demonstrate its potential.

4. Fight against ageism is going from strength to strength

Age discrimination is an age-old psychological, cultural barrier hard to defeat in the short term not only in the workplace but also in society in general. However, reflecting upon aging or an aged society as a reality and the increasing importance of active aging, the fight against ageism is progressing, with the number of institutions and activists against age discrimination rising. The American Psychological

Association (APA) is one of many such institutions, and various media and advocacy groups like MySilverAge, one of California's largest non-profit providers of senior living communities, are championing anti-ageism campaigns. Melissa Dittmann, an award-winning writer, says in a feature article for APA, "Geropsychologists are striving to stop negative age stereotypes."[91] Ashton Applewhite, an activist at the forefront of the fight against ageism says her mission "is to put ageism on the same page as racism and sexism and homophobia, as grounds on which people are discriminated against all the time."[92] On the other hand, many experts recognize that that "age discrimination is still seen as okay in the workplace."[93] Most employers believe that a significant change in the youth centric corporate culture cannot occur soon enough to substantially discourage age discrimination in the workplace.[94]

Whatever the present reality of ageism, we will be seeing a rising number of older workers performing their tasks vigorously in the workplace in an increasing number of countries in the years ahead. As indicated above, both the ability to survive and the competitiveness of most companies will come to depend greatly upon not only their willingness to aggressively recruit and retain older workers but also their capacity to foster working conditions that fit the elderly workforce by providing, among others, a shield against ageism.

"Ageism" is an old term originally coined as early as 1968 by Robert Neil Butler, a US gerontologist and psychiatrist, and has become an old-fashioned word now. Such a protective mechanism will alleviate a combination of three connected elements the renowned gerontologist noted when he invented the term—prejudicial attitudes towards older people, discriminatory practices against the elderly, and institutional practices and policies that perpetuate stereotypes about elderly people.[95] As the changing demographic realities demand the workplace expand its efforts to defeat ageism, younger workers, for their own benefits, must call to mind the time-honored saying that goes, "You can understand and utilize the new only when you value, explore and learn the merits of the old." This proverb resonates with the recent WHO warning that pervasive misconceptions, negative attitudes, and assumptions about older people are serious barriers to developing good public policy that can capitalize on the great human capacity that older people represent.[96]

Finally, we need to look at the aging workforce in aging societies from an additional perspective. The elderly workforce will continue to grow in advanced, rich, and dynamic nations with low birth rates but not in most underdeveloped, poor, lethargic countries where life expectancy remains very low and fertility rates are very high. The fertility rate refers to the average number of children a woman gives birth to in her childbearing years. Among the top twenty countries with the highest fertility rates in the world in 2016 (They are in order: 1. Niger, 2. Burundi, 3. Mali, 4. Somalia, 5. Uganda, 6. Burkina Faso, 7. Zambia, 8. Malawi, 9. Angola, 10. Afghanistan, 11. South Sudan, 12. Mozambique, 13. Nigeria, 14. Ethiopia, 15. East Timor, 16. Benin, 17. Tanzania, 18. Guinea, 19. Sierra Leone, 20. Cameroon),[97] eighteen countries are located in sub-Saharan Africa and two states—Afghanistan and East Timor—are in South and Southeast Asia, respectively. The fertility rate of the top twenty countries ranges approximately from seven to five births per woman.[98] All of them are among the poorest countries in the world. This reality is likely to result in a megatrend in which aging countries will have to develop new immigration policies to attract a young labor force from poor countries in Africa, Asia, and elsewhere as well as to work out long-term policies to raise their own birth rates. No economy will be able to perform well without a young workforce at scale anyway. This prospect will stimulate us once again to rethink the need for advanced countries to pay more attention to the dire realities faced by poor, sluggish economies, notably those in Africa and South Asia where working-age populations are growing.

CHAPTER 10

Climate Change

1. Climate change is pushing the Doomsday Clock closer to midnight

> Two planets meet. The first one asks, "How are you?"
> "Not so well," the second answers. "I've got human species."
> "Don't worry," the other replies, "I had the same. That won't
> last long.'"

Could this conversation be considered as a soft comic dialogue for today? Since the turn of the century at least, climate change scientists and celebrities have cautioned political leaders against global warming in earnest. In January 2007 when US president George W. Bush decided to send an extra twenty thousand troops into Iraq four years into the Iraq war, David Letterman, a US talk show host and comedian, quipped,

> Here's good news: George W. Bush says that he is committed
> to fighting global warming. Yeah, well, he nipped that in
> the bud, didn't he? ... President Bush says he's really going
> to buckle down now and fight global warming. In fact, he
> announced today he's sending 20,000 troops to the sun.

In 2010, the National Research Council (NRC), the working arm of the United States National Academies, concluded that "Climate change is occurring, is very likely caused by human activities, and poses significant risks for a broad range of human and natural systems."[1] Even though the NRC was not 100 percent sure about the causes of climate change as it said, "very likely," we are experiencing an unparalleled recurrence of extreme weather events, such as heavy precipitation, heat waves, droughts and tropical cyclones. The science linking extreme weather to climate change is still developing, but projections through computer modeling suggest changes in the frequency and intensity of extreme weather events. For example, scientists have studied a relationship between climate change and deadly hurricanes as described below. They have found that the number of very intense storms has been increasing in a warmer world.[2]

Hurricane Harvey devastated many parts of Texas and its neighboring areas in August 2017 and was classified as a once-in-five-hundred-years storm or "the costliest weather disaster in US history."[3] Lethal hurricanes followed Harvey shortly. Irma severely damaged the Caribbean islands and Florida in early September 2017. Only ten days later, Maria ruined Puerto Rico, leaving the US territory in a complete power outage for over seven months.[4] Hurricane Florence harshly hit South and North Carolina in September 2018. Shortly after this, hurricane Michael ruined beach towns of Florida and its neighboring states in early October 2018.

Many worries that climate change may endanger the existence of all human beings on the globe. Reflecting this worry, major media across the world has contended that extreme weather events like these monster storms should be a warning to US president Donald Trump, a disbeliever of climate change, that climate change is a global threat.[5]

Since the two terms "global warming" and "climate change" are closely related and often used interchangeably, it seems necessary to explain the difference between the two.

> Global warming refers only to the Earth's rising surface temperature, while climate change includes warming and

the "side effects" of warming—like melting glaciers, heavier rainstorms, or more frequent droughts. Said another way, global warming is one symptom of the much larger problem of human-caused climate change. (C. Kennedy and R. Lindsey, "What's the difference between global warming and climate change?" Climate.gov [2015], available at: https://www.climate.gov/, accessed June 17, 2015)

An increasing number of people from around the world feel that climate change is an urgent life-and-death issue[6] and are calling for a global leadership to address this escalating threat to humanity much more aggressively than is being done at present. They have been staging fierce protests to call for climate justice and a strong global deal. The demonstrations in Paris on December 10, 2015, defied a government ban on such campaigns due to the terrorist attacks in the French capital that happened shortly before the rallies protesting the lack of a global leadership to deal with climate change. The protesters seemed to suggest that it didn't matter how the last breath of one's life came, whether from climate change or from a terror attack. Oddly enough though, many major world leaders seem to prefer an ostrich policy or believe that tomorrow's climate will not be so destructive as to put humanity at risk or might even get better.

Climate change skeptics may argue that the issue of climate change cannot qualify as a megatrend for an in-depth analysis since climate is fundamentally not changing in the way climate change believers suggest or even if it is changing, the change is not due to human activities but thanks to natural causes over which humanity has no control. To elaborate, this stance amounts to claiming there has always been climate change throughout the history of this planet and to advising mainstream climate change scientists to stop their research on this issue and to just wait and see how nature will take its course. This contention sounds defeatist and reckless since humans should normally do their best even when they deal with unknown unknowns (unexpected or unforeseeable conditions), if they are suspected of posing a potential danger to humanity. In fact, leading research organizations are putting increasing emphasis on climate change when they handle megatrends. For example, the NIC includes climate change in the six categories of megatrends in its latest report and addresses the issue in depth everywhere relevant throughout the report.[7]

The Doomsday Clock represents a countdown to possible global catastrophe. It has been maintained since 1947 by the members of the Science and Security Board of the *Bulletin of the Atomic Scientists* (BAS), who are in turn advised by the governing board and the board of sponsors, including eighteen Nobel laureates. The BAS was founded by some of the people who worked on the Manhattan Project, which was a research and development project that produced the first atomic bombs used during World War II. The closer they set the Clock to "midnight," the closer they say the world is to global disaster. As a result, "midnight" is also known as the End of Humanity or Doomsday.

The Clock hangs on a wall in the *Bulletin's* office in the University of Chicago, where Nobel Prize–winning Italian American physicist Enrico Fermi and his colleagues engineered the first controlled, self-sustaining nuclear chain reaction on December 2, 1942. The Clock's hands have been adjusted twenty-three times since then, ranging from two minutes to midnight to seventeen minutes before midnight. The Clock had been at five minutes to midnight since 2012, but the BAS announced at a news conference held on January 22, 2015, that it was adjusting the countdown to Doomsday by taking away two minutes. So, the Clock ticked then at three minutes to midnight, which was a warning that the End of Humanity might be near. It was the closest the Clock had been to Doomsday since 1984.

To add insult to injury, scientists pushed the Clock thirty seconds closer to midnight on January 26, 2017. One of the principal reasons for the move, which BAS scientists wrote about in an op-ed in the *New York Times*, was the ascent of US president Donald Trump. They wrote, "Never before has the Bulletin decided to advance the clock largely because of the statements of a single person. Mr. Trump's statements and actions have been unsettling."[8] In a tweet in December 2016, then US president-elect Trump wrote, "The United States must greatly strengthen and expand its nuclear capability until such time as the world comes to its senses regarding nukes."[9] Earlier, on September 27, 2016, he tweeted that "The concept of global warming was created by and for the Chinese in order to make U.S. manufacturing non-competitive."[10] The Clock's closest approach to midnight since its inception happened in 1953 when the United States and the Soviets tested their own first hydrogen bomb, a weapon far more powerful than any atomic bomb. It was set at two minutes to midnight then.

The symbolic Clock has thus represented an analogy for the threat of a global nuclear war. However, since 2007 the Clock has also reflected climate change, together with new developments in life sciences and technologies that could inflict irrevocable harm on humanity. When the Clock was moved two minutes forward to midnight in 2015, Kennette Benedict, BAS executive director, said that world leaders had failed to act with the speed or on the scale required to protect citizens from potential global catastrophe due to climate change. BAS scientists called on people to demand action from their leaders to curb fossil fuel pollution that they believe is endangering the planet.[11] The series of massive protests against global leaders' failure to take serious action to fight climate change that have occurred since the turn of the century in many countries across the world, including the United Kingdom, the United States, France, Belgium, Australia, Kenya, Chile, Morocco, and others can thus be considered to have been in accordance with the BAS call. The number of analysts who observe that global warming is "the most serious currently active challenge facing humanity, comparable in scope of impact to global nuclear war, if such were to occur" is increasing.[12]

Under current conditions, the world is likely warm by two degrees Celsius as early as 2040 and by four degree Celsius by the end of the century, according to World Bank Group (WBG) predictions.[13] The WBG warned that such increases would impact across key human support systems, such as agriculture and food production, water resources, ecosystems and biodiversity, and human health.[14] To put in detail, for warming of 2°C to 3°C, summers that are among the warmest recorded or the warmest experienced in people's lifetimes would become frequent. For warming levels of 1°C to 2°C, the area burned by wildfire in parts of western North America is expected to increase by 2 to 4 times for each degree (°C) of global warming. ("Climate stabilization targets," National Research Council [2017], available at: https://www.scribd.com/, accessed August 30, 2010)

Wildfires in California have been occurring more severely and frequently as if proving the WBG predictions are correct.

The 2016 United Nations Climate Change Conference (UNCCC), also known as COP 22, which was held in Morocco, November 7–18, issued a report that said carbon emissions from burning fossil fuels have been nearly flat for three years in a row—a "great help" but not enough to stave off dangerous global warming. Earlier on December 12, 2015, COP 21 negotiated the Paris Agreement—a global consensus among representatives of 196 parties on the slowing down of climate change. The agreement is scheduled to start to deal with greenhouse gas emissions mitigation, adaptation, and finance from 2020. The accord sets out a global action plan to put the world on track to avoid dangerous climate change by limiting global warming to well below two degrees Celsius above preindustrial levels by the middle of this century and beyond. As of June 2017, 195 members of the United Nations Framework Convention on Climate Change (UNFCCC), which convenes the UNCCC, have signed the agreement, 152 of which have ratified it. On the face of it, the Paris consensus seemed to have reached a significant milestone to fight against climate change. To attain the threshold goal of two degrees Celsius, "greenhouse gas emissions in 2050 will have to be 40 to 70 percent lower than what they were in 2010. By the end of the century, they will need to be at zero," according to the Intergovernmental Panel on Climate Change (IPCC).[15]

However, the Paris accord, like all other preceding conferences and the Kyoto Protocol of 1997, produced only ambiguous and non–legally binding results. The 195 participating countries agreed to reduce their carbon output "as soon as possible" and to do their best to keep global warming "to well below 2 degrees C."[16] Many criticisms on the accord have naturally surfaced. At the core of the reproaches was the lack of binding enforcement mechanism. James Hansen, a former scientist of the National Aeronautics and Space Administration (NASA) and a climate change expert, voiced anger that most of the Paris agreement consists of "promises" or aims and not firm commitments.[17]

To add insult to injury, as if he were in a battle against critics like James Hansen, US president Donald Trump turned his back on the nearly two hundred countries that are still committed to reducing greenhouse gas emissions, dealing a devastating blow to the non–legally binding accord. On June 1, 2017, Trump announced that the United States will withdraw from the Paris agreement. "Embracing isolationist voices," Trump argued that "the agreement was a pernicious threat to the economy and American sovereignty."[18] The United States as the world's most powerful country and second largest emitter of greenhouse gases or 17.89 percent of the world's total, following China's 20.09 percent (as of April 22, 2016), should ideally be at the forefront of the fight against climate change.

As their name suggests, greenhouse gases act much like the roof of a greenhouse as they trap heat on Earth. This process happens in two steps. First, greenhouse gases let the visible and ultraviolet light in sunlight to pass through Earth's atmosphere unimpeded and reach the Earth's surface. But then, when light strikes Earth's surface and is reflected to the atmosphere as infrared energy or heat, greenhouse gases absorb this heat and warm the planet. Besides carbon dioxide that we hear of most frequently, there are other types of greenhouse gases that result from human activities. We produce more carbon dioxide (54.7% of the total) than any other greenhouse gases—namely, followed by methane, nitrous oxide, and fluorinated gas that constitute 30, 4.9, and 0.6 percent, respectively. Other man-made greenhouse gases make up 9.8 percent. Why is methane, which constitutes 30 percent of the total, less threatening than carbon dioxide? While methane is a more potent greenhouse gas than carbon dioxide, the quantity of carbon dioxide in the atmosphere is over two hundred times more than methane. Hence, the warming due to methane is 28 percent that of the warming due to carbon dioxide.

Carbon dioxide volumes are now 140 percent above the levels found before the Industrial Revolution of 1750.[19] Human activities since the beginning of the Industrial Revolution until 2016 are assessed to have produced more than a 40 percent increase in the atmospheric concentration of carbon dioxide. The process involved large-scale deforestation that adds to the problem. Greenhouse gases come from all sorts of everyday activities, such as using electricity, heating our homes, and driving around town. In the United States, for example, "sources of greenhouse gas emissions are electricity (31%), transportation (27%), industry (21%), commercial and residential (12%), and agriculture (9%)," the United States Environmental Protection Agency (EPA) says.[20]

Now, seeing the general situation here, many might question what immediate, concrete, and effective actions could the global community take to save humanity from the deteriorating climate. People are not inclined to believe events like the COP 23, which was organized by Fiji, one of the Pacific island nations most physically vulnerable to climate change and extreme weather events in the world, and held in Bonn, Germany, November 6–17, 2017, can ever yield global action programs that can be put into practice for real effects for a sustainable Earth. They only keep being told of warnings like the following: Robert Glasser, the UN's head of disaster planning, says,

> The world's failure to prepare for natural disasters will have "inconceivably bad" consequences as climate change fuels a huge increase in catastrophic droughts and floods, and the humanitarian crises that follow. (S. Jones, "'World heading for catastrophe over natural disasters,' risk expert warns," *Guardian* [2016], available at: https://www.theguardian.com/, accessed April 24, 2016)

The essential point here is that the amount of international effort currently being made to combat climate change betrays the global reality, which requires a drastic increase in humanity's efforts to make our ailing planet healthy again. The alerts from the BAS, IPCC, WBG, and so on coincide with what we are already experiencing. For example, reports on climate change like the following have already become too commonplace these days to become news.

1. Report 1: The government of Kiribati, a tiny island nation in the central Pacific Ocean, bought about six thousand acres in Fiji, an archipelago country in the South Pacific with a population of some 860,000, as "Fiji's higher elevation and more stable shoreline make it less vulnerable." Kiribati "has essentially been drawing up plans for its demise." Five small Pacific islands, including part of the Solomon Islands, have already disappeared due to rising seas and erosion.[21]

2. Report 2: A US$17 million massive study of climate change that started in the Canadian Arctic in May 2017 has been canceled because of climate change. The study of how climate change is affecting the areas around the Hudson Bay has been nixed for now because hazardous sea ice is traveling farther south than usual due to warmer temperatures in the Arctic.[22]

3. Report 3: The California wildfire season in 2017 was the most devastating one on record, which saw many wildfires burning across California. California is suffering a ravaging climate change–induced drought, which could be a harbinger of devastating change. "Much of the state is facing an exceptional drought, which is characterized by exceptional and widespread crop losses; shortages of water in reservoirs, streams and wells creating water emergencies."[23] California isn't the only state at risk. According to a survey of the US Government Accountability Office, state water managers expect forty of fifty states will suffer water shortages in some portions of their states in the next ten years.[24]

According to an EPA guide on climate change released in 2016,

Glaciers all over the world have been melting for the last 50 years at least, and the rate of melting is speeding up. Many glaciers in Alaska and other parts of the United States have shrunk dramatically. If temperatures keep rising, glaciers will continue melting, and some could disappear completely. As glaciers and the giant ice sheets on Greenland and Antarctica melt, they add more water into the ocean, which causes sea level to rise. ("Melting glaciers," United States Environmental Protection Agency (EPA) [2016], available at: https://www.epa.gov/, accessed March 3, 2016)

According to National Geographic, if these trends continue, sea levels could rise between 2.5 and 6.5 feet by the end of the century, and even at the lower end of the estimate, coastal cities like Miami would be devastated.[25]

Richard Somerville, a distinguished professor emeritus and research professor at Scripps Institution of Oceanography of the University of California at San Diego, says,

Unless much greater emissions reductions occur very soon, the countries of the world will have emitted enough carbon dioxide and other greenhouse gases by the end of this century to profoundly transform the Earth's climate. ("Press release: It is now 3 minutes to midnight," *Bulletin of the Atomic Scientist* [2015], available at: http://thebulletin. org/, accessed January 22, 2015)

Despite this horrible prospect, "efforts at reducing global emissions of heat-trapping gases have so far been entirely insufficient."[26] Somerville notes that 2014 was the hottest on record and that the tipping point of ice loss in West Antarctica has been reached, meaning the melt is now unstoppable.[27] In the summer of 2017, "a trillion-ton iceberg, one of the biggest ever recorded, splintered off western Antarctica and is now floating at sea."[28]

2. Skeptics' opposing arguments and mainstream scientists' own weaknesses

Some scientists don't believe carbon dioxide emissions are the prime culprit behind global warming. These dissenting scientists include Nobel Prize winners and are affiliated with world-famous universities and research institutions in the United States, the United Kingdom, Canada, Australia, and other advanced countries, including MIT, Harvard, Princeton, the National Academy of Sciences, the Smithsonian Institution, and the Royal Society of London. A tiny minority or only about 3 percent of climate scientists takes a skeptical stance, while about 97 percent agree with the consensus position that humans are causing global warming.[29] The skeptics challenge the apocalyptic predictions, arguing that the observed warming is more likely to be attributable to natural causes—that is, sunlight and volcanic eruptions—than to human activities. In short, they believe that all climate problems are natural.[30]

There have been several efforts to compile lists of dissenting scientists, including a 2008 US senate minority report, the Oregon Petition, and a 2007 list by the Heartland Institute—a Chicago-based conservative and libertarian public policy think tank. The Center for Research on Globalization (CRG), a renowned scientific research body in Canada, said in September 2014 that "More than 1,000 dissenting scientists from around the globe have now challenged man-made global warming claims made by the IPCC."[31] The CRG continued that the number of dissenting scientists was increasing. Interestingly, the skeptical voices of these over one thousand international scientists included many former and current IPCC scientists, who have turned against the IPCC.[32]

Earlier, the so-called Climategate scandal[33] that began in November 2009 with the hacking of a server at the Climatic Research Unit of the University of East Anglia—a public research university in the United Kingdom—by an external attacker contributed to strengthening the position of climate change critics, who argue that science is all about testing hypotheses with real-world data and that climate change is a complete and total scientific lie that started as an outright fraud. The Climategate controversy started several weeks before the Copenhagen Summit on climate change—held December 7–18, 2009, at the Bella Center in Copenhagen, Denmark—as the hacker copied thousands of e-mails and computer files to various locations on the Internet. The critics and others denying the significance of human-caused climate change claimed that the e-mails showed global warming was a scientific conspiracy or fraud.[34] They alleged that scientists manipulated climate data and attempted to suppress critics.[35]

However, the coverage of the controversy by most media outlets criticized the allegations of the dissenting scientists, and the investigations that followed the scandal cleared the mainstream scientists involved of any wrongdoings. Nonetheless, it aggravated public confusion about scientific facts on climate change. A. A. Leiserowitz, director of the Yale University Project on Climate Change, and his colleagues found in 2010 that "Climategate had a significant effect on public beliefs in global warming and trust in scientists."[36]

The views of dissenting scientists that had subsequently brought about much media coverage significantly understated the perspectives that support anthropogenic (APC) climate change. Public opinion polls that followed also found much of the public was skeptical of APC views. After all, the Climategate scandal has led many people to have second thoughts about the consensus mainstream scientists of climate change have reached.[37] They came to question, Is our climate really changing at an unprecedented pace to the extent that the Earth will face a catastrophe anytime soon, unless we take urgent and strong measures to drastically reduce greenhouse gas emissions? Most startling perhaps was the results of a Pew Research Center survey released in September 2014, which showed only 40 percent of Americans believed there was solid evidence of APC.[38] A subsequent 2016 Pew survey showed only 48 percent of Americans believed that humans were causing global warming, while at least 95 percent of climate scientists believed in APC.[39]

The dissenting scientists have tried to give details on how changes in sunlight and volcanic eruptions cause climate change. A report published by the NASA Earth Observatory introduces a part of the dissenting view as follows.

> Variations in the Sun itself have alternately increased and decreased the amount of solar energy reaching the Earth. Volcanic eruptions have generated particles that reflect sunlight, brightening the planet, and cooling the climate. Volcanic activity has also, in the deep past, increased greenhouse gases over millions of years, contributing to episodes of global warming. (H. Riebeek, "Global warming," Earth Observatory of the National Aeronautics and Space Administration [2010], available at: http://earthobservatory.nasa.gov/, accessed December 23, 2010)

The NASA report, however, unequivocally said,

> The current warming trend is of particular significance because most of it is extremely likely (greater than 95 percent probability) to be the result of human activity since the mid-twentieth century and proceeding at a rate that is unprecedented over decades to millennia. ... There is no question that increased levels of greenhouse gases must cause the Earth to warm in response. ("Climate change: How do we know?" NASA [2017], available at: https://climate.nasa.gov/, accessed April 18, 2017)

History shows that the views of the minority in the scientific community have proved correct now and then. When the Italian polymath Galileo Galilei championed the astronomical model in which the Earth and planets revolve around the sun at the center of the solar system, he was tried by the Holy Office, then found "vehemently suspect of heresy," was forced to recant in 1635, and spent the last nine years of his life under house arrest. After being forced to recant his scientific conviction that the Earth moves around the sun, Galileo allegedly muttered the rebellious phrase, "And yet it moves." In the Catholic world prior to Galileo's conflict with the Church, the majority of the educated subscribed to the Aristotelian geocentric view that the earth was the center of the universe and that all heavenly bodies revolved around the Earth. The Galileo affair was forgotten among the public after his death.

It was as late as October 31, 1992, that Pope John Paul II expressed regret for how the Galileo affair was handled and issued a declaration acknowledging the errors committed by the Catholic Church tribunal that judged the scientific viewpoints of Galileo. In March 2008, Nicola Cabibbo, the head of the Pontifical Academy of Sciences, announced a plan to honor Galileo by erecting a statue of him inside the Vatican walls. The Galileo affair as one of the examples that demonstrate that the stances of the majority in the scientific community can at times turn out to be wrong makes it impossible that the views of the dissenting scientists on climate change may prove correct sometime in the future.

Although mainstream scientists by far outnumber the dissenting scientists, the scientific community is not supposed to function like a political democracy. Scientists do not reach conclusions on critical issues by the majority rule or a plurality voting system. Although scientific validations through rigorous research are at the core of all scientific efforts, such verifications turn out incorrect from time to time. Historically, quite a few scientific findings from painstaking, long-lasting studies have in fact proved wrong. Climate change is not an exact science, and it is, if anything, in the stage of relatively early development. As things stand now, climate change science needs to collect more hard facts and evidences enough to validate either of the two competing viewpoints. Some dissenting scientists take a firm position that climate change science will never be an exact science. They contend that it is fundamentally impossible to project global climate accurately to justify the ranges projected for temperature and sea-level rise over the next century.[40]

True, climate change science has yet to qualify as an exact science due to its limited capacity for scientific verification and its need to "deal with subjective uncertainties."[41] And, "few issues in science are as controversial as global warming."[42] This implies that all the existing projections for human activity–caused climate change may be incorrect. This controversial situation, distinctive in climate change science, has fueled dissenting scientists' challenges to mainstreamers. Nobel Prize–winning US theoretical physicist Richard Phillips Feynman observes that "it doesn't matter how beautiful your theory is; it doesn't matter how smart you are. If it doesn't agree with experiment, it's wrong." Stewart Franks, a professor of environmental engineering at the University of Tasmania in Australia, thinks along the same line. He argues that "perhaps the most frustrating aspect of the science of climate change is the lack of any real substance in attempts to justify the hypothesis."

The skeptics, for their own part, have failed to offer decisive scientific findings that could clearly establish that, say, the current IPCC projections are either too high or too low, or completely wrong. They have argued that the IPCC projections are likely to be inaccurate due to inadequacies of the current global climate modeling.[43] They have used equivocal expressions like "almost certain," "improbable," "doubtful," and so on. The dissenting scientists include some thirty-one thousand who have signed Global Warming Petition Project and have stated that "there is no convincing scientific evidence that human release of carbon dioxide will soon cause catastrophic heating of the Earth's atmosphere."[44] This dissent amounts to saying that all international conferences on climate change have been held without conclusive facts and findings, which should have been the keystone of any such conference. However, the skeptics have, for their part, failed to fully validate their opposing stance scientifically.

The EPA admits, at least in part, the natural causes that the dissenting scientists suggest are responsible for global warming. The environmental agency concedes the Earth does go through natural cycles of warming and cooling, caused by factors such as changes in the sun or volcanic activity. The EPA also recognizes some positive effects of moderate global warming. For instance, global warming is beneficial, as it serves improved agriculture at high latitudes and increased vegetation growth in some circumstances. However, the agency fundamentally agrees with, for example, the National Oceanic and Atmospheric Administration (NOAA) that says "climate change will dramatically change patterns of global agriculture."[45] The basic stance of the EPA on climate change has been that the negatives of global warming far outweigh its positives. The EPA has supported the IPCC's position that the global warming the world has seen in the past fifty years cannot be explained by natural causes alone, "especially warming since the mid-twentieth century. Rather, it is extremely likely that human activities have been the dominant cause of that warming."[46] According to the US agency, the global average temperature increased by more than 1.5°F over the last century.[47]

Likewise, NOAA takes notice of the increment in global temperatures and its consequences. Rising global temperatures have been accompanied by other changes in weather. Many places around the world have experienced changes in rainfall resulting in more floods or droughts, as well as more frequent and severe heat waves.[48] The planet's oceans and glaciers have also experienced changes: oceans are not only warming but also becoming more acidic, only proving that global climate is deteriorating.[49] The EPA, the NOAA, and other major organizations engaged in climate change research have updated their research results that show that the Earth is getting warmer. Likewise, the UK-based Committee on Climate Change (CCC)—an independent, statutory body established under the Climate Change Act 2008—also warns, "Climate change will become more pronounced in the future as emissions continue."[50]

The key problem, however, is that all the data and studies released by these research bodies still fail to fully verify the hypothesis that climate change is primarily due to human activities. In the last analysis, there is yet no perfect consensus among scientists on what causes global warming. Most skeptics of climate change too concede, at least, that the planet has been getting warmer for years, although some disbelievers have gone out of their way as to argue that the world is cooling. As a result, they are worsening the public confusion over climate change. The key point is that either of the two contending perspectives on the causes of global warming, man-made or natural, is equally menacing.

As for the former, it is realistically impossible that all governments and human beings in the world could start soon enough to make an all-out collective effort to radically reduce greenhouse gases. The latter sounds fatalistic as it argues that climate works according to the law of Mother Nature, even if it is often producing weather events too extreme for humans to endure. With the two similarly intimidating positions, the former may look less hopeless since there seems to remain the possibility that humanity's desperate efforts, if manifested soon enough, may forestall a global catastrophe. However, for the public, the views of dissenting scientists may be more appealing than that of the mainstreamers, as they argue Mother Nature has so far worked for humans' survival rather than destruction.[51] In fact, those who believe the skeptics, be they country leaders, corporate tycoons, academics, or ordinary citizens, have little reason to pay serious attention to the causes of global warming most scientists suggest.[52]

Whatever the public attitudes toward climate change, recent studies show that climate change is happening faster than predicted, and that the number of people who believe global warming is man-made is increasing.[53] "Globally, 78 percent of the public now believe we're heading towards an environmental disaster unless we change our habits quickly."[54] According to the studies of mainstream scientists, about 80 percent of human-induced carbon dioxide emissions comes from the burning of fossil fuels globally, while about 20 percent results from deforestation. One of the main features that make it hard to lessen the impact of greenhouse gases on climate in a short time span is that "some will remain in the atmosphere for thousands of years, due in part to the very slow process by which carbon is transferred to ocean sediments."[55] The scientists with IPCC elaborate,

> Moreover, if we stabilized concentrations and the composition of today's atmosphere remained steady, which would require a dramatic reduction in current greenhouse gas emissions, surface air temperatures would continue to warm. This is because the oceans, which store heat, take many decades to fully respond to higher greenhouse gas

concentrations. (Intergovernmental Panel on Climate Change [IPCC], *Climate Change 2014: Mitigation of Climate Change*, 1st ed. [IPCC, 2015], available at: https://www.ipcc.ch/, accessed February 20, 2015)

The ocean's response to higher greenhouse gas concentrations and higher temperatures will continue to impact climate over the next several decades to hundreds of years.[56] ... Ground-level air temperatures are expected to continue to warm more rapidly over land than oceans. Some parts of the world are projected to see larger temperature increases than the global average. ("Future of Climate Change," EPA [2017], available at: https://www.epa.gov/, accessed January 19, 2017)

The EPA, based on IPCC's 2014 Assessment Report on representative concentration pathways (RCP), introduces four pathways, of which RCP 2.6 or RCP3-PD (PD stands for "peak" and "decline") is a very low emissions pathway, which suggests curbing global temperature increases a way below two degrees Celsius (3.6°F) by 2050 and beyond.[57] The remaining three scenarios, RCP 4.5, RCP 6.0, and RCP 8.5 (the numbers refer to forcings for each RCP) are far more frightening, as they assume no or little action on climate change, with global temperatures rising to much higher levels in the same period.[58] A lot of scientists say that to achieve the goal as conceived in RCP 2.6 is unlikely,[59] as it would require active and speedy policies to decrease the billions of tons of our present annual greenhouse gas emissions to a marvelous extent, or 40–70 percent below 2010 levels, by 2050. On top of that, they argue that even if global temperature could be curbed by two degrees Celsius or more by 2050 and beyond, the world is unlikely to avoid frequent, extreme climate events as we are already experiencing.[60] In short, even the RCP 2.6 trajectory is an unpleasant scenario.[61]

Also unsavory is the fact that climate scientists, in the majority, remain a house divided inside, further complicating the battlefield against climate change. For example, many of them question among themselves the accuracy of the projections. Most of them recognize the weaknesses of their own claims. Some top climate scientists with IPCC have even confessed that their global warming forecasts are wrong and that the world is not heating at the rate they claimed it was in a key report.[62] Mainstream scientists admit that there will be no effective national or global policies on global warming until they discover more detailed facts about the Earth's changing climate. Those with the IPCC, EPA, and other major institutions say that they are still researching critical questions, including exactly how much the Earth will warm, how quickly it will warm, and what the consequences of the warming will be in specific regions of the world. "They continue to research these questions so society can be better informed about how to plan for a changing climate."[63] Besides, some scientists focus primarily on deforestation as the key cause of global warming, noting that trees as a natural carbon dioxide regulator play a huge role in converting the carbon dioxide in the air to oxygen.[64]

At the policy level, their different views have led to a variety of approaches to how to tackle climate change. The mainstreamers have yet to prioritize the policies under their consideration and show how they should be enforced to best reduce global greenhouse gas emissions. For instance, some of them advocate a national carbon tax, some prefer to mandate companies to disclose their climate risks, and still others want to push investors to divest from fossil fuel companies and to make a major shift in investments from fossil fuels to renewable energy. Such lack of consensus remains a major obstacle to working out policies to fight global warming.

Therefore, when it comes to the issue of public policy on climate change, all institutions concerned, including the IPCC, have a long way to go before mainstream scientists reach a unified agreement and recommend consensus-based public policies that could be implemented for economies, organizations, groups, and individuals emitting greenhouse gases. More seriously, all global institutions that have evolved since the late twentieth century to fight global warming are all consensus-driven deliberative forums with no binding legal force. The Paris Agreement is no exception in this respect. There is no mechanism in the climate agreement to force a country to set a specific target by a specific date. It is out of their authority and power to enforce public policies even if the mainstream scientists could ever reach an unqualified agreement on a set of policies to decrease greenhouse gas emissions. All this means that the total situation of the combat against climate change remains highly complicated and practically ineffective at present. The battle in disarray against climate change reminds us of all the difficult economic and political problems that developed and developing countries of the world have faced.[65] In sum, the world community is not expected to be able to build a powerful united front capable of enforcing action programs to cope with climate change anytime soon.

3. Climate change and national security

It matters little to humankind whose perspective on the causes of global warming is correct. If we can detect climate is changing in unprecedented patterns as NASA shows in its investigation of vital signs of global climate change,[66] we cannot but try our best to fight this. To put it another way, our ultimate question should be whether there is anything humans can do to avoid a possible catastrophe as soon as possible. *Forbes* reported in March 2017 that fifty years after the first groundbreaking paper on climate change was made public, the study predicted global warming almost perfectly.[67]

To reiterate, the scientific community has no rule that says that the views of mainstream scientists almost always prove right. Nonetheless, it is sensible for us to pay more attention to the majority view of the scientists. We cannot afford to neglect what we should do, only believing non-APC global warming, which humanity has no control over. Today we do feel that global warming is real and posing a fundamental threat to human survival. At this moment, all we need to do may be to follow Martin Luther's dictum: "Even if I knew that tomorrow the world would go to pieces, I would still plant my apple tree."

Climatologist Stephen H. Schneider at Stanford University observed that speculation by scientists can be a good thing, especially when the future of the planet is at stake. Schneider seems to offer a reasonable way to approach the two contesting stances of mainstream scientists and skeptics. The environmental expert maintains,

> political leaders are not able to judge the likelihood of a certain climate scenario any more than a patient is competent to judge which metal should be in the blade of the scalpel used by her or his surgeon. (Quoted in M. Shwartz and D. Levy, "Global warming: It's not an exact science, but it's science all the same," Stanford University [News Release] [2000], available at: http://news.stanford.edu/, accessed February 11, 2012)

If nobody on Earth can completely preclude a looming apocalypse due to climate change and time is obviously not on our side, we cannot afford to waste time, trying to find out whose view on climate change is right.

The issue of national security seems to provide a useful analogy for a global fight against climate change. Let's imagine the following theoretical situation: Most experts of national security in your country contend that your present ally is likely to be your future adversary, while those in the minority claim your friend of today will remain your collaborator forever. Under the circumstances, national security policies should normally prepare for even the least likely event, even if they involve a substantial amount of defense expenditures that could otherwise be used for, say, improving social welfare, public education, and so on. If we cannot substantiate that the causes of global warming are not anthropogenic, we cannot but do our best to diminish man-made causes to keep the world sustainable.

Otherwise, humanity might find it too late to do anything to save our planet and only watch the End of Humanity emerge as a reality. Humanity needs to be reminded of the notion that "People have been talking apocalypses for millennia, but few have tried to prevent them.

Humans are also bad at doing anything about problems that have not occurred yet."[68] To reemphasize, most imperative is a unified global leadership deeply committed to the battle against climate change. Global leaders, if united, are expected to encourage mainstream scientists to iron out their differences on all issues of climate change and public policies involved. However, most leaders of major countries—for example, the United States—do not remain devoted to the campaign, as BAS scientists note.

The *Washington Post* editorialized in May 2014 the view on climate change of US senator Marco Rubio under the title, "Marco Rubio's rhetoric on climate change casts questions about his judgment."[69] Senator Rubio said,

> I do not believe that human activity is causing these dramatic changes to our climate the way these scientists are portraying it, and I do not believe that the laws that they propose we pass will do anything about it, except it will destroy our economy.(Editorial Board, "Marco Rubio's rhetoric on climate change casts questions about his judgment," *Washington Post* [2014], available at: https://www.washingtonpost.com/, accessed May 12, 2014)

US president Donald Trump obviously shares this notion.[70] Since he won the race for the White House in November 2016, Trump has maintained the stance that global warming is a concept invented by China.[71] Trump picked in December 2016, Scott Pruitt, a prominent skeptic of climate science and an ardent foe of government action on climate change, to head the EPA.[72] His selection as EPA chief outraged environmental activists and organizations. In late April 2017, the EPA removed most climate change information from its website, saying that language on the website is being updated to "reflect the approach of new leadership." Environmental groups were disappointed by the EPA's step.[73] Earlier, on March 28, 2017, President Trump signed a sweeping new executive order aimed at demolishing central parts of Barack Obama's efforts to fight climate change.[74] Wrapping up the 2017 G20

Summit held July 7–8 in Hamburg, Germany, nineteen of the twenty leaders could agree on all points made in the joint declaration, but US president Donald Trump did not, as he announced in June.[75] Skeptics of climate change seem to believe that "climate change, no matter how scary, is unlikely to make the entire planet uninhabitable."[76] Professor Schneider indicated politicians' lack of responsibility for climate change, emphasizing the importance of scientists' warning of global warming. He asked, "If we don't offer a carefully hedged but nonetheless expert judgment on global warming, then who's going to do it? Politicians? Special interests?"[77] Considering the issue of climate change from the perspective of national security, climate change should be regarded at least as a phenomenon of known unknowns, if not of known knowns, never of unknown unknowns.[78]

If we could ever see our planet stop further warming for any reason, we will not have to move the Doomsday Clock closer to midnight. Hopefully, it will move backward for that matter. Contrary to such hope, however, most scientists warn repeatedly that climate change is likely to become the utmost fear of humankind, a possible Doomsday scenario, as time goes by.[79] Distinguished physicist Stephen Hawking warned in May 2017 that "humanity needs to become a multi-planetary species within the next century to avoid extinction."[80] The first in the existential risks he mentions in the warning is climate change. Earlier in 2016, Hawking predicted that the chance of a species-ending event on Earth was a "near certainty."[81]

Despite dire warnings of this kind, the good news is that the number of concerned citizens calling for climate justice is growing across the world. The bad news, however, is that many key world leaders still don't believe that Earth's climate can change to a level that will end humanity due to human activities. As things stand now, the general pattern of thought of world leaders seem to be not only one of indifference to the increasing apocalyptic warnings but also one of weakening the global potential for a united fight against climate change. In short, they lack motivation.[82] As a result, all the warnings, projections, and agreements about climate change look like a barking dog that never bites: they are not legally binding.

Notwithstanding all the dire realities and disappointing prospects for an intense fight against climate change, we cannot completely exclude the possibility that climate change will be recognized among all human beings as a life-or-death issue before it is too late. Already, signs of concerned citizens' strong determination to fight climate change have surfaced in all six continents of the world. They are championing the hope for the future.[83] Last but not least, we may find some comfort when we remember the double-edged nature of advances in technology. Advances in technology since the Industrial Revolution could be to blame for climate change, but they can also provide solutions to the problem. For example, the aforementioned technology called "Zero-Carbon Natural Gas," which is expected to be available in the next three to five years "would mean the world has a way to produce carbon-free energy from a fossil fuel at a reasonable cost."[84] Also, MTR selected "carbon dioxide catcher" as one of the "10 breakthrough technologies 2019," which will be able to remove carbon dioxide from the air in the next five to ten years.[85] In short, advancing technology could offer great ways to reduce greenhouse gases.

This amazing century should be "amazing" in a positive sense that would have no real relevance to a Doomsday scenario that contemporary great minds, such as BAS scientists and Stephen Hawking, suggest as a constructive warning to humanity. All members of the global community, especially world leaders, are called to double their efforts to combat climate change right from this moment. Otherwise, all discussions of other megatrends are meaningless.

Endnotes

Introduction

1. See, for example, M. Burrows, "The future, strategy and fiction," *The Art of the Future* (2014), available at: http://artoffuturewarfare.org/, accessed December 9, 2014.

2. P. Leskin, "'A.I. could be the "worst thing ever to happen to humanity,' Stephen Hawking says," Inverse (2017), available at: https://www.inverse.com/, accessed November 7, 2017.

3. A. Cuthbertson, "Stephen Hawking will show how humans can move planet in 100 years," *Newsweek* (2017), available at: http://www.newsweek.com/, accessed May 3, 2017. According to Hawking, "We should have spread out into space and to other stars, so a disaster on Earth would not mean the end of the human race."

4. *Global Trends: The Paradox of Progress*, 1st ed., NIC (Washington, DC: Office of the Director of National Intelligence, 2017), available at: https://www.dni.gov/, accessed February 2, 2017.

5. B. Page, "Foreword," in *Global Trends Survey 2017: Fragmentation, Cohesion & Uncertainty*, 1st ed. (Paris, France: Ipsos Group S.A., 2017), available at: https://www.ipsos.com/, accessed May 2, 2017.

6. See, for example, C. Macphail, I. Sturgis and *Telegraph* Film, "What is Back to the Future Day - and what did the film get right and wrong about October 21 2015?" *Telegraph* (2015), available at: http://www.telegraph.co.uk/, accessed October 27, 2015.

7. Such books include A. Toffler's *The Third Wave* (New York: Bantam Books, 1980) and *Power Shift: Knowledge. Wealth, and Violence at the Edge of the 21st Century* (Bantam Books, 1990), J. Naisbitt's *Megatrends: Ten New Directions Transforming Our Lives* (New York: Warner Books, 1982) and *Megatrends 2000: Ten new directions for the 1990's* (New York: William Morrow and Company, 1990), and P. Dixon's *Futurewise: The Six Faces of Global Change* (London: HarperCollins, 1998).

8. Mainly for this purpose, NIC, for instance, has released since 1997 quadrennial reports on global trends which the US president-elect is supposed to receive shortly after the presidential election is over. NIC's latest edition, the sixth in the series, was released in January 2017.

Chapter 1: Civicracy

1. R. Stewart, "Why democracy matters," TED (2012), available at: http://www.ted.com/, accessed December 30, 2012.

2. D. Cameron, "The next age of government," TED (2010), available at: http://www.ted.com/, accessed December 15, 2010.

3. A. Swift, "Congress approval remains at 16% in September," *Gallup News* (2017), available at: http://news.gallup.com/, accessed September 13, 2017.

4. L. Madison, "Congressional approval at all-time low of 9%," *CBS News/New York Times Poll* (2012), available at: http://www.cbsnews.com/, accessed December 14, 2012; F. Newport, "Congress job approval jumps to 28%, highest since 2009," *Gallup News* (2017), available at: http://www.gallup.com/, accessed February 7, 2017.

5. Institute of Politics, *Survey Report 2013: Survey of Young Americans' Attitudes Toward Politics and Public Service*, 24th ed. (Cambridge, MA: Harvard University, 2014), available at: http:// www.iop.harvard. edu/, accessed March 20, 2015.

6. B. Schieffer, "Face the Nation," *CBS* (2014), available at: http://www.cbsnews.com/, accessed February 16, 2014.

7. C. Silva, "Trump new approval ratings show he's the least popular president to enter a second year in office and it's not even close," *Newsweek* (January 8, 2018), available at: http://www.newsweek.com/, accessed January 8, 2018.

8. H. Enten, "It's not just CNN's poll. All polling shows Trump's approval rating dropping," *CNN* (2018), available at: https://edition.cnn.com/, accessed September 11, 2018.

9. A. Lockie, "The countries with the most prisoners," *Business Insider* (2016), available at: http://www.businessinsider.com/, accessed February 3, 2016.

10. *An Economy For the 1%*, 210 Oxfam Briefing Paper, Oxfam (2016), available at: https://www-cdn.oxfam.org/, accessed January 18, 2016.

11. M. Kelley, "Wealth inequality is much worse than you realize," *Business Insider* (2013), available at: http://www.businessinsider.com/, accessed March 6, 2013.

12. "Report for Selected Countries and Subjects," IMF (2017), https://www.imf.org/, accessed May 5, 2017.

13. *The World Factbook*, "List of government budgets by country," CIA (2017), available at: https://www.cia.gov/, accessed March 26, 2017.

14. See, for example, R. Boccia, "How the United States' high debt will weaken the economy and hurt Americans," Heritage Foundation (2013), available at: http://www.heritage.org/, accessed February 12, 2013. See also K. Amadeo, "The U.S. debt and how it got so big," The Balance (2017), available at: https://www.thebalance.com/, accessed May 19, 2017.

15. "Top 10 Countries with Largest National Debt-to-GDP in 2018," StashLearn (2017), available at: https://learn.stashinvest.com/, accessed July 26, 2017.

16. See, for instance, C. A. Kupchan, "The decline of the West: Why America must prepare for the end of dominance," *Atlantic* (2012), available at: https://www.theatlantic.com/, accessed December 15, 2014.

17. See, for instance, *Survey of Young Americans' Attitude Toward Politics and Public Service*, 24th ed., Institute of Politics (IOP) (Cambridge, MA: Harvard University, 2013). A Harvard IOP survey conducted October 30–November 11, 2013, available at: http://iop.harvard.edu/, accessed January 15, 2014.

18. D. Jackson, "Bush ran aground over Trump anti-establishment politics," *USA TODAY* (2016), available at: http://www.usatoday.com/, accessed February 22, 2016.

19. Ibid.

20. C. Cillizza, "Michelle Obama really, really doesn't like Donald Trump," *Washington Post* (2016), available at: https://www.washingtonpost.com/, accessed October 25, 2016.

21. J. Calmes, "Why is First Lady scarce in campaign?" *New York Times* (2014), available at: https://www.nytimes.com/, accessed October 3, 2014.

22. K. Liptak, "Michelle Obama: 'The Clinton surrogate that could finish off Trump,'" *CNN* (2016), available at: http://edition.cnn.com/, accessed October 14, 2016.

23. AFP, "French citizens' movement calls for worldwide demos," *Local France* (2017), available at: https://www.thelocal.fr/, accessed May 8, 2017.

24. See, for instance, A. Cieslik, "France seriously wants Obama to run for president, even though he's not French," *Daily Break* (2017), available at: https://www.dailybreak.com/, accessed February 26, 2017.

25. Ibid.

26. J. Toyer and S. Edwards, "Spain's political crisis deepens as Catalonia rules out snap election," *Global News* (2017), available at: https://globalnews.ca/, accessed October 26, 2017.

27. A. Soto and A. Boadle, "Brazil's Temer deploys army as protesters battle police," Reuters (2017), available at: https://www.reuters.com/, accessed May 24, 2017.

28. "Top 10 trends of 2015," WEF (2015), available at: https://www.weforum.org/, accessed February 26, 2015.

29. "Freedom in the world 2016," Freedom House (2016), available at: https://freedomhouse.org/, accessed December 2, 2016.

30. J. Soto, "The weakening of representative democracy," *Outlook on the Global Agenda 2015*, WEF (2015), available at: https://www.weforum.org/, accessed February 26, 2015.

31. Ibid.

32. C. Jose, "10 maps and charts that predict how the world will be in 2015," World.Mic (2014), available at: https://mic.com/, accessed November 7, 2014.

33. E. Li, "A tale of two political systems," TED (2013), available at: http://www.ted.com/, accessed July 4, 2013.

34. E. Li, "Why China's political model is superior," *New York Times* (2012), available at: https://www.nytimes.com/, accessed February 16, 2012.

35. "Economies of emerging markets better rated during difficult times," Pew Research Center (2013), available at: http://www.pewresearch.org/, accessed May 23, 2013.

36. J. Yu, "China: High Trust, But Skepticism Toward Business," Edelman (2018), available at: https://www.edelman.com/, accessed April 11, 2018.

37. Li, "Why China's political model is superior."

38. Ibid.

39. L. Cook, "'China will replace U.S. as global superpower,' says the world," *U.S. News & World Report* (2015), available at: https://www.usnews.com/, accessed June 30, 2015.

40. "Freedom in the world 2016," Freedom House (2016).

41. "The WJP Rule of Law Index 2016," World Justice Project (WJP)'s research team (2016), available at: https://worldjusticeproject.org/, accessed November 14, 2016. WJP is a US-based nonprofit organization. Its "Rule of Law Index" is "the world's leading source for original, independent data on the rule of law."

42. Human Development Indices and Indicators 2018 Statistical Update," UNDP (2018), available at: http://www.undp.org/, accessed September 29, 2018.

43. "GDP per capita, PPP (current international $)," World Bank (2017). available at: https://data.worldbank.org/, accessed July 27, 2017.

44. "Rankings & Distance to Frontier," World Bank (2018). available at: https://data.worldbank.org/, accessed October 10, 2018.

45. "2018 Index of Economic Freedom," Heritage Foundation (2018), available at: https://www.heritage.org/, accessed March 24, 2018.

46. The International Telecommunication Union (ITU), *ICT Development Index* (2016), available at: http://www.itu.int/, accessed May 6, 2016.

47. "GDP per capita, PPP (current international $)," World Bank (2017).

48. C. Johnson, *MITI and the Japanese Miracle* (Redwood City, CA: Stanford University Press, 1982), 412. MITI used to be one of the most powerful ministries of the Japanese government. At the height of its influence, it governed much of Japanese industrial policy. In 2001, its

role was taken over by the newly created Ministry of Economy, Trade and Industry (METI) as its power declined.

49. Some analysts regard Chalmers Johnson as a revisionist. See, for instance, T. Watanabe, "Piercing Japan 'myths': Maverick scholar Chalmers Johnson inspires a new generation of critics who dispute traditional theories about the Japanese," *Los Angeles Times* (1989), available at: http://articles.latimes.com/, accessed November 27, 1989.

50. *World Economic Outlook Database*, IMF (2017), available at: https://www.imf.org/, accessed April 18, 2017.

51. J. Nye, *Is the American Century Over?* (Oxford and Boston: Polity, 2015).

52. See, for example, "Government eyes making permanent residency easier for 'Cool Japan' talent," *Japan Times* (2018), available at: https://www.japantimes.co.jp/, accessed February 26, 2018.

53. F. Zakaria, *Commencement Speech* (2012), Harvard University.

54. J. Hays, "Political reform and socialist democracy under Deng Xiaoping," Facts and Details (2009), available at: http://factsanddetails.com/, accessed March 10, 2012.

55. As for an incipient study supporting this view, see S. Huntington, "Will more countries become democratic?" *Political Science Quarterly* 99, no. 2 (1984): 193–218.

56. For the prospects for this downtrend, see, for example, J. Nie and Y. Jia, "Has China's growth reached a turning point?" Federal Reserve Bank of Kansas City (2017), available at: https://www.kansascityfed.org/, accessed August 30, 2017.

57. *The Global Risks Report 2016*, 11th ed. WEF (2016), available at: https://www.weforum.org/, accessed October 25, 2016.

58. A. Browne, "China loses control of the economic story line," *Wall Street Journal* (2016), available at: https://www.wsj.com/, accessed February 16, 2016.

59. "China—economic forecast summary," OECD (November 2017), available at: http://www.oecd.org/economy/china-economic-forecast-summary.htm, accessed December 31, 2017.

60. I. Armstrong, "Forecasting China's anti-corruption campaign," *Global Risk Insights* (2015), available at: http://globalriskinsights.com/, accessed August 30, 2015.

61. Stewart, "Why democracy matters." Stewart remarks, "If democracy is to be rebuilt …"

62. Ipsos, *Global Trends Survey 2017: Fragmentation, Cohesion & Uncertainty*, 1st ed. (Paris, France: Ipsos Group S.A., 2017), available at: https://www.ipsos.com/, accessed May 2, 2017.

63. Ibid.

64. J. Barro, "A resolution for the establishment in 2017: No more no-choice politics," *Business Insider* (2016), available at: http://www.businessinsider.com/, accessed December 30, 2016.

65. See for example, C. Callaghan, "Social media news—social media as government watchdog," Social Songbird (2014), available at: http://www.socialsongbird.com/, accessed March 14, 2014. Callaghan writes, "This trend of social media as a government watchdog will only increase."

66. See, for instance, I. Goldin, "Navigating our global future," TED (2009), available at: http://www.ted.com/, accessed July 31, 2009.

67. For the last decade at least, experts have explored the development and use of social media in influencing politics and society. See, for instance, A. Auvinen, "Social Media and Politics - The New Power of Political Influence," Wilfried Martens Centre for European Studies (2012), available at: https://martenscentre.eu/, accessed May 5, 2017.

68. Cameron, "The next age of government."

69. Ibid.

70. G. Colvin, "4 reasons to truly hate everything about the 2016 election," *Fortune* (2016), available at: http://fortune.com/, accessed November 8, 2016.

71. C. Fishwick, "Why did people vote for Donald Trump? Voters explain," *Guardian* (2016), available at: https://www.theguardian.com/, accessed November 9, 2016.

72. See, for example, Editorial, "The *Guardian* view on Trump's behavior: Tyrannical not presidential," *Guardian* (2017), available at: https://www.theguardian.com/, accessed May 10, 2017.

73. See, for instance, M. Reis, "Letter: Why Donald Trump was the wrong choice," *Herald-News* (2016), available at: http://www.theherald-news.com/, accessed November 26, 2016.

74. R. Wike, B. Stokes, J. Poushter, and J. Fetterolf, "U.S. Image Suffers as Publics Around World Question Trump's Leadership," Pew Research Center (2017), available at: http://www.pewglobal.org/, accessed June 26, 2017.

75. *NBC News* exit poll desk, "Exit polls: Voters still don't like either of these candidates," *NBC News* (2016), available at: http://www.cnbc.com/, accessed November 9, 2016. See also N. Vladimirov, "Poll: Americans want alternative to Trump, Clinton," *Hill* (2016), available at: https://www.thehill.com/, accessed September 7, 2016.

76. See, for instance, Z. Blay, and L. Workneh, "55 reasons Obama will go down as one of our best presidents," *Huffington Post* (2017), available at: http://www.huffingtonpost.com/, accessed January 12, 2017.

77. "South Korea's parliament impeaches President Park Geun-hye," *Public Radio International* (2016), available at: https://www.pri.org/, accessed December 9, 2016.

78. I. Tharoor, "South Korea's president is hardly the only leader to turn to mystics and shamans," *Washington Post* (2016), available at: https://www.washingtonpost.com/, accessed November 2, 2016.

79. Ibid.

80. Ibid.

81. Ibid.

82. B. Lee and L. Glass, "We're psychiatrists. It's our duty to question the president's mental state," *Politico Magazine* (2018), available at: https://www.politico.com/, accessed January 10, 2018.

83. Tharoor, "South Korea's president is hardly the only leader to turn to mystics and shamans."

84. See, for example, R. Reilly, "The Mueller Investigation, Explained. Here's Your Guide To The Trump-Russia Probe," *Huffington Post* (2018), available at: https://www.huffingtonpost.com/, accessed September 14, 2018.

85. W. Cummings, "Rudy Giuliani: Americans would 'revolt' if Trump impeached 'for political reasons'," *USA TODAY* (2018), available at: http://www.usatoday.com/, accessed August 24, 2018.

86. M. McArdle, "Poll by sinking poll, Trump inches toward impeachment," *Washington Post* (2018), available at: https://www.washing-

tonpost.com/, accessed August 31, 2008. The *Post* article introduces the results of a *Washington Post-ABC News* poll and says, "In January 1974, well into the Watergate scandal, Richard Nixon's poll numbers on impeachment were better than President Trump's are now." See also A. Buncombe, "Majority of Americans back Trump's impeachment, finds new poll," *Independent* (2018), available at: https://www.independent.co.uk/, accessed August 31, 2018.

87. The *Economist* Intelligence Unit, "Democracy Index 2017: Free speech under attack," *Economist* (2018).

88. *Corruption Perceptions Index 2016*, Transparency International (2018), available at: http://www.transparency.org/, accessed June 20, 2018. In 2016, TI studied a total of 176 countries for the index.

89. M. Roser, "Democracy. Our world in data" (2017), available at: https://ourworldindata.org/, accessed August 20, 2017.

90. Benjamin Lawsky is an American attorney and served as New York State's first superintendent of Financial Services, 2011–15. The *New York Times* reviewed his "polarizing four-year tenure" positively, saying that the state's banks would not miss the Columbia graduate. "He threatened to pull their licenses, fined them hundreds of millions of dollars and forced dozens of their employees to resign." J. Silver-Greenberg and B. Protessm, "Benjamin Lawsky, sheriff of Wall Street, is taking off his badge," *New York Times* (2015), available at: http://www.nytimes.com/, accessed May 20, 2015.

91. For the latest development of the Occupy movement, see, for example, A. Gabbatt, "The growing Occupy Ice movement: 'We're here for the long haul'" *Guardian* (2018), available at: https://www.theguardian.com/, accessed July 6, 2018.

92. K. Heuvel, "Will Occupy Wall Street's spark reshape our politics?" *Washington Post* (2011), available at: https://www.washingtonpost.com/, accessed October 11, 2011.

93. J. Kirkup, "Occupy protesters were right, says Bank of England official," *Telegraph* (2012), https://www.telegraph.co.uk/, accessed October 30, 2012.

94. Ford Media, "Looking further with Ford," *Ford's Sixth Annual Trend Report*, 1st ed. (Dearborn, MI: Ford Motor Company, 2018), available at: https://media.ford.com, accessed February 3, 2018.

95. P. Catapano, "Can you hear them now?" *New York Times* (2011), available at: https://opinionator.blogs.nytimes.com/, accessed September 30, 2011.

96. Soto, "The weakening of representative democracy."

97. Ibid.

98. "Switzerland's voters reject basic income plan," *BBC News* (2016), available at: http://www.bbc.com/, accessed June 6, 2016.

99. According to Peter Marber, author of *Seeing the Elephant* (2009), the seven countries are as follows: BRICs, Indonesia, Mexico, and South Korea—as opposed to Turkey.

100. S. Ülgen, "The anatomy of Turkey's botched coup," Carnegie Europe (2016), available at: http://carnegieeurope.eu/, accessed July 19, 2016.

101. "The vote that will determine the fate of Turkey's democracy," *Economist* (2017), available at: http://www.economist.com/, accessed April 15, 2017.

Chapter 2: The Triumph of Wisdom

1. Adapted from a humorous story of an unknown source.

2. Aristotle's *Rhetoric* is an ancient Greek treatise on the art of persuasion, dating from the fourth century BC.

3. For this line of reasoning, see, for instance, S. Renshon, "Leadership: The bridge from good judgement to successful enactment," in *Good Judgment in Foreign Policy: Theory and Application*. 1st ed., eds. S. Renshon and D. Welch (New York: Rowman and Littlefield, 2003), 46.

4. See, for example, J. Mearsheimer, "Can China Rise Peacefully?" *National Interest* (2014), https://nationalinterest.org/, accessed October 25, 2014. Mearsheimer considers that China's growing power will likely bring it into conflict with the United States. However, critics charge him with having an outdated zero-sum view of the world. See, J. Read, "Is Power Zero-Sum or Variable-Sum? Old Arguments and

New Beginnings," *Political Science Faculty Publications* (2012), College of Saint Benedict and Saint John's University.

5. P. Hruby, "Experts' predictions of the future have a history of being wrong," *Washington Times* (2012), available at: http://www.washingtontimes.com/, accessed December 12, 2012.

6. For a view on a professional body of knowledge, see, for instance, G. Romme, *The Quest for Professionalism: The Case of Management and Entrepreneurship* (Oxford: Oxford University Press, 2016), 211.

7. D. Sornette and G. Ouillon, "Dragon-kings: Mechanisms, statistical methods, and empirical evidence," *European Physical Journal*, Special Topics 205 no. 1 (2012): 1–26.

8. D. Majumdar, "New report details why a war between China and America would be catastrophic," *National Interest* (2016), available at: http://nationalinterest.org/, accessed August 1, 2016.

9. Many analysts do not preclude a possible third world war, especially a Sino-US conflict likely to break out in the near future. See, for example, R. Farley, "5 Places Where World War III Could Start in 2019," *National Interest* (2018), available at: https://nationalinterest.org/, accessed December 22, 2018.

10. R. Farley, "Asia's greatest fear: A U.S.-China war," *National Interest* (2014), available at: http://nationalinterest.org/, accessed June 9, 2014.

11. G. Allison, "The Thucydides trap: Are the U.S. and China headed for war?" *Atlantic* (2015), available at: https://www.theatlantic.com/, accessed September 24, 2015.

12. "Why the Cold War didn't turn hot," *Telegraph* (2001), available at: http://www.telegraph.co.uk/, accessed January 20, 2001.

13. William Ellery Channing, the foremost Unitarian preacher in the United States, observed during his "Baltimore Sermon" on May 5, 1819: "Error is discipline through which we advance."

14. See, for example, L. Edwards, *Ronald Reagan and the Fall of Communism*, 1st ed. (Washington, DC: Heritage Foundation, 2010), available at: http://www.heritage.org/, accessed March 8, 2010.

15. R. Hilton, "The collapse of the Soviet Union and Ronald Reagan: A history study released by Stanford University" (2017), available at: https://wais.stanford.edu//History, accessed May 24, 2017.

16. Ibid.

17. *World Economic Outlook Database*, IMF (2018), available at: https://www.imf.org/, accessed August 14, 2018.

18. Allison, "The Thucydides trap."

19. J. Weston, "The moral arc reconsidered: Empirical evidence that the arc of the moral universe bends toward justice," *UU World* (2013), available at: http://archive.uuworld.org/, accessed April 20, 2013.

20. N. Kristof, "Why 2017 was the best year in human history," *New York Times* (2018), available at: https://www.nytimes.com/, accessed January 8, 2018.

21. J. Johnson, "More than 60 house dems denounce Trump for 'raising the specter of nuclear war,'" Common Dreams (2017), available at: https://www.commondreams.org/, accessed August 10, 2017.

22. Scientist John Gofman, for instance, was one of America's most prominent antinuclear activists. He was a member of the Manhattan Project group. P. Stone, "John Gofman: Nuclear and anti-nuclear scientist," *Mother Earth News* (March/April 1981), available at: http://www.motherearthnews.com/, accessed April 25, 2013.

23. *Global Trends: The Paradox of Progress*, NIC (2017). This NIC report, for example, uses the expression, the paradox of progress, as follows: "As the paradox of progress implies, the same trends generating near-term risks also can create opportunities for better outcomes over the long term" (p. xi).

24. A. J. Nathan, *Peking Politics, 1918–1923* (Berkeley and Los Angeles: University of California Press, 1976), 28.

25. "A pessimist's guide to the world in 2015," *Bloomberg* (2014), available at: https://www.bloomberg.com/, accessed December 17, 2014.

26. B. Obama, Remarks by President Obama to the United Nations General Assembly, The White House (2015). The president's remarks were delivered at United Nations Headquarters on September 28, 2015.

27. J. Perlezsept, "Xi Jinping pledges to work with U.S.," *New York Times* (2015), available at: https://www.nytimes.com/, accessed September 22, 2015.

28. Some analysts note globalism seems to be being discouraged in some parts of the world, including Europe. However, they say that over-

all globalism isn't going away. M. Meehan, "The top trends shaping business for 2017," *Forbes* (2016), available at: https://www.forbes.com/, accessed December 17, 2017.

29. C. Binkley, "Beyond China: US colleges look afield for foreign students," *Seattle Times* (2016), available at: http://www.seattletimes.com/, accessed November 14, 2016.

30. D. H. Rosen and T. Hanemann, "The rise in Chinese overseas investment and what it means for American businesses," Rhodium Group (2012), available at: http://rhg.com/, accessed July 5, 2012.

31. Ibid.

32. J. Mullen, "China is America's biggest creditor once again," *CNN* (2017), available at: http://money.cnn.com/, accessed August 16, 2017.

33. As for a possible trade war between the U.S. and China, see, for instance, M. Pei, "A trade war with China is likely under Donald Trump," *Fortune* (2016), available at: http://fortune.com/, accessed November 10, 2016.

34. "US exports to China (2006–16)," The US-China Business Council (2017), available at: https://www.uschina.org/, accessed June 30, 2017.

35. L. Shaffer, "'Trump trade policy will likely swing balance of power toward China,' economists say," *CNBC* (2017), available at: http://www.cnbc.com/, accessed February 23, 2017.

36. A. Blake, "How Trump's trade war with China could go sideways on him," *Washington Post* (2018), available at: https://www.washingtonpost.com/, accessed July 7, 2018.

37. "Trouble ahead: What's next for the Chinese economy?" The Wharton School of the University of Pennsylvania (2016), available at: http://knowledge.wharton.upenn.edu/, accessed March 9, 2016.

38. *The Global Risks Report 2016*, WEF (2016).

39. *The Global Risks Report 2017*, WEF Insight Report (2017), 12th ed., available at: https://www.weforum.org/, accessed January 10, 2017.

40. D. Palmer, "'Company debt swelling in China,' warns S&P," *Herald Sun* (2016), available at: http://www.heraldsun.com/.au/, accessed October 11, 2016.

41. "Income inequality in China" (A report of *China Daily*), The Institute of Social Science Survey of Peking University (2014), available at: http://www.chinadaily.com/.cn/, accessed July 26, 2014.

42. S. Hsu, "China is set to lose its 'emerging market' status as growth continues to decline," *Forbes* (2018), available at: https://www.forbes.com/, accessed January 25, 2018.

43. B. Bryan, "China's economic problems are everyone's economic problems," *Business Insider* (2015), available at: http://www.businessinsider.com/, accessed June 21, 2015.

44. L. Gensler, "Global 2000: The largest companies in China in 2017," *Forbes* (2017), available at: https://www.forbes.com/, accessed May 24, 2017.

45. See, for example, "Chernobyl: Ten Years Later," *Bulletin of the Atomic Scientists* (May/June 1996). "Castle Bravo" was the code name given to the first US test of a dry fuel hydrogen bomb detonated on March 1, 1954. It was the most powerful US test (at that time) with yields of sixty-three thousand terajoules, compared with sixty-three terajoules of energy that was released by the atomic bomb that exploded over Hiroshima on August 6, 1945, during World War II.

46. H. Kristensen and R. Norris, "Status of world nuclear forces," Federation of American Scientists (FAS) (2017), available at: https://fas.org/, accessed December 12, 2017.

47. See, for example, "Nuclear Notebook," *Bulletin of the Atomic Scientists* (2017).

48. "Where the wisdom is in the planning," Kiker Wealth Management (2013), available at: http://www.kikerwealth.com/, accessed December 12, 2013.

49. "World Economic Outlook (WEO) April 2013: Statistical Appendix," IMF (2013).

50. J. B. DeLong, "Estimating World GDP, One Million B.C. – Present," Brad DeLong's Home Page (1998), available at: http://www.j-bradford-delong.net/, accessed February 12, 2013.

51. Ibid.

52. "Gross Domestic Product 2014," World Bank Open Data (2018), available at: https://data.worldbank.org/, accessed October 10, 2018.

53. F. Ferreira, C. Lakner, and C. Sanchez "The 2017 global poverty update from the World. Bank," World Bank (2017), available at: https://www.worldbank.org/, accessed October 16, 2017.

54. "Zakaria shares message of hope in commencement speech," *Harvard Magazine* (2012), available at: http://harvardmagazine.com/, accessed May 24, 2012.

55. A. Furnham, "Are men really more intelligent than women?" *Psychology Today* (2014), available at: https://www.psychologytoday.com/, accessed June 22, 2014.

56. "The role of women is changing in the Arab World," *U.S. News & World Report* (1983), available at: https://www.usnews.com/, accessed October 10, 1983.

57. See, for instance, Jamal Al Shalabi, "Political participation of Jordanian women," ResearchGate (2012), available at: https://www.researchgate.net/, accessed December 10, 2012.

58. M. Etehad and N. Bulos, "Allowing women to drive is expected to boost Saudi Arabia's economy," *Los Angeles Times* (2017), available at: http://www.latimes.com/, accessed October 1, 2017.

59. K. Hewitt, "My 21st century leaders experience," 21st Century Leaders (2016), available at: https://www.21stcenturyleaders.org/, accessed December 16, 2016.

60. Karl Zinsmeister, "15 years later, Iraq is a modest success," *Wall Street Journal* (2018), available at: https://www.wsj.com/, accessed April 8, 2018.

61. "Commit to Compassion," The Foundation for Developing Compassion and Wisdom (2018), available at: http://www.compassionandwisdom.org/, accessed January 26, 2018.

62. Ford Media, "Looking further with Ford."

Chapter 3: Informal Education

1. "Informal learning, home education and homeschooling," Infed (2015), available at: http://infed.org/, accessed September 26, 2016. Infed is a not-for-profit site run by the YMCA George Williams College.

2. J. Dewey, *Democracy and Education: An Introduction to the Philosophy of Education* (New York: Macmillan, 1916).

3. S. Jobs, "You've got to find what you love," Commencement Address at Stanford University (2005), available at: http://news.stanford.edu/, accessed June 15, 2005.

4. Ibid.

5. Ibid.

6. Ibid.

7. S. Levy, "Steve Jobs," Encyclopedia Britannica (2018), available at: https://www.britannica.com/, accessed October 1, 2018.

8. J. Wang, "Rags to riches 2016: Wealthiest self-made billionaires.," *Forbes* (2016), available at: https://www.forbes.com/, accessed March 1, 2016.

9. R. Klein, "18 successful home-school alums," *Huffington Post* (2013), available at: http://www.huffingtonpost.com/, accessed August 23, 2013.

10. "Pearl S. Buck," Teachers College Columbia University (2000), available at: http://www.tc.columbia.edu/, accessed August 25, 2013.

11. S. Williams and B. Hilary, *Venus and Serena: Serving From The Hip: 10 Rules for Living, Loving, and Winning* (New York: Houghton Mifflin Harcourt, 2005).

12. A. Kerstein, "7 traits of philanthropic people who see success," Borgen Project (2015), available at: https://borgenproject.org/, accessed August 16, 2015.

13. M. Biro, "5 traits of leaders who are ready for social good," *Forbes* (2012), available at: https://www.forbes.com/, accessed December 9, 2013.

14. Quoted in K. Stern, "Why the rich don't give to charity," *Atlantic* (April 2013), available at: https://www.theatlantic.com, accessed May 5, 2013.

15. "Serena Williams Biography," Bio (2017), available at: http://www.biography.com/, accessed December 21, 2017.

16. See, for instance, "Final report: Fifth international conference on adult education at Hamburg, Germany," UNESCO (July 14–18, 1997), available at: http://www.unesco.org/, accessed March 12, 2014.

17. A. Paudel, "Scope and importance of non-formal education," *Academia* (2015), available at: https://www.academia.edu/, accessed December 2, 2015.

18. G. Fischer, "Lifelong Learning - More than Training," *Journal of Interactive Learning Research* (2000), 11, 3–4, 265–294.

19. See, for instance, K. Sloan, "Whittier Law School's collapse won't be the last: Experts," Law.com (2017), available at: http://www.law.com/, accessed April 20, 2017. The final section of chapter 10 of this book discusses the prospects for school education.

20. V. Strauss, "How schools kill creativity in kids," *Washington Post* (2011), available at: https://www.washingtonpost.com/, accessed April 14, 2011.

21. D. L. Chandler, "MIT and Harvard launch a 'revolution in education,'" *MIT News* (2012), available at: http://news.mit.edu/, accessed May 2, 2012.

22. "'Four out of 10 recent college grads are underemployed,' new Accenture research finds," Accenture News Room (2013), available at: https://newsroom.accenture.com/, accessed April 30, 2013.

23. M. Bois-Reymond, *Study on the Links between Formal and Non-formal Education,* 1st ed. (Strasbourg, France: The Council of Europe, 2003), available at: http://www.coe.int/, accessed March 31, 2003.

24. SPACE.com Staff, "Dwarf planet: Science & Facts About the Solar System's Smaller Worlds," SPACE.com (2017), available at: https://www.space.com/, accessed October 27, 2017.

25. J. Griffiths, "Lonely planet: Astronomers find galaxy's largest solar system," *CNN* (2016), available at: http://www.cnn.com/, accessed January 28, 2016.

26. "Gravitational waves detected 100 years after Einstein's prediction," A LIGO news release, LIGO (2016), available at: https://ligo.caltech.edu/, accessed February 11, 2016.

27. S. Arbesman, *The Half-Life of Facts: Why Everything We Know Has an Expiration Date* (London: Penguin Group, 2012).

28. For references about programming languages, refer to the following. "Theory of Programming languages," FreeComputerBooks.com

(2017), available at: http://freecomputerbooks.com/, accessed April 25, 2017.

29. See, for instance, "Mexico, Russia and China anticipate changed U.S. relations under Trump," An *NPR* news transcript, *National Public Radio* (2017), available at: http://www.npr.org/, accessed January 20, 2017.

30. A. Sajjanhar, "How will US foreign policy change under Trump?" Observer Research Foundation (2016), available at: http://www.orfonline.org/, accessed November 14, 2016.

31. See, for instance, I. Hossein-zadeh, *Beyond Mainstream Explanations of the Financial Crisis* (New York: Routledge, 2014), 8.

32. L. Eisgruber, "Life's journey and the value of learning," Commencement Address at Princeton University (2014).

33. An expression quoted in *Global Trends: The Paradox of Progress*, NIC (2017).

34. "Digging in: The university is pushing toward the digital horizon," Progress Report 2015 of the Johns Hopkins University, 10x2020 (2015), available at: https://10x2020progress.jhu.edu/, accessed November 25, 2015.

35. See, for example, B. Handwerk, "Five incredible—and real— mind-control applications," National Geographic (2013), available at: http://news.nationalgeographic.com/, accessed August 29, 2013.

36. "How to become a Wall Street outlier without a target school degree," Life on the Buy Side (2015), available at: http://www.lifeonthebuyside.com/, accessed March 20, 2015.

37. L. Pope, *Colleges That Change Lives* (London: Penguin Books, 1996).

38. M. Bernick, "It doesn't matter where you go to college," *TIME* (2014), available at: http://time.com/, accessed April 10, 2014.

39. Page, "Foreword," in *Global Trends Survey 2017*.

40. Ajou University said this is a "very challenging semester program" designed to help students carry out the tasks they designed themselves without limitation in all areas of disciplines. "YTN introduces Ajou's Paran (Blue in English) semester," Ajou University (2016), available at: http://www.ajou.ac.kr/en/news/, accessed July 20, 2016.

41. As for the need for the fusion of disciplines, see, for instance, P. Holmgren, "'GLF brings "fusion of disciplines" at turning point for climate and development,' says CIFOR's DG," Global Landscapes Forum (GLF) (2014), available at: http://www.landscapes.org/, accessed January 31, 2014.

42. "Ivy league grade inflation: Grade expectations," *Economist* (2014), available at: http://www.economist.com/, accessed September 6, 2014.

43. Quite a few major news media, including *Boston Globe*, *Christian Science Monitor*, *New York Times* and *Forbes*, criticized the Harvard cheating scandal. See for example, R. Perez-Pena, "Students Disciplined in Harvard Scandal," *New York Times* (2013), available at: https://www.nytimes.com/, accessed February 1, 2013.

44. See, for instance, R. D. Robbins, "Harvard investigates 'unprecedented' academic dishonesty case," *Harvard Crimson* (2012), available at: https://www.thecrimson.com/, accessed August 30, 2012.

45. *Global Trends: The Paradox of Progress*, NIC (2017).

46. J. Monahan and J. Clancy, "Lifelong learning is the secret to happiness in old age," *Guardian* (2011), available at: https://www.theguardian.com/, accessed May 17, 2011.

47. See, for example, W. Erstad, "Online vs. traditional education: What you need to know," Rasmussen College (2017), available at: https://www.rasmussen.edu/, accessed August 16, 2017.

48. A lot of studies and reports show numerous such personalities. See, for instance, T. Loudenback and E. Martin, "The 20 most generous people in the world," *Business Insider* (2015), available at: http://www.businessinsider.com/, accessed October 12, 2015. See also A. Antunes, "The 30 most generous celebrities," *Forbes* (2012), available at: http://www.forbes.com/, accessed January 11, 2012.

49. R. Susskind and D. Susskind, "Technology will replace many doctors, lawyers, and other professionals," *Harvard Business Review* (2016), available at: https://hbr.org/, accessed October 11, 2016.

Chapter 4: Innovative Teens

1. J. Birch, "Teens who are changing the world," Mom.me (2012), available at: https://mom.me/, accessed July 13, 2012.

2. L. Penny, "Laurie Penny on today's teenagers: Smarter, tougher and braver than my generation—and yours, too," *New Statesman* (2013), available at: http://www.newstatesman.com/, accessed July 15, 2013.

3. K. Robinson, "Do schools kill creativity?" TED (2006), available at: http://www.ted.com/, accessed February 28, 2006.

4. Ibid.

5. B. Osotimehin, "Young people have the power to change the world," *Atlantic* (2012), available at: https://www.theatlantic.com/, accessed November 30, 2012.

6. See, for example, *TIME* Staff, "The 30 most influential teens of 2017," *TIME* (2017), available at: http://time.com/, accessed November 3, 2017.

7. P. Marinova, "18 under 18: Meet the young innovators who are changing the world," *Fortune* (2016), available at: http://fortune.com/, accessed September 15, 2015.

8. Birch, "Teens who are changing the world."

9. I. Tucker, "Nick D'Aloisio: 'I dream of a virtual brain. It's coming in 10 or 20 years,'" *Guardian* (2015), available at: https://www.theguardian.com/, accessed January 12, 2015. For updated news about Nick D'Aloisio, see, for example, S. Shead, "Yahoo is shutting down the news app it bought from a 17-year-old Brit for a reported $30 million," *Business Insider* (2017), available at: http://uk.businessinsider.com/, accessed June 23, 2017.

10. "The teen who made a revolutionary robot arm," *BBC News* (2015), available at: http://www.bbc.com/, accessed October 26, 2015.

11. Ibid.

12. "Aidan Dwyer: Better solar designs," PopTech (2011), available at: https://poptech.org/, accessed November 16, 2011.

13. T. Singh, "A 15-year-old is developing a 3D printer that's 10 times faster than anything on the market!" *inhabitat* (2014), available at: http://inhabitat.com/, accessed July 14, 2014.

14. "Jack Andraka, the teen prodigy of pancreatic cancer," Smithsonian (2012), available at: http://www.smithsonianmag.com/, accessed December 12, 2012.

15. *TIME* Staff, "The 30 most influential teens of 2016," *TIME* (2016), available at: http://time.com/, accessed October 19, 2016.

16. "The world's billionaires," *Forbes* (2017 Ranking [Real Time]), available at: https://www.forbes.com/, accessed June 12, 2017.

17. D. M. Ewalt, "The world's most powerful people," *Forbes* (2016), available at: https://www.forbes.com/, accessed December 14, 2016.

18. "The story of Kelvin Doe: The poor Sierra Leone teen who wowed MIT's engineers," Idea to Value (2017), available at: https://www.ideatovalue.com/, accessed June 5, 2017.

19. "Croydon boy Laurence Rook invents phone-linked doorbell," *BBC News* (2011), available at: http://www.bbc.com/, accessed June 7, 2011.

20. See, for instance, B. Brumfield, "Malala's journey from near death to the Nobel Peace Prize," *CNN* (2014), available at: http://www.cnn.com/, accessed October 10, 2014.

21. D. Jones, "Five teenage producers starting a DIY revolution," DAZED (2015), available at: http://www.dazeddigital.com/, accessed December 4, 2015.

22. M. Levinson, "The digital lives of teens: Revolutionary 'Bliss'?" Edutopia (2013), available at: https://www.edutopia.org/, accessed May 22, 2013.

23. See, for example, B. Stebner, "Are you smarter than an 8th grader? Rare test from 1912 shows what students were quizzed over," *New York Daily News* (2013), available at: http://www.nydailynews.com/, accessed August 13, 2013. See also P. Mashegoane, "Are We More Intelligent Than Our Grandparents?" *Huffington Post* (2017), available at: https://www.huffingtonpost.com/, accessed June 22, 2017.

24. As for the characteristics of today's kids, see, for example, T. Parker-Pope, "Are Today's Teenagers Smarter and Better Than We Think?" *New York Times* (2018), available at: https://www.nytimes.com/, accessed March 30, 2018.

25. For an example of memory-based questions, see M. Alonso, "Warning: This Eighth Grade Exam May Make You Feel Bad About Yourself,"

ABC News (2013), available at: https://abcnews.go.com/, accessed August 14, 2014.

26. W. Klemm, "What good is learning if you don't remember it?" *Journal of Effective Teaching* 7, no. 1 (2007): 61–73.

27. See, for example, "Critical thinking vs. rote memorization," A Pass Educational Group (2013), available at: http://apasseducation.com/, accessed July 2, 2013.

28. See, for example, R. Sternberg, "Teach creativity, not memorization," *Chronicle of Higher Education* (2010), available at: http://www.chronicle.com/, accessed October 10, 2010.

29. "Guinness Book IQ (Category removal)," Hmolpedia (2015), available at: http://www.eoht.info/, accessed July 15, 2015.

30. H. Brown, "Good question: Are today's kids smarter than we were?" *CBS Minnesota* (2013), available at: http://minnesota.cbslocal.com/, accessed August 8, 2013.

31. Penny, "Laurie Penny on today's teenagers."

32. "Why kids should learn how to program," RELSIG (2016), available at: http://relsig.com/, accessed May 5, 2016.

33. Ibid.

34. P. Wyman, *Amazing Grades: 101 Best Ways to Improve Your Grades Faster* (Las Vegas: The Center for New Discoveries in Learning, 2012).

35. Ibid.

36. M. Safer, "Boy wonder: Jack Andraka," *CBS 60 Minutes* (2013), available at: https://www.cbs.com/, accessed October 13, 2013.

37. Ibid.

38. A. Mulholland, "Teen cancer researcher says all good discoveries start with 1 small idea," *CTVNews* (2013), available at: http://www.ctvnews.ca/, accessed June 21, 2013.

39. Safer, "Boy wonder: Jack Andraka."

40. S. Cortez, "What a tween startup founder learned when she went to college," *Business Insider* (2012), available at: http://www.businessinsider.com/, accessed June 28, 2012.

41. As for this view, see, for instance, D. Hambrick, "What Makes a Prodigy?" *Scientific American* (2015), https://www.scientificamerican.com/, accessed September 22, 2015.

42. S. Vincent-Lancrin, "Creativity in schools: What countries do (or could do)," OECD Education Today (2013), available at: http://oecdeducationtoday.blogspot.kr/, accessed January 30, 2013.

43. J. Davidson, "How sending your child to private school can save you $53,000," *TIME* (2014), available at: http://time.com/, accessed August 18, 2014.

44. H. Robinson, "Is Any High School Really Worth $136,000? *Huffington Post* (2011), available at: http://www.huffingtonpost.com/, accessed May 25, 2011.

45. A. Wong, "Living Hawaii: Many families sacrifice to put kids in private schools," *Honolulu Civil Beat* (2014), available at: http://www.civilbeat.org/, accessed March 17, 2014.

46. W. Gu, "Chinese parents push kids to elite Western summer schools," *Wall Street Journal* (2013), available at: https://www.wsj.com/, accessed June 28, 2013.

47. Y. Ahn, "Educational tyranny kills creativity," *Korea Times* (2014), available at: http://www.koreatimes.co.kr/, accessed February 23, 2014.

48. See, for instance, "'Kyoiku Mama': Educating offspring is full-time job," Education Week (2017), available at: http://www.edweek.org/, accessed April 18, 2017.

49. See, for example, D. Fricke, "Frances Bean Cobain on Life After Kurt's Death: An Exclusive Q&A," *Rolling Stone* (2015), available at: https://www.rollingstone.com/, accessed April 8, 2015.

50. Rolling Stone, "100 Greatest Guitarists – David Fricke's Picks: 12) Kurt Cobain," *Rolling Stone* (2010), available at: https://www.rollingstone.com/, accessed April 21, 2016.

51. See, for example, F. Cronin, and L. Turner, "Six reasons why we still love Kurt Cobain," *BBC News* (2017), available at: http://www.bbc.com/news/, accessed April 21, 2017.

Chapter 5: Popullectuals

1. B. Sisario, A. Alter, and S. Chan, "Bob Dylan wins Nobel Prize, redefining boundaries of literature," *New York Times* (2016), available at: https://www.nytimes.com/, accessed October 13, 2016.

2. Ibid.

3. "The Nobel Prize in literature 2016," The Royal Swedish Academy (2016), available at: https://www.nobelprize.org/, accessed December 15, 2016.

4. K. Ferguson, "Angelina Jolie appointed as professor at the London School of Economics," *Independent* (2016), available at: http://www. independent.co.uk/, accessed May 24, 2016.

5. As for various negative reactions from the public, see, for instance, Voices "Outrage at the LSE's appointment of Angelina Jolie is nothing more than academic snobbery," *Independent* (2016), available at: http://www.independent.co.uk/, accessed May 24, 2016.

6. E. Addley, "Angelina Jolie gets new role as visiting professor at LSE," *Guardian* (2016), available at: https://www.theguardian.com/, accessed May 23, 2016.

7. S. Briggs, "Refuse to be a boring teacher: 15 ways to have more fun," informED (2015), available at: http://www.opencolleges.edu/.au/, accessed October 10, 2015.

8. D. Drezner, "Am I defining public intellectuals down?" *Foreign Policy* (2008), available at: http://foreignpolicy.com/, accessed June 12, 2008.

9. A. Lightman, "The role of the public intellectual," MIT Communication Forum (1999).

10. Ibid.

11. R. Emerson, "The American scholar," An oration delivered before the Phi Beta Kappa Society at Cambridge, Massachusetts, on August 31, 1837.

12. Lightman, "The role of the public intellectual."

13. Ibid.

14. F. Furedi, *Where Have All the Intellectuals Gone?* (New York: Continuum, 2004), 32.

15. E. Said, "A series of lectures named 'Representations of the intellectual,'" quoted in Lightman, "The role of the public intellectual."

16. E. Faure, F. Herrera, A. Kaddoura, H. Lopes, A. Petrovsky, M. Frederick, and C. Ward, *Learning to Be: The World of Education Today and Tomorrow*, 1st ed. (Paris: UNESCO, 1972).

17. N. McIntosh, "The widening digital divide," *Guardian* (2002), available at: https://www.theguardian.com/, accessed July 3, 2002.

18. *Top 10 Emerging Technologies of 2016*, WEF (2016), available at: https://www.weforum.org/, accessed July 30, 2016.

19. See, for example, D. Rotman, "Technology and inequality," *MIT Technology Review* (2014), available at: https://www.technologyreview.com/, accessed October 21, 2014.

20. M. Crider, "What is bitcoin, and how does it work?" How-To Geek (2017), available at: https://www.howtogeek.com/, accessed December 7, 2017.

21. Editors of *MIT Technology Review*, "10 breakthrough technologies 2018," *MIT Technology Review* (2018), available at: https://www.technologyreview.com/, accessed February 23, 2018.

22. See, for example, Editors at Cybersecurity Ventures, Cybersecurity Market (2016), available at: http://cybersecurityventures.com/, accessed November 20, 2016.

23. K. Dickerson, "Here's why we should be really excited about quantum computers," *Business Insider* (2015), available at: http://www.businessinsider.com/, accessed April 21, 2015.

24. K. Dolan, "Forbes 2017 billionaires list," *Forbes* (2017), available at: http://www.forbes.com/, accessed March 20, 2017.

25. See, for instance, A. Orlowski, "Avoid Wikipedia, warns Wikipedia chief," The Register (2006), available at: https://www.theregister.co.uk/, accessed October 17, 2015.

26. G. Satell, "Here's how quantum computing will change the world," *Forbes* (2016), available at: https://www.forbes.com/, accessed October 2, 2016.

27. See, for example, D. Serdaroglu, "Student teachers," Humanising Language Teaching (2009), available at: http://www.hltmag.co.uk/, accessed February 26, 2012.

28. Webopedia: Online Tech Dictionary for Students, Educators and IT Professionals, available at: http://www.webopedia.com/, accessed October 10, 2016.

29. Quoted in *Forbes* (2017), available at: https://www.forbes.com/, accessed March 29, 2017.

30. M. O'Hara, "How comedy makes us better people," *BBC News* (2016), available at: http://www.bbc.com, accessed August 30, 2016.

31. A. Borges, "16 genius ways to be less pessimistic," *BuzzFeed* (2015), available at: https://www.buzzfeed.com/, accessed May 12, 2015.

32. As for sense of humor, see, for example, R. Martin, *The Psychology of Humor: An Integrative Approach*, (Burlington, MA: Elsevier Academic Press, 2007), 2–30. See also H. Goldstein and E. McGhee, eds., "Overview and conclusions," in *The Psychology of Humor: Theoretical Perspectives and Empirical Issues* (Cambridge, MA: Academic Press, 1972), 243–57.

33. O. Khazan, "The dark psychology of being a good comedian," *Atlantic* (2014), available at: https://www.theatlantic.com/, accessed February 27, 2014.

34. K. Lawrence, "How do we develop our sense of humor?" SOTT.net (2015), available at: https://www.sott.net/, accessed December 4, 2015.

35. W. Christensen, "What does it mean to be self-taught?" Treehouse (2015), available at: http://blog.teamtreehouse.com/, accessed August 13, 2015.

36. Ibid.

37. B. Martin, *Information Liberation* (London: Freedom Press, 1998), 168.

38. P. Conway, "9 celebrity role models we love," Common Sense (2017), available at: https://www.commonsensemedia.org/, accessed January 2, 2017.

39. See, for instance, N. Simek, "This death which is not one: The first colonial author as public intellectual," in *The New Public Intellectual: Politics, Theory, and the Public Sphere*, 1st ed., eds. D. Leo, R. Jeffrey, and P. Hitchcock (New York: Palgrave Macmillan, 2016), 79–93.

40. See, for example, as for the shortcomings of genuine intellectuals, G. Trung, "What is the role of intellectuals in society?" WEF (2013), available at: https://www.weforum.org/, accessed March 15, 2013.

41. "What went wrong with economics," *Economist* (2009), available at: http://www.economist.com/, accessed July 16, 2009.

42. See, for example, S. Patton, "The Ph.D. now comes with food stamps," *Chronicle of Higher Education* (2012), available at: https://www.chronicle.com, accessed May 6, 2012.

43. J. Oliver, "Teach every child about food," TED (2010), available at: https://www.ted.com/, accessed February 15, 2010.

44. See, for instance, "10 ordinary people who became social media celebrities overnight," Indian Social Media (2016), available at: https://www.socialsamosa.com/, accessed October 20, 2016.

45. See, for example, T. Smale, "Lessons from 7 people who got rich and famous on social media," (2015), available at: https://www.entrepreneur.com/, accessed July 1, 2015.

46. M. McLuhan, *The Medium Is the Massage: An Inventory of Effects* (New York: Bantam Books, 1967).

47. See, for instance, "New graduation skills," *Economist* (2007), available at: http://www.economist.com/, accessed May 10, 2007.

48. J. L. Lehmiller, "Tips from a self-taught teacher," *Observer* 27, no. 7 (2014): 1–2. *Observer* is a publication of the Association for Psychological Science.

49. As for this view and profile of the musician professor, J. Roig-Francolí, "Why is it so hard to teach yourself?" The Art of Freedom (2016), available at: http://www.artoffreedom.me/, accessed February 16, 2016.

50. See, for example, S. Higgins and R. Coe, "Seven 'great' teaching methods not backed up by evidence," *Conversation* (2014), available at: https://theconversation.com/, accessed October 31, 2014.

51. See, for example, W. Reville, "The reason why modern teaching methods don't work," *Irish Times* (2015), available at: https://www.irishtimes.com/, accessed March 2, 2015.

52. B. Lenon, "What really makes a good teacher?" *Telegraph* (2015), available at: http://www.telegraph.co.uk/, accessed January 15, 2015.

53. B. Brende, "Why education is the key to development," WEF (2015), available at: https://www.weforum.org/, accessed July 2, 2015.

54. M. Korn, "Imagine discovering that your teaching assistant really is a robot," *Wall Street Journal* (2016), available at: https://buy.wsj.com/, accessed May 6, 2015.

55. D. Beres, "'Robots will never replace humanity,' Matthieu Ricard explains," *Huffington Post* (2016), available at: http://www.huffingtonpost.com/, accessed January 22, 2016.

56. See, for example, M. Wehner, "Scientists have developed AI that can read your mind and predict your thoughts," *Fox News* (2017), available at: http://www.foxnews.com/, accessed July 3, 2017.

57. *Global Trends: The Paradox of Progress*, NIC (2017). "Without regulatory standards, the development and deployment of AI—even if less capable than human intellect—is likely to be inherently dangerous to humans," according to the NIC report (p. 16).

58. M. Liccione, "Here's why robots will never achieve consciousness," *Intellectual Takeout* (2016), available at: http://www.intellectualtakeout.org/, accessed April 4, 2016.

59. R. Pierson, "Kids don't learn from people they don't like," Brainspace (2014), available at: https://brainspacemagazine.com/, accessed November 22, 2014.

60. S. Huntington, *American Politics: The Promise of Disharmony* (Cambridge, MA: Harvard University Press, 1981), v.

61. A. Pollack, "Scientists talk privately about creating a synthetic human genome," *New York Times* (2016), available at: https://www.nytimes.com/, accessed May 13, 2016.

62. Ibid.

Chapter 6: Hutechciety

1. See, for example, D. Mackay, "Pyeongchang 2018 set to offer AI automatic translation services after signing new deals," *Inside the Games* (2016), available at: http://www.insidethegames.biz/, accessed July 2, 2016.

2. Editors of *MIT Technology Review*, "10 breakthrough technologies 2018."

3. Ibid.

4. J. Temple, "10 Breakthrough Technologies 2017," *MIT Technology Review* (2017), available at: https://www.technologyreview.com/, accessed February 12, 2017.

5. O. Cann, "These are the top 10 emerging technologies of 2018," WEF (2018), available at: https://www.weforum.org/, accessed September 14, 2018.

6. O. Cann, "These are the top 10 emerging technologies of 2017," WEF (2017), available at: https://www.weforum.org/, accessed June 26, 2017.

7. O. Cann, "These are the top 10 emerging technologies of 2016," WEF (2016), available at: https://www.weforum.org/, accessed June 10, 2016.

8. Editors of *MIT Technology Review,* "10 breakthrough technologies 2018."

9. F. FitzGerald, *Way Out There In the Blue: Reagan, Star Wars and the End of the Cold War* (New York: Simon & Schuster, 2001).

10. See, for instance, "The CEA: A key player in technological research," French Alternative Energies and Atomic Energy Commission (CEA) (2017), available at: http://www.cea.fr/, accessed March 31, 2017.

11. *Global Trends 2030: Alternative Worlds,* NIC (2012), 86–100.

12. M. Liedtke and B. Ortutay, "The problem is humans can't keep up with all the technology they have created," *Business Insider* (2015), available at: http://www.businessinsider.com/, accessed July 9, 2015. The authors work with the Associated Press.

13. For initial understanding of the IoT, see, for instance, J. Morgan, "A simple explanation of 'The Internet of Things,'" *Forbes* (2014), available at: https://www.forbes.com/, accessed May 13, 2014.

14. R. Juskalian, "Practical quantum computers," *MIT Technology Review* (2017), available at: https://www.technologyreview.com/, accessed February 23, 2017.

15. See, for example, G. Satell, "5 trends that will drive the future of technology," *Forbes* (2013), available at: http://www.forbes.com/, accessed March 12, 2013.

16. See, for example, N. Kobie, "The quantum clock is ticking on encryption—and your data is under threat," *WIRED* (2016), available at: http://www.wired.co.uk/, accessed October 4, 2016.

17. "10 breakthrough technologies 2015," *MIT Technology Review* (2015), available at: https://www.technologyreview.com/, accessed November 15, 2015.

18. A. Petroff, "U.S. workers face higher risk of being replaced by robots. Here's why," *CNN* (2017), available at: http://money.cnn.com/, accessed March 24, 2017.

19. Ibid.

20. "The future of jobs," Global Challenge Insight Report, WEF (2016), available at: https://www.weforum.org/, accessed, January 15, 2016.

See also "Five million jobs by 2020: The real challenge of the fourth Industrial Revolution," WEF (2016), available at: https://www.weforum.org/, accessed January 18, 2016.

21. Ibid.

22. M. Ferkoun, "Cloud computing and big data: An ideal combination," IBM Cloud (2014), available at: https://www.ibm.com/blogs/, accessed February 10, 2014.

23. For a guide to big data, see, for example, "What is big data?" Oracle (2019), available at: https://www.oracle.com/, accessed January 5, 2019.

24. Ferkoun, "Cloud computing and big data: An ideal combination."

25. K. Bent, "8 ways big data will change our lives," *CRN* (2013), available at: http://www.crn.com/, accessed January 29, 2013.

26. R. Smolan, *The Human Face of Big Data.* Lebanon (CT: Against All Odds Productions 2012).

27. A. Zaharia, "10 alarming cyber security facts that threaten your data," Heimdal (2016), available at: https://heimdalsecurity.com/, accessed May 12, 2016.

28. Center for Strategic and International Studies (CSIS), *Net Losses: Estimating the Global Cost of Cybercrime,* 1st ed., A CSIS Report Sponsored by McAfee (2014), available at: http://www.cyberriskinsuranceforum.com/, accessed June 30, 2014.

29. Ibid. See also Ponemon Institute, "The rising costs of cyber crime: 2016 Ponemon Institute cost of cyber crime study," Hewlett Packard Enterprise (2016), available at: https://saas.hpe.com/, accessed March 29, 2016.

30. See, for example, S. White, "FBI's top 10 most wanted cybercriminals," *CIO* (2017), available at: http://www.cio.com/, accessed May 30, 2016. See also "What we investigate," and "Evgeniy Mikhailovich Bogachev," both from FBI (2017), available at: https://www.fbi.gov/, accessed December 29, 2017.

31. Zaharia, "10 alarming cyber security facts that threaten your data."

32. Ibid.

33. "What we investigate," FBI.

34. White, "FBI's top 10 most wanted cybercriminals."

35. Zaharia, "10 alarming cyber security facts that threaten your data."

36. J. Linshi, "U.S. offers $3 million reward for information on Russian hacker," *TIME* (2015), available at: http://time.com/, accessed February 25, 2015.

37. C. Nachreiner, "Our governments are making us more vulnerable," *Dark Reading* (2015), available at: http://www.darkreading.com/, accessed February 19, 2015.

38. Zaharia, "10 alarming cyber security facts that threaten your data."

39. Ibid.

40. Ibid.

41. J. Finkle, "Exclusive: FBI warns of 'destructive' malware in wake of Sony attack," Reuters (2014), available at: http://www.reuters.com/, accessed December 2, 2014.

42. *Global Trends: The Paradox of Progress*, NIC (2017), 42. This report says, "Technology will be a double-edged sword." I began to use the quoted expression to write this book years before the NIC report was released.

43. Ibid.

44. Ibid.

45. Ibid.

46. Ibid.

47. "What is the differences between automation and robotics?" Granta (2019), https://www.granta-automation.co.uk/, accessed August 16, 2017.

48. See, for example, A. Kooser, "Elektro: 1939 smoking robot saved from oblivion," *CNET* (2012), available at: https://www.cnet.com/, accessed April 5, 2012.

49. E. Holodny, "This map shows which countries are being taken over by robots. *Business Insider* (2016), available at: http://www.businessinsider.com/, accessed March 28, 2016.

50. See, for example, C. Arthur, "I, Cyborg, by Kevin Warwick," *Independent* (2002), available at: https://www.independent.co.uk/, accessed September 30, 2002. See also K. Warwick, *I, Cyborg* (Champaign, IL: University of Illinois Press, 2004).

51. K. Warwick, *I, Cyborg.*

52. Sara P., "20 Interesting And Bizarre Facts About Robots To Learn Before They Take Over The World," Knowable (2016), available at: https://www.knowable.com/, accessed November 9, 2016.

53. D. Shewan, "Robots will destroy our jobs—and we're not ready for it," *Guardian* (2017), available at: https://www.theguardian.com/, accessed January 11, 2017.

54. See, for example, "What is 3D printing?" 3dprinting.com (2017), available at: https://3dprinting.com/, accessed June 6, 2017.

55. MakerBot 3D printers are manufactured by MakerBot Industries, an American business. https://www.makerbot.com/, accessed August 7, 2016.

56. "What is a 3D bio printer?" MyLikes (2016), available at: https://mylikes.com/, accessed September 1, 2016.

57. See, for instance, M. Day, "Doomed penguin offered second chance by 3D printer," *Telegraph* (2014), available at: http://www.telegraph.co.uk/, accessed March 21, 2014.

58. Editors of *MIT Technology Review*, "10 breakthrough technologies 2018."

59. R. Morelle, "Working gun made with 3D printer," *BBC News* (2013), available at: http://www.bbc.com/, accessed May 6, 2013.

60. See, for instance, S. Cullinane, "3D guns: Untraceable, undetectable and unstoppable?" *CNN* (2018), available at: https://edition.cnn.com/, accessed July 31, 2018.

61. Temple, "10 breakthrough technologies 2017."

62. V. Fthenakis, H. Kim, and A. Alsema, "Emissions from photovoltaic life cycles," *Environmental Science & Technology* 42, no. 6 (New York: the American Chemical Society, 2008): 2168–74.

63. *Global Trends 2030: Alternative Worlds*, NIC (2012), 99.

64. See, for instance, "DNA profiling," Better Health (2017), available at: https://www.betterhealth.vic.gov.au/, accessed September 7, 2017.

65. See, for example, *Global Trends 2030: Alternative Worlds*, NIC (2012), 99.

66. C. Lytal, "New health facility aims to translate stem cell science into therapies," *USC News* (2014), available at: https://news.usc.edu/, accessed October 9, 2016.

67. B. Agnew, "Xenotransplants: Using animal organs to save human lives," University of Texas at Austin (2017), available at: http://apps. engr.utexas.edu/, accessed October 11, 2017.

68. Ibid.

69. "8 crucial pros and cons of xenotransplantation," Connect US (2017), available at: https://connectusfund.org/, accessed September 18, 2017.

70. See, for example, K. Loria, "10 Amazing Superpowers Humans Will Be Able To Get From Brain Implants," *Business Insider* (2014), available at: https://www.businessinsider.com/, accessed May 8, 2014.

71. Pollack, "Scientists talk privately about creating a synthetic human genome."

72. R. Bal, "Public perceptions of fairness in NBIC technologies," in *Nanotechnology and the Challenges of Equity, Equality and Development*, eds. S. Cozzens and J. Wetmore (New York: Springer, 2011), 236.

73. "Country comparison: Infant mortality rate," *The World Factbook*, CIA (2016), available at: https://www.cia.gov/, accessed October 11, 2016.

74. Pollack, "Scientists talk privately about creating a synthetic human genome."

75. M. Hanks, "'Human lifespan may be extended indefinitely within two decades,' Futurist claims," Mysterious Universe (2015), available at: http://mysteriousuniverse.org/, accessed May 18, 2015.

76. M. Mountain, "How seven billion humans lead to mass extinction," Earth in Transition (2011), available at: http://www.earthintransition.org/, accessed November 1, 2011.

77. K. Serena, "How One Reckless Surgeon Killed His Patient – Plus Two Bystanders," ati (2017), available at: https://allthatsinteresting.com/, accessed December 20, 2017.

78. Ibid.

79. MIT Program in Science, Technology, and Society, available at: http://sts-program.mit.edu/, accessed March 30, 2017.

80. Ibid.

81. "Professor Elting E. Morison dies at 85," *MIT News* (1995), available at: http://news.mit.edu/, accessed April 26, 1995.

82. The *Times* article adds, "If we cannot sleep, nearly half of us play with our phones before the night is out. Such is our obsession that if we are separated from our phone, we feel lost."

83. Ibid.

84. For Dave Barry's quotes, see, for instance, P. Dave, "SQLAuthority news—funny technology quotes—humor," SQL Authority.com (2010), available at: https://se.ambafrance.org/, accessed July 23, 2010.

85. J. Kantor, "Obama girls' role: Not to speak, but to be spoken of," *New York Times* (2012), available at: http://www.nytimes.com/, accessed September 6, 2012.

86. *Global Trends: The Paradox of Progress*, NIC (2017), ix.

87. B. Marr, "The 4th Industrial Revolution and a jobless future—a good thing?" *Forbes* (2017), available at: https://www.forbes.com/, accessed March 3, 2017.

88. For a cross reference, see "Technology and People: The Great job-creating machine," Deloitte Touche Tohmatsu (2015), https://www2.deloitte.com/, accessed August 18, 2015.

89. Marr, "The 4th Industrial Revolution and a jobless future—a good thing?"

90. For this line of argument, see, for example, B. Erford, "What the future holds for the counseling profession," *Counseling Today* (2012), available at: https://ct.counseling.org/, accessed March 1, 2012.

91. E. Dans, "Machines will never replace men (Danger: Slippery slope ahead)," *Forbes* (2016), available at: https://www.forbes.com/, accessed March 8, 2016.

92. G. Press, "Breaking news: Humans will forever triumph over the machines," *Forbes* (2015), available at: https://www.forbes.com/, accessed June 30, 2015.

Chapter 7: Publivacy

1. R. Hooijdonk, "In this digital age, your privacy is continuously invaded," (2016), available at: https://www.richardvanhooijdonk.com/, accessed February 18, 2016.

2. Harvard University's Justice with Michael Sandel, "Episode 12: Debating same-sex marriage," Justice: What is the right thing to do? (2009), available at: http://justiceharvard.org/, accessed December 29, 2010.

3. "Privacy," *Online Etymology Dictionary* (2015), available at: http://www.etymonline.com/, accessed February 15, 2015.

4. A Terry Fox Quote, Quotefancy (2018), available at: https://quotefancy.com/, accessed May 20, 2018.

5. R. Gilbey, "Olivia Wilde: 'People thought I could only play the badass,'" *Guardian* (2013), available at: https://www.theguardian.com/, accessed October 31, 2013.

6. G. Miller, "eWave: Is privacy dying? Technology is pervasive and invasive," *Providence Journal* (2013). See also G. Miller, "eWave: Public opinion shifting after NSA revelations," *Providence Journal* (2013), both available at: http://www.providencejournal.com/, accessed July 27, 2013.

7. For a series of privacy-related surveys, see "Privacy and safety, 2013–16," Pew Research Center (2016), available at: http://www.pewresearch.org/, accessed June 15, 2016.

8. G. Alexia and G. Caterina, "The effect of privacy concerns on social network formation," *Journal of Economic Behavior & Organization* (2017), 141, 233–253.

9. Miller, "eWave: Is privacy dying?"

10. Ibid.

11. Quoted in Miller, "eWave: Is privacy dying?"

12. Miller, "eWave: Is privacy dying?"

13. Statcounter Global Stats (2017), available at: http://gs.statcounter.com, accessed January 2, 2018.

14. C. Miller, "F.T.C. fines Google $22.5 million for Safari privacy violations," *New York Times* (2012), available at: https://www.nytimes.com/, accessed August 9, 2012.

15. J. Martin, "Lower Merion district's laptop saga ends with $610,000 settlement," *Philadelphia Inquirer* (2010), available at: http://www.philly.com/, accessed December 12, 2010.

16. Ibid.

17. Miller, "eWave: Is privacy dying?"

18. S. Greenwood, A. Perrin, and M. Duggan, "Social media update 2016," Pew Research Center (2016), available at: http://www.pewresearch.org/, accessed November 11, 2016.

19. Ibid.

20. "Baidu's Internal Monitoring and Censorship Document leaked (1) and (2)," *China Digital Times* (2009), available at: http://chinadigitaltimes.net/, accessed December 19, 2009.

21. J. Stempel, "Baidu, China sued in U.S. for Internet censorship," Reuters (2011), available at: http://www.reuters.com/, accessed May 18, 2011.

22. Editors of *MIT Technology Review*, "10 breakthrough technologies 2018."

23. W. Elder, "Electronic surveillance: Unlawful invasion of privacy or justifiable law enforcement," Yale-New Haven Teachers Institute (2016), available at: http://teachersinstitute.yale.edu/, accessed December 23, 2016.

24. R. Goud and M. Mookherjee, *India–Sri Lanka Relations* (New Delhi, India: Allied Publishers, 2013), 297.

25. Ibid.

26. E. Rosenbach and A. Peritz, "The role of private corporations in the intelligence community," Belfer Center for Science and International Affairs, Harvard Kennedy School (2009), available at: http://www.belfercenter.org/, accessed July 11, 2009.

27. L. Rainie and J. Anderson, "The future of privacy," Pew Research Center (2014), available at: http://www.pewresearch.org/, accessed March 20, 2015.

28. See, for example, D. Perera, "Blaming Snowden for Paris," *POLITICO* (2015), available at: https://www.politico.com/, accessed November 18, 2015.

29. See, for instance, G. Greenwald, E. MacAskill, and L. Poitras, "Edward Snowden: The whistleblower behind the NSA surveillance revelations," *Guardian* (2013), available at: https://www.theguardian.com/, accessed June 11, 2013.

30. B. Gellman and A. Soltani, "'NSA infiltrates links to Yahoo, Google data centers worldwide,' Snowden documents say," *Washington Post* (2013), available at: https://www.washingtonpost.com/, accessed October 30, 2013.

31. J. Watts, "NSA accused of spying on Brazilian oil company Petrobras," *Guardian* (2013), available at: https://www.theguardian.com/, accessed September 9, 2013.

32. J. Ball and N. Hopkins, "GCHQ and NSA targeted charities, Germans, Israeli PM and EU chief," *Guardian* (2013), available at: https://www.theguardian.com/, accessed December 20, 2013.

33. L. Poitras, "GCHQ and NSA targeted private German companies and Merkel," *Der Spiegel* (2014), available at: http://www.spiegel.de/, accessed March 29, 2014.

34. S. Shane and D. Sanger, "N.S.A. suspect is a hoarder. But a leaker? Investigators aren't sure," *New York Times* (2016), available at: https://www.nytimes.com/, accessed October 6, 2016.

35. "Foreign Intelligence Surveillance Act," Federation of American Scientists (2018), available at: https://fas.org/, accessed October 9, 2018.

36. For this criticism, see, for instance, S. Ackerman, "Fisa chief judge defends integrity of court over Verizon records collection," *Guardian* (2013), available at: https://www.theguardian.com/, accessed June 6, 2013.

37. News Desk, "FISA court reauthorizes NSA phone surveillance program," *PBS NewsHour* (2014), available at: http://www.pbs.org/newshour/, January 3, 2014.

38. See, for example, "Terrorist Attacks," esri (2018), available at: https://storymaps.esri.com, accessed October 14, 2018.

39. The Editors, "Biometric security poses huge privacy risks," *Scientific American* 310 no. 1 (Berlin, Germany: Springer, 2014), available at: https://www.scientificamerican.com/, accessed January 1, 2014.

40. Editors of *MIT Technology Review*, "10 breakthrough technologies 2018."

41. M. Ruppert, "The troubling privacy implications of increasingly common eye tracking technology," *Activist Post* (2013), available at: http://www.activistpost.com/, accessed May 6, 2013.

42. R. Ross, "Robotic insect takes off," *MIT Technology Review* (2007), available at: https://www.technologyreview.com/, accessed July 19, 2007.

43. E. Palermo, "Drones could grow to \$11 billion industry by 2024," Live Science (2014), available at: http://www.livescience.com/, accessed July 29, 2014.

44. R. Johnson, "Micro-drones combined with DNA hacking could create a very scary future," *Business Insider* (2012), available at: http://www.businessinsider.com/, accessed October 28, 2012.

45. Editors of *MIT Technology Review*, "10 breakthrough technologies 2018."

46. See, for instance, "Privacy is dead, invasive technology is here to stay," AFP (2015), available at: http://www.industryweek.com/, accessed January 22, 2015.

47. "Swiss endorse new surveillance powers," *BBC News* (2016), available at: http://www.bbc.com/, accessed September 25, 2016.

48. See, for example, W. Marmon, "European affairs: Main cyber threats now coming from governments as 'state actors.'" European Institute (2011), available at: https://www.europeaninstitute.org/, accessed June 15, 2012.

49. T. Friedman, "Four Words Going Bye-Bye," *New York Times* (2014), available at: https://www.nytimes.com/, accessed May 20, 2014.

50. N. Richards, "Privacy is not dead—it's inevitable," *Boston Review* (2014), available at: http://bostonreview.net, accessed May 28, 2014.

Chapter 8: Widening Life-Expectancy Divide

1. Jobs, "You've got to find what you love."

2. S. Boseley, "Global life expectancy increases to 71.4 years," *Guardian* (2016), available at: https://www.theguardian.com/, accessed May 19, 2016.

3. "Chapter 1: Setting the scene," United Nations Population Fund (UN-FPA) (2012), available at: https://www.unfpa.org/, accessed March 8, 2013.

4. Ibid.

5. R. Stepler, "World's centenarian population projected to grow eight-fold by 2050," Pew Research Center (2016), available at: http://www.pewresearch.org/, accessed April 21, 2016.

6. Ibid.

7. W. Santrock, *A Topical Approach to Lifespan Development*, 8th ed. (New York: McGraw Hill, 2010), 168.

8. See, for instance, M. Battersby, *Is That a Fact?* (Calgary, Canada: Broadview Press, 2010), 206.

9. S. Jones and M. Kennedy, "'More than a third of babies born in 2012 will live to 100,' report predicts," *Guardian* (2012), available at: https://www.theguardian.com/, accessed March 26, 2012.

10. *The World Factbook*, CIA (2018), available at: https://www.cia.gov/, accessed April 18, 2018.

11. Ibid.

12. WHO has raised this issue since 1995. See, for example, *World Health Report*, WHO (1995), available at: http://www.who.int/, accessed March 17, 2017.

13. Ibid.

14. *World Health Statistics 2016*, WHO (2016).

15. *World Health Statistics 2014*, WHO (2014).

16. *World Health Statistics 2015*, WHO (2015).

17. See, for example, B. Briggs, "American men finally closing the longevity gender gap," *NBC* (2012), available at: http://www.nbcnews.com/, accessed May 21, 2012.

18. *The World Factbook*, CIA (2018).

19. *World Economic Outlook Database*, IMF (2018).

20. *The World Factbook*, CIA (2018).

21. Ibid.

22. *World Economic Outlook Database*, IMF (2018).

23. "The evolution of life expectancy in the world," Inequality Watch (2014), available at: http://www.inequalitywatch.eu/, accessed May 14, 2012.

24. B. Mason, "World health report: Life expectancy falls in poorest countries," derived from O. Fayehun, "Household Environmental Health Hazards and Child Survival in Sub-Saharan Africa," Demographic and Health Surveys (DHS) *Working Paper* no. 74 (US Agency for International Development, 2010).

25. The Centers for Disease Control and Prevention, "Ten great public health achievements—United States, 1900–1999," *MMWR Weekly*, available at: mmwrq@cdc.gov/, accessed April 2, 1999.

26. Ibid.

27. L. Kishore, "China, India show a seven-year jump in average life expectancy: WHO," *Merinews* (2013), available at: http://www.merinews.com/, accessed May 29, 2013.

28. See, for instance, "Global life expectancy stands at 72 years: Lancet," *Times of India* (2016), available at: http://timesofindia.indiatimes.com/, accessed October 7, 2016.

29. *The World Factbook*, CIA (2018).

30. "Ebola virus: New case emerges in Sierra Leone," *BBC News* (2016), available at: http://www.bbc.com/, accessed February 18, 2016.

31. J. Zumbrun, "The richer you are the older you'll get," *Wall Street Journal* (2014), available at: https://www.wsj.com/, accessed April 18, 2014.

32. Ibid.

33. A. Garcia, "Life expectancy gap for rich and poor is widening," *CNN* (2016), available at: http://money.cnn.com/, accessed February 18, 2016, quoted in B. Bosworth, G. Burtless, and K. Zhang, *Later Retirement, Inequality in Old Age, and the Growing gap in Longevity between Rich and Poor*, 1st ed. (Washington, DC: Brookings Institution, 2016), available at: https://www.brookings.edu/, accessed January 31, 2016.

34. D. Whitmore, S. Nunn, and L. Bauer (2016), "The changing landscape of American life expectancy," Brookings Institution (2016), available at: https://www.brookings.edu/, accessed June 30, 2016.

35. R. Pells, "Life expectancy gap between rich and poor widening for first time in 150 years," *Independent* (2016), available at: http://www.independent.co.uk/, accessed May 3, 2016. See also S. Boseley, "Life expectancy increases but gap widens between rich and poor," *Guardian* (2015), available at: https://www.theguardian.com/, accessed April 30, 2015.

36. S. Wong, "'People will live longer than official estimates predict,' say researchers," Imperial College of London (2015), available at: http://www3.imperial.ac.uk/, accessed April 30, 2015.

37. Editors of Publications International, Ltd (PIL), "Top 10 countries with the highest life expectancy," How Stuff Works (2016), Publications International, Ltd., available at: http://health.howstuffworks.com/, accessed May 25, 2015.

38. See, for instance, "Operational plan 2011–2015," UK Department for International Development (2010), available at: https://www.gov./uk/, accessed June 25, 2010.

39. "Sub-Saharan Africa time for a policy reset," *Regional Economic Outlook*, IMF (2016), available at: http://www.imf.org/, accessed April 16, 2016.

40. J. Gregson, "The poorest countries in the world," *Global Finance* (2017), available at: https://www.gfmag.com/, accessed January 1, 2017.

41. *IMF Working Paper*, IMF (2015), available at: http://www.imf.org/, accessed June 10, 2015. IMF releases a variety of reports in various years, including World Economic Outlook, Regional Economic Outlook, and Working Papers.

42. See, for example, G. Burtless, "Life expectancy and rising income inequality: Why the connection matters for fixing entitlements," Brookings Institution (2012), available at: https://www.brookings.edu/, accessed October 23, 2012.

43. C. Okojie and A. Shimeles, *Inequality in Sub-Saharan Africa*, 1st ed. (London: The Inter-Regional Inequality Facility, 2006), available at: https://www.odi.org/, accessed June 20, 2010.

44. "GINI index—country ranking," World Bank Development Research Group (2016), available at: http://iresearch.worldbank.org/ and https://www.indexmundi.com/, accessed April 20, 2016.

45. *The World Factbook*, CIA (2018).

46. Ibid.

47. "Humanity divided: Confronting inequality in developing countries," UNDP (2014), available at: http://www.undp.org/, accessed January 29, 2014.

48. *The World Factbook*, CIA (2018).

49. For the global distribution of terrorist groups and their regional relationships, see, for instance, "Mapping militant organizations," Stanford University (2012), available at: http://web.stanford.edu/, accessed June 6, 2012.

50. A quote from Luc de Clapiers, a French writer and moralist of the eighteenth century.

51. In 2008, the World Bank came out with a figure (revised largely due to inflation) of US$1.25 as the poverty line at 2005 purchasing power parity (PPP). M. Ravallion, S. Chen and P. Sangraula, "Dollar a day revisited," *World Bank Economic Review* (2009), 23, 2, 163–84.

52. "Sustainable development goals," United Nations (2016), available at: http://www.un.org/, accessed May 15, 2016.

53. In September 2015, the World Bank updated the international poverty line to US$1.90 a day. "FAQs: Global Poverty Line Update," World Bank (2015), available at: http://www.worldbank.org/, accessed September 30, 2015.

54. See, for instance, "The IMF and the World Bank," IMF (2016), available at: http://www.imf.org/, accessed September 26, 2016.

55. K. Tate, "The Borgen Project: Working to downsize poverty," *Huffington Post* (2011), available at: http://www.huffingtonpost.com/, accessed May 25, 2011.

56. E. Riley, "How much money would end global poverty?" *Borgen Magazine* (2014), available at: http://www.borgenmagazine.com/, accessed June 5, 2014.

57. S. Perlo-freeman, A. Fleurant, P. Wezeman and S. Wezeman, "Trends in world military expenditure, 2015," Stockholm International Peace Research Institute (SIPRI), *SIPRI Fact Sheet* (2016), available at: https://www.sipri.org/, accessed April 30, 2016.

58. "How to end global poverty," Borgen Project (2014), available at: http://borgenproject.org/, accessed July 12, 2014.

59. The four countries and others, including China and India, have gone from poor to rich nations thanks to structural transformation of the economy, etc. See, for example, L. Whitfield, "How countries become rich and reduce poverty," a working paper of Danish Institute for International Studies (2011), available at: https://www.diis.dk/, accessed April 15, 2012.

60. S. Huntington, "Cultures Count," in *Culture Matters: How Values Shape Human Progress.* 1st ed., eds. L. Harrison and S. Huntington (New York: Basic Books, 2000), xiii.

61. "GDP per capita (current US$)," World Bank (2018), available at: http://www.worldbank.org/, accessed July 30, 2018.

62. "Freedom in the World 2017," Freedom House (2017), available at: https://freedomhouse.org/, accessed April 15, 2017.

63. See, for instance, A. Lopez-Claros, "Does culture matter for development?" Let's Talk Development (a blog of the World Bank Group)

(2014), available at: http://blogs.worldbank.org/, accessed December 9, 2014.

64. B. Tasch, "The 25 poorest countries in the world," *Business Insider* (2016), available at: http://uk.businessinsider.com/, accessed April 3, 2016.

65. See, for example, S. Devarajan, "What will it take to end poverty in Africa?" World Bank: Africa Can End Poverty (2012), available at: http://blogs.worldbank.org, accessed October 10, 2012.

66. F. Hezel, *The Role of Culture in Economic Development*, 1st ed., Micronesian Counselor, no. 77, Micronesian seminar (MicSem) (2009), available at: http://www.micsem.org/, accessed June 30, 2009.

67. "Freedom in the World 2016," Freedom House (2017), available at: https://freedomhouse.org/, accessed April 12, 2017.

68. *Corruption Perceptions Index 2017*, Transparency International (2018), available at: http://www.transparency.org/, accessed February 21, 2018.

69. D. Moyo, "Why foreign aid is hurting Africa," *Wall Street Journal* (2009), available at: https://www.wsj.com/, accessed March 21, 2009.

70. D. Acemoglu and J. Robinson, "Why foreign aid fails—and how to really help Africa," *Spectator* (2014), available at: http://www.spectator.co.uk/, accessed January 25, 2014.

71. Moyo, "Why foreign aid is hurting Africa."

72. M. Nsehe, "The five worst leaders in Africa," *Forbes* (2012), available at: http://www.forbes.com/, accessed February 9, 2012.

73. R. Hodler, "Why African leaders like Chinese aid," *World Finance* (2016), available at: http://www.worldfinance.com/, accessed February 1, 2016.

74. See, for instance, Baobab, "Civil wars: The picture in Africa," *Economist* (2013), available at: https://www.economist.com/, accessed November 13, 2013.

75. I. Elbadawi and N. Sambanis, "Why are there so many civil wars in Africa? Understanding and preventing violent conflict," *Journal of African Economies (JAE)* 9, no. 3 (2000): 3–13. *JAE* is a World Bank publication.

76. A. Oyeniyi, "Conflict and violence in Africa: Causes, sources and types," *TRANSCEND Media Service* (2011), available at: https://www.transcend.org/, accessed February 28, 2011.

77. P. Collier and A. Hoeffler, "Greed and grievance in civil war," *Oxford Economic Papers* 56 (Oxford: Oxford University Press, 2004): 563–95.

78. See, for instance, M. Basedau and T. Wegenast, "Oil and diamonds as causes of civil war in sub-Saharan Africa under what conditions?" *Colombia International*, no. 70 (July–December 2009): 15.

79. E. Banfield, *The Moral Basis of a Backward Society* (New York: Free Press, 1958), 10.

80. Ibid., 19.

81. Ibid., 85–87.

82. See, for instance, "The life expectancy myth, and why many ancient humans lived long healthy lives," Ancient Origins (2014), available at: http://www.ancient-origins.net/, accessed April 24, 2014.

83. See, for instance, T. Miles, "'Global life expectancy: Life spans continue to lengthen around the world,' WHO says," *Huffington Post* (2013), available at: http://www.huffingtonpost.com/, accessed July 15, 2013.

84. "The evolution of life expectancy in the world," Inequality Watch.

85. Ibid.

86. E. Hirsch, J. Kett, and J. Trefil, *The Dictionary of Cultural Literacy*, 3rd ed. (Boston: Houghton Mifflin, 2002), 123.

87. M. Fusco, "'World faces challenge as life expectancies lengthen,' scientist says," *Stanford News Service* (2006), available at: http://news.stanford.edu/, accessed February 17, 2006.

88. Ibid.

89. See, for instance, *Newsletter* (December, 2016), McGowan Institute For Regenerative Medicine (2016), available at: https://www.mirm.pitt.edu/, accessed December 20, 2016.

90. Ibid.

91. M. Pena, "Stem cells: The solution to living over 100 years?" *Dartmouth Undergraduate Journal of Science* (2013), available at: http://dujs.dartmouth.edu/, accessed January 29, 2013.

92. See, for instance, "Stem cells and miracles," *BBC News* (2009), available at: http://news.bbc.co.uk/, accessed January 15, 2009.

93. A. Stevenson, "Explainer: What is a stem cell," *Science News for Students* (2013), available at: https://www.sciencenewsforstudents.org/, accessed June 27, 2013.

94. "Embryonic stem cell research: An ethical dilemma," Euro Stem Cell (2015), available at: http://www.eurostemcell.org/, accessed November 5, 2015.

95. "What are stem cells?" University of Rochester Medical Center (2018), available at: https://www.urmc.rochester.edu/, accessed July 18, 2018.

96. Ibid.

97. Stevenson, "Explainer: What is a stem cell," *Science News for Students* (2013), available at: https://www.sciencenewsforstudents.org/, accessed July 7, 2018.

98. Editors of *MIT Technology Review*, "10 breakthrough technologies 2018."

99. Z. Corbyn, "Live forever: Scientists say they'll soon extend life 'well beyond 120,'" *Guardian* (2015), available at: https://www.theguardian.com/, accessed January 11, 2015.

100. Goldin, "Navigating our global future."

101. Ibid.

102. "The wealth report," Knight Frank (2016), available at: http://www.knightfrank.com/, accessed June 18, 2017.

103. See also R. Neate, "More than a million people join ranks of very wealthy after stock markets boom," *Guardian* (2017), available at: https://www.theguardian.com/, accessed September 28, 2017.

104. "The wealth report," Knight Frank (2016).

105. "Exclusive UHNWI analysis: The world ultra wealth report 2017," Wealth-X (2017), available at: http://www.wealthx.com/, accessed June 27, 2017.

106. "Ultra-High Net-Worth Individual (UHNWI)," Investopedia (2018), available at: https://www.investopedia.com/, accessed September 19, 2018.

107. N. McCarthy, "The global pyramid of wealth," Statista (2015), available at: https://www.statista.com/, accessed April 10, 2015.

108. Ibid.

109. "'62 people own the same as half the world,' reveals Oxfam Davos report," Oxfam International (2016), available at: https://www.oxfam.org/, accessed January 16, 2017.

110. Ibid.

111. Ibid.

112. "Richest 1% will own more than all the rest by 2016," Oxfam International (2015), available at: https://www.oxfam.org/, accessed July 7, 2018.

113. "'62 people have as much wealth as world's 3.6B poorest,' Oxfam finds ahead of Davos," *CNBC* (2016), available at: https://www.cnbc.com/, accessed January 16, 2016.

114. "The world's 8 richest men are now as wealthy as half the world's population," *Fortune* (2017), available at: http://fortune.com/, accessed January 16, 2017.

115. R. Frank, "Richest 1% now owns half the world's wealth," *CNBC* (2017), available at: https://www.cnbc.com, accessed November 14, 2017.

116. Ibid. See also "10 facts on malaria," WHO (2016), available at: http://www.who.int/, accessed December 29, 2016.

117. Hirsch, Kett, and Trefil, *The Dictionary of Cultural Literacy.*

Chapter 9: The Aging Workforce

1. *World Economic Outlook Database*, IMF (2016).

2. Ibid.

3. A. Kiersz, "THE GLOBAL 20: Twenty big stories that define the world right now," *Business Insider* (2015), available at: http://www.businessinsider.com/, accessed May 13, 2015.

4. "The world population prospects: 2015 Revision," United Nations (2015), available at: http://www.un.org/, accessed July 29, 2015.

5. K. Rapoza, "China's aging population becoming more of a problem," *Forbes* (2017), available at: https://www.forbes.com/, accessed 21 February 21, 2017.

6. See, for example, G. Nargund, "Declining birth rate in developed countries: A radical policy re-think is required," The National Center for Biotechnology Information (2009), available at: https://www.ncbi.nlm.nih.gov/, accessed December 23, 2015.

7. "Lowest birth rates in the world by country," World Atlas (2017), available at: http://www.worldatlas.com/, accessed February 21, 2017.

8. "Birth dearth: 20 countries with lowest birth rates," *CBS News* (2017), available at: http://www.cbsnews.com/, accessed January 1, 2017.

Country rankings in low birth rates vary a little according to different survey organizations, but the variance is insignificant.

9. A. Evans-Pritchard, "Germany dominance over as demographic crunch worsens," *Telegraph* (2015), available at: http://www.telegraph.co.uk/, accessed June 1, 2015.

10. "Fueled by aging baby boomers, nation's older population to nearly double in the next 20 years, Census Bureau Reports," United States Census Bureau (2017), available at: http://www.census.gov/, accessed May 6, 2014.

11. M. Mather, "Fact sheet: Aging in the United States," Population Reference Bureau (2016), available at: http://www.prb.org/, accessed January 31, 2016.

12. See, for example, M. Horvath, "The silver tsunami is coming, are we ready?" *Huffington Post* (2013), available at: https://www.huffingtonpost.com/, accessed August 11, 2013.

13. J. Coleman, *Unfinished Work: The Struggle to Build an Aging American Workforce* (Oxford: Oxford University Press, 2015), 208–12.

14. R. Williams, "The silver tsunami—why we will need aging workers," *Psychology Today* (2011), available at: https://www.psychologytoday.com/, accessed July 16, 2011.

15. "Birth dearth: 20 countries with lowest birth rates," *CBS News*.

16. *World Health Statistics 2016*, WHO (2016).

17. "Countries With The Largest Aging Population In The World," World Atlas (2018), available at: https://www.worldatlas.com/, accessed June 5, 2018.

18. Y. Takeda, "Will the sun also rise?" in *Postwar Japan: Growth, Security, and Uncertainty since 1945*, eds. M. Green and Z. Cooper (Lanham, MD: Rowman & Littlefield, 2017), 121.

19. Williams, "The silver tsunami—why we will need aging workers."

20. "Increase opportunities for elderly to remain active in aging society" (an editorial reported on September 22, 2015), *Yomiuri Shimbun* (2015), available at: http://www.yomiuri.co.jp/, accessed October 31, 2015.

21. Ibid.

22. S. Oda, "Silver gifts to centenarians get cheaper as ranks rise," *Japan Times* (2016), available at: https://www.japantimes.co.jp/, accessed September 17, 2016.

23. W. He, D. Goodkind, and P. Kowalet, *An Aging World: 2015*, 1st ed. (Washington, DC: US Census Bureau, 2016), available at: https://www.census.gov/, accessed March 30, 2016.

24. "Global health and aging," WHO (2016), available at: http://www.who.int/, accessed May 30, 2016.

25. O. Balch, "Age discrimination is still seen as okay in the workplace," *Guardian* (2015), available at: https://www.theguardian.com/, accessed April 2, 2015.

26. Ibid.

27. "Labor force statistics from the current population survey," US Bureau of Labor Statistics (2011), available at: https://www.bls.gov/, accessed May 11, 2015.

28. See, for example, K. Johnston, "Is the hot tech job market leaving its veterans behind?" *Boston Globe* (2016), available at: https://www.bostonglobe.com/, accessed March 6, 2016.

29. "General aging," Division 20, Adult Development and Aging, American Psychological Association (2017), available at: http://www.apadivisions.org/, accessed April 22, 2017.

30. J. Ortman, V. Velkoff, and H. Hoganet, *An Aging Nation: The Older Population in the United States*, 1st ed. (Washington, DC: US Census Bureau, 2014), available at: http://www.census.gov/, accessed May 15, 2014.

31. M. Toossi, *Labor Force Projections to 2020: A More Slowly Growing Workforce*, 1st ed. (Washington, DC: US Bureau of Labor Statistics, 2012), available at: https://www.bls.gov/, accessed January 3, 2012.

32. "Median age of the labor force, by sex, race and ethnicity," US Bureau of Labor Statistics (2017), available at: https://www.bls.gov/, accessed October 24, 2017.

33. B. Drake, "Number of older Americans in the workforce is on the rise," Pew Research Center (2014), available at: http://www.pewresearch.org/, accessed January 7, 2014.

34. "Demographic and Social Change," PWC (2017), available at: http://www.pwc.co.uk/, accessed August 28, 2017.

35. Ibid.

36. For coming "silver tsunami," see, for instance, P. Perry, "Can the World Sustain 9 Billion People by 2050?" Big Think (2016), available at: https://bigthink.com/, accessed July 24, 2016.

37. C. Chosewood, "Safer and healthier at any age: Strategies for an aging workforce," Center for Disease Control and Prevention (2012), available at: https://blogs.cdc.gov/, accessed July 19, 2012.

38. R. Das, "A silver tsunami invades the health of nations," *Forbes* (2015), available at: https://www.forbes.com/, accessed August 11, 2015.

39. J. Celeste, "7 ways businesses can surf the silver tsunami and survive," *Huffington Post* (2016), available at: http://www.huffingtonpost.com/, accessed September 8, 2016.

40. "Global age watch index: Norway best for older people," *BBC News* (2014), available at: http://www.bbc.com/news/, accessed October 1, 2014.

41. H. Alexander, "Why Norway is the best place in the world to grow old," *Telegraph* (2014), available at: http://www.telegraph.co.uk/, accessed October 1, 2014.

42. O. Petter, "World's best countries to grow old in revealed," *Independent* (2017), available at: http://www.independent.co.uk/, accessed July 26, 2017.

43. "The 'Silver tsunami': Why older workers offer better value than younger ones," Knowledge@Wharton (2010), available at: http://knowledge.wharton.upenn.edu/, accessed December 6, 2010.

44. "Aging," National Institute on Aging (NIA) (2016), available at: https://www.nia.nih.gov/, accessed March 28, 2016.

45. "Old-age dependency ratios," *Economist* (2009), available at: http://www.economist.com/, accessed May 7, 2009.

46. "Age dependency ratio, old (% of working-age population)," World Bank (2017), available at: https://data.worldbank.org/, accessed November 16, 2017.

47. Quoted in P. Moeller, "Challenges of an aging American workforce," Center on Aging and Work of Boston College (2013), available at: http://agingandwork.bc.edu/, accessed July 24, 2013.

48. T. Sightings, "How to boost your retirement confidence," *U.S. News & World Report* (2015), available at: http://money.usnews.com/, accessed June 8, 2015.

49. D. Parkinson, J. McFarland, and B. McKenna, "Boom, bust and economic headaches," *Globe and Mail* (2015), available at: https://beta.theglobeandmail.com/, accessed November 6, 2015.

50. Ibid.

51. Moeller, "Challenges of an aging American workforce."

52. See, for example, "Aging workers," Canadian Centre for Occupational Health and Safety (2017), available at: https://www.ccohs.ca/, accessed September 1, 2017.

53. N. Rot, *Injuries at Work Are Fewer among Older Employees*, 1st ed. (Washington, DC: US Bureau of Labor Statistics, 2011).

54. "Labor force statistics from the current population survey," US Bureau of Labor Statistics (2011).

55. Moeller, "Challenges of an aging American workforce."

56. Ibid.

57. "The changing brain in healthy aging," NIA (2015), available at: https://www.nia.nih.gov/, accessed December 12, 2016.

58. Ibid.

59. Ibid.

60. Ibid.

61. See, for instance, "Some areas of the brain slow with aging," Care Builders at Home (2016), available at: http://www.carebuildersathome.com/, accessed December 2, 2016.

62. See, for example, "Some areas of the brain slow with aging," CareBuilders at Home (2017), available at: https://www.carebuildersathome.com/, accessed August 21, 2017.

63. See, for example, S. Johnson, "How can older people play a bigger role in society?" *Guardian* (2015), available at: https://www.theguardian.com/, accessed March 30, 2015.

64. UN Department of Economic and Social Affairs (DESA), *Development in an Ageing World,* 1st ed. (New York: United Nations, 2007), available at: http://www.un.org, accessed December 20, 2007.

65. N. Pimlott, "Failure and the aging of society," *Official Journal of the College of Family Physicians of Canada* 61, no. 3 (Ontario, Canada: College of Family Physicians of Canada, 2015), available at: http://www.cfp.ca/, accessed March 20, 2015.

66. "The changing brain in healthy aging," NIA (2015).

67. Ibid.

68. Ibid.

69. See, a series of reports titled "Issue Brief" released since 2007 by the Employee Benefit Research Institute, available at: https://www.ebri.org/, accessed May 1, 2017.

70. T. Harbert, "Age bias in IT: The reality behind the rumors," *Computerworld* (2011), available at: http://www.computerworld.com/, accessed September 1, 2011.

71. Ibid.

72. Harbert, "Age bias in IT: The reality behind the rumors."

73. Ibid.

74. Ashoka, "10 ways universities can improve entrepreneurship education," *Forbes* (2014), available at: http://www.forbes.com/, accessed September 10, 2014.

75. Ibid.

76. Miller, "Computers designed specifically for seniors," *Huffington Post* (2013), available at: http://www.huffingtonpost.com/, accessed November 10, 2013.

77. 42Gears Team, "How to make mobile devices friendly for elderly individuals?" 42Gears(2016), available at: https://www.42gears.com/, accessed April 21, 2016.

78. C. Gustke, "Making technology easier for older people to use," *New York Times* (2016), available at: https://www.nytimes.com/, accessed March 11, 2016.

79. Ibid.

80. Ibid.

81. See, for example, "The new old age," *Atlantic* (2017), available at: https://www.theatlantic.com/, accessed October 4, 2017. The *Atlantic* offers New Old Age forum.

82. See, for example, J. Bakewell, "Working into old age like Prince Philip is becoming the new normal. Here's how to plough on," *Telegraph* (2017), available at: http://www.telegraph.co.uk/, accessed May 5, 2017. The *Atlantic*'s New Old Age forum.

83. Guest Contributor, "Technology is making seniors' lives easier," Social Media Scoop for Seniors (2014), available at: http://seniornet.org/, accessed July 17, 2014.

84. M. Egan, "Best phone for the elderly," *TechAdvisor* (2017), available at: http://www.pcadvisor.co.uk/, accessed January 4, 2017.

85. L. Orlov, "Top 10 technology devices for seniors," HomeCare (2016), available at: http://www.homecaremag.com/, accessed December 15, 2016.

86. "Innovative technology for seniors: How the evolving digital era is influencing the way we age," Institute on Aging (2015), available at: https://blog.ioaging.org/, accessed November 25, 2015.

87. O. Rudgard, "Older workers healthier and more reliable," *Telegraph* (2015), available at: http://www.telegraph.co.uk/, accessed May 14, 2015.

88. D. Hyde, "Older workers 'do not steal jobs from young,'" *Telegraph* (2015), available at: http://www.telegraph.co.uk/, accessed March 11, 2015.

89. See, for instance, J. Burton, "Healthy workplace framework and model," WHO (2010), available at: http://www.who.int, accessed February 25, 2010.

90. R. Fernández-Ballesteros, J. Robine, A. Walker, and A. Kalache, "Active aging: A global goal," *Current Gerontology and Geriatrics Research* (2013), available at: https://www.ncbi.nlm.nih.gov/, accessed February 13, 2013.

91. M. Dittmann, "Fighting ageism," *American Psychological Association* (2003), available at: http://www.apa.org/, accessed May 31, 2003.

92. J. Tarnoff, "3 tips on combating ageism from an anti-ageism activist," *Huffington Post* (2015), https://www.huffingtonpost.com/, accessed March 8, 2015.

93. Balch, "Age discrimination is still seen as okay in the workplace."

94. Ibid.

95. "Ageism," OMICS International (2016), available at: http://research. omicsgroup.org/, accessed February 20, 2016.

96. A. Officer, M. Schneiders, D. Wu, P. Nash, J. Thiyagarajan, and J. Beard, "Valuing older people: time for a global campaign to combat ageism," *Bulletin of the World Health Organization* (2016), available at: http://www.who.int/, accessed December 27, 2016.

97. "The 20 countries with the highest fertility rates in 2016," Statista (2017), available at: https://www.statista.com/, accessed January 7, 2017.

98. Ibid.

Chapter 10: Climate Change

1. "Advancing the science of climate change," National Research Council (2010), available at: http://www.nationalacademies.org/, accessed March 12, 2010.

2. See, for example, J. Schwartz, "The Relationship Between Hurricanes and Climate Change," *New York Times* (2017), available at: https:// www.nytimes.com/ accessed Aug. 25, 2017.

3. "AccuWeather predicts Hurricane Harvey to be more costly than Katrina, Sandy combined," AccuWeather (2017), available at: https:// www.accuweather.com/, accessed September 1, 2017.

4. See, for example, Jessica Conditt, "How Puerto Rico's power crisis ends," Engadget (2017), available at: https://www.engadget.com/, accessed September 30, 2017.

5. The Times Editorial Board, "Harvey should be a warning to Trump that climate change is a global threat," *Los Angeles Times* (2017), available at: http://www.latimes.com/opinion/, accessed August 30, 2017.

6. See, for example, J. Broome, "KlimaCampus colloquium: 'Climate change: life and death,' CliSAP (2016), available at: https://www.clisap.de/, accessed May 26, 2016.

7. *Global Trends: The Paradox of Progress*, NIC (2017), 21–25.

8. R. Lallensack, "Doomsday Clock ticks 30 seconds closer to midnight, thanks to Trump," *Science* (2017), available at: http://www.science-mag.org/, accessed January 26, 2017.

9. Ibid.

10. A. Ohlheiser, "Trump didn't delete his tweet calling global warming a Chinese hoax," *Washington Post* (2016), available at: https://www.washingtonpost.com/, accessed September 27, 2016.

11. "Climate change and nuclear tensions push Doomsday Clock hands forward," *Bulletin of Atomic Scientists* (2015), available at: http://thebulletin.org/, accessed January 22, 2015.

12. "Pledge to stop Saying 'climate change,'" Job One for Humanity (2017), available at: http://www.joboneforhumanity.org/, accessed September 10, 2017.

13. "World Bank online open course on climate change," World Bank (2014), available at: http://www.worldbank.org/, accessed February 21, 2014.

14. Ibid.

15. A. Thompson, "Major greenhouse gas reductions needed by 2050: IPCC," Climate Central (2014), available at: http://www.climatecentral.org/, accessed May 12, 2014.

16. J. Boyle, "Gathering in the gloom of Warsaw: Assessing the outcomes of COP19," in *A Climate Insights Product*, 1st ed. (Winnipeg, Canada: International Institute for Sustainable Development, 2013), available at: http://www.iisd.org/, accessed February 25, 2013.

17. M. Oliver, "James Hansen, father of climate change awareness, calls Paris talks 'a fraud,'" *Guardian* (2015), available at: https://www.theguardian.com/, accessed December 12, 2015.

18. M. Shear, "Trump will withdraw U.S. from Paris Climate Agreement," *New York Times* (2017), available at: https://www.nytimes.com/, accessed June 1, 2017.

19. J. Horton, "Greenhouse gases rise by 260% since Industrial Revolution," *Scotsman* (2012), available at: http://www.scotsman.com/, accessed November 20, 2012.

20. "Sources of greenhouse gas emissions," EPA (2014), available at: https://www.epa.gov/, accessed November 30, 2016.

21. See, for example, M. Ives, "A remote Pacific nation, threatened by rising seas," *New York Times* (2016), available at: https://www.nytimes.com/, accessed July 2, 2016.

22. D. Criss, "A massive climate change study is canceled ... because of climate change," *CNN* (2017), available at: http://edition.cnn.com/, accessed June 20, 2017.

23. Kiersz, "THE GLOBAL 20."

24. United States Government Accountability Office (GAO), "Freshwater: Supply concerns continue, and uncertainties complicate planning," GAO–14–430, 1st ed. (Washington, DC: GAO, 2014), available at: http://www.gao.gov/, accessed May 21, 2014.

25. Kiersz, "THE GLOBAL 20."

26. "Press release: It is now 3 minutes to midnight," *Bulletin of the Atomic Scientist* (2015), available at: http://thebulletin.org/, accessed January 22, 2015.

27. Ibid.

28. M. Park, "Q&A: A trillion-ton iceberg is floating in the sea. Now what?" *CNN* (2017), available at: http://edition.cnn.com/, accessed July 13, 2017.

29. "The 97% consensus on global warming," Skeptical Science (2017), available at: https://www.skepticalscience.com/, accessed May 23, 2017.

30. Skeptics suggest numerous reasons that climate change is natural. See, for example, C. Meredith, "100 reasons why climate change is natural," *Express* (2012) available at: http://www.express.co.uk/, accessed November 20, 2012.

31. "More than 1000 international scientists dissent over man-made global warming claims," Global Research (2014), available at: http://www.globalresearch.ca/, accessed September 21, 2014.

32. Ibid.

33. For Climategate scandal, see, for instance, J. Henig, "Climategate," FactCheck.org (2009), available at: http://www.factcheck.org/, accessed December 22, 2009.

34. Meredith, "100 reasons why climate change is natural."

35. For questions and answers about Climategate, see, D. Carrington, "Q&A: Climategate," *Guardian* (2011), available at: https://www.theguardian.com/, accessed November 30, 2011.

36. A. Leiserowitz, E. Maibach, C. Roser-Renouf, and N. Smith, "Climategate, public opinion, and the loss of trust," *American Behavioral Scientist* (2012), available at: http://journals.sagepub.com/, accessed September 13, 2013.

37. See, for example, D. Carrington, "Q&A: 'Climategate,'" *Guardian* (2011), available at: https://www.theguardian.com/, accessed November 22, 2011.

38. S. Motel, "Polls show most Americans believe in climate change, but give it low priority," Pew Research Center (2014), available at: http://www.pewresearch.org/, accessed September 23, 2014.

39. C. Funk and B. Kennedy, "Public views on climate change and climate scientists," Pew Research Center (2016), available at: http://www.pewresearch.org/, accessed October 4, 2017. See also W. Anderegga, J. Prallb, J. Harold, and S. Schneider, "Expert credibility in climate change," *Proceedings of the National Academy of Sciences of the United States of America* (April 9, 2010), available at: http://www.pnas.org/, accessed November 16, 2011. This study says, "97–98% of the climate researchers most actively publishing in the field surveyed here support the tenets of ACC (Anthropogenic Climate Change) outlined by the Intergovernmental Panel on Climate Change."

40. "How reliable are climate models?" Skeptical Science (2017), available at: https://www.skepticalscience.com/, accessed August 15, 2017.

41. M. Shwartz and D. Levy, "Global warming: It's not an exact science, but it's science all the same," Stanford University (News Release) (2000), available at: http://news.stanford.edu/, accessed February 11, 2012.

42. Ibid.

43. "How reliable are climate models?" Skeptical Science.

44. "The 97% consensus on global warming," Skeptical Science.

45. Kiersz, "THE GLOBAL 20."

46. "Causes of climate change," EPA (2017), available at: https://www.epa.gov/, accessed February 22, 2017.

47. "Climate change: Basic information," EPA (2017), available at: https://www.epa.gov/, accessed February 22, 2017.

48. "NOAA: Past decade warmest on record according to scientists in 48 countries," National Oceanic and Atmospheric Administration (NOAA) (2010), available at: http://www.noaanews.noaa.gov/, accessed July 28, 2010.

49. Ibid.

50. "The science of climate change," Committee on Climate Change (2016), available at: https://www.theccc.org/.uk/, accessed November 23, 2016.

51. For notions following this line of reasoning, see, for example, P. Gwynne, "Human-caused climate change has a partner in crime: Mother nature herself," *Inside Science* (2016), available at: https://www.insidescience.org/, accessed December 7, 2016.

52. See, for instance, D. Markham, "Global warming effects and causes: A top 10 List," Planetsave (2009), available at: http://planetsave.com/, accessed June 7, 2009.

53. Ipsos, *Global Trends Survey 2017*, 17.

54. Ibid., 125.

55. "Climate change indicators: Greenhouse gases," EPA (2017), available at: https://www.epa.gov/, accessed February 20, 2017.

56. See, for example, "Future of climate change," EPA (2017), available at: https://www.epa.gov/, accessed January 19, 2017.

57. Ibid.

58. Ibid.

59. "Ecology, climate change and related news," Point Blue (2017), available at: http://www.pointblue.org/, accessed July 31, 2017.

60. A. Luers, M. Mastrandrea, K. Hayhoe, and P. Frumhoff, *How to Avoid Dangerous Climate Change: A Target for U.S. Emissions Reductions*, 1st ed. (Cambridge, MA.: Union of Concerned Scientists, 2007), available at: http://www.ucsusa.org/, accessed January 31, 2017.

61. Ibid.

62. H. Dixon, "Top climate scientists admit global warming forecasts were wrong," *Telegraph* (2013), available at: http://www.telegraph.co.uk/, accessed September 15, 2013.

63. "Climate change facts: Answers to common questions," EPA (2016), available at: https://www.epa.gov/. See also A. Spiewak, "Mo' carbon, mo' problems—a rap guide to climate chaos," *Rand Magazine* (2016), available at: http://www.rdmag.com/, accessed June 3, 2016.

64. S. Jakuboski, "Green science: Deforestation and global warming," Scitable by Nature Education (2012), available at: http://www.nature.com/scitable/blog/, accessed June 12, 2014.

65. As for the politics of global warming, see, for example, J. Gillis, "Short Answers to Hard Questions About Climate Change," *New York Times* (2015), available at: https://www.nytimes.com/, accessed November 29, 2015.

66. "Climate change: How do we know?" NASA (2017).

67. E. Siegel, "The first climate model turns 50, and predicted global warming almost perfectly," *Forbes* (2017), available at: https://www.forbes.com/, accessed March 15, 2017.

68. A. Sandberg, "The five biggest threats to human existence," *Conversation* (2014), available at: http://theconversation.com/, accessed May 29, 2014. Sandberg regards climate change as an "unknown unknown."

69. Editorial Board, "Marco Rubio's rhetoric on climate change casts questions about his judgment," *Washington Post* (2014), available at: https://www.washingtonpost.com/, accessed May 12, 2014.

70. Ohlheiser, "Trump didn't delete his tweet calling global warming a Chinese hoax."

71. See, for instance, L. Dodgson, "The biggest threat to Earth has been dismissed by Trump as a Chinese hoax," *Business Insider* (2016), available at: http://www.businessinsider.com/, accessed November 11, 2016.

72. On July 5, 2018, Scott Pruitt resigned as EPA head amid scandals. Pruitt stoked anger among Democrats and environmentalists for casting doubt on humanity's role in climate change. See, for example, T. DiChristopher, "EPA Leader Scott Pruitt resigns after scandals engulf his agency," *CNBC* (2018), available at: https://www.cnbc.com/, accessed July 5, 2018.

73. R. Marsh, "EPA removes climate change information from website," *CNN* (2017), available at: http://edition.cnn.com/, accessed May 1, 2017.

74. B. Plumer, "'Trump's big new executive order to tear up Obama's climate policies,' explained," *Vox* (2017), available at: http://www.vox.com/, accessed March 28, 2017.

75. N. Slawson, "G20 summit: 'G19' leave Trump alone in joint statement on climate change—as it happened," *Guardian* (2017), available at: https://www.theguardian.com/, accessed July 8, 2017.

76. Quoted in Sandberg, "The five biggest threats to human existence." Sandberg notes that we have "a huge moral reason to work hard to prevent existential threats from becoming reality."

77. Ibid.

78. For this line of reasoning, see, for example, J. Romm, "What are the 'unknown unknowns' of global warming," *ThinkProgress* (2011), available at: https://thinkprogress.org/, accessed October 1, 2011.

79. For this concern, see, for instance, "Coastal consequences of sea level rise," NASA (2017), available at: https://climate.nasa.gov/, accessed April 18, 2017.

80. A. Cuthbertson, "Stephen Hawking will show how humans can move planet in 100 years."

81. Ibid.

82. For the inadequacy of political leaders' response to climate change, see, for example, G. Readfearn, "Tragic lack of leadership puts red hot climate change out in the cold," *Guardian* (2016), available at: https://www.theguardian.com/, accessed June 29, 2016.

83. As for the signs, see, for example, 350.org, "10 reasons you should have hope for the future," EcoWatch (2016), available at: https://www.ecowatch.com/, accessed May 18, 2016.

84. Editors of *MIT Technology Review,* "10 breakthrough technologies 2018."

85. Editors of *MIT Technology Review,* "10 breakthrough technologies 2019." The rest of the "10 breakthroughs 2019" are robot dexterity, new-wave nuclear power, predicting preemies, gut probe in a pill, custom cancer vaccines, the cow-free burger, an ECG on your wrist, sanitation without sewers and smooth-talking AI assistants.

Index

B

Babel-Fish Earbuds 114, 115
baby boomers
  baby boomer generation 190
Baidu
  censorship 147
Banfield, Edward 176
BAS 206, 207, 211, 224, 226
bin Laden, Osama
  al-Qaeda 117
bioeconomy 131
biofuel 131
biometric authentication system 147
biometric database 158
bioprinting 129
biotechnology 100, 131, 133, 178,
    180
blockchain
  bitcoin 97
BLS 189, 190
Bode, Maximilian 41
Bosworth, Barry 169
Brende, Borge 109
Brexit 18, 41, 59
BRICs 168, 173, 236
Brindak, Juliette 84
  Miss O & Friends 83
Brookings Institution 169, 266, 267
Brooks, Joanna 195
Buck, Pearl S. 51
  Buck 242
Buffet, Warren 99
Bulletin of the Atomic Scientists
    See BAS
Bush, George W. 203
Butler, Robert Neil 201
Butrimas, Vytautas 152

C

Cameron, David 5, 18
Canadian Arctic, the 211
carbon dioxide 209, 210, 212, 213,
    217, 219, 221
CARE 172
Carnegie, Andrew 49
Castle Bravo
  nuclear bomb 41
centenarian 164
Center for Research on
    Globalization. *See* CRG
Centers for Disease Control and
    Prevention 168
China's one-party system 11
Chomsky, Noam 92
Church, George
  Human Genome Synthesis Project
    2 112
Churchill, Winston 17
CIA 42, 117, 134, 153, 165, 166,
    171, 259, 265-267
Cicero, Marcus 33
civicracy 19-24, 26, 27, 28
climate change 2, 36, 41, 203-205,
    207-211, 213, 214, 216-226,
    279-285
  believers, skeptics 205
  scientists 205
Climategate
  conspiracy or fraud 213
  public opinion 214
Clinton, Hillary 8, 20
Cobain, Kurt
  Nirvana 87
Coelho, Paulo 85
Cold War 13, 31, 32, 41, 237

F

Fallon, Lynnette 197
FBI 123, 124, 156, 158, 256, 257
Federal Bureau of Investigation.
       See FBI
Federal Trade Commission. *See* FTC
Federation of American Scientists 41
Fermi, Enrico 206
fertility rate 202
Feynman, Richard Phillips 217
FISA 155, 156, 263
Flynn effect 78
Foreign Intelligence Surveillance
       Act. *See* FISA
formal education 47, 49, 51, 53-57,
       60, 62, 64-66, 243
Fountain of Youth
  mythical spring 178
Fox, Terry 142
Franklin, Benjamin 49
Franks, Stewart 217
Freedom House 9, 12, 230, 231,
       268, 269
Friedman, Thomas 161
Friends of the Internet 24
FTC 145
Furedi, Frank 93

G

Galilei, Galileo 215
Garland, Stacia 84
Gartner 98
Gates, Bill 50, 80
gene drive 115
Generations X and Y 69, 87
Generation Z 69, 78
genetically modified. *See* GM

genetic fortune telling 115
Genie Talk
  automatic translation app 113
Global Age Watch Index 191
Global Financial Crisis 42
Global Risk Insights 39, 233
global warming 132, 171, 203-205,
       207-209, 213-215, 217-219,
       221-224, 280-285
Global Warming Petition Project
       217
GM 130
Goldin, Ian 181
Google
  strongest cyberimperial power 145
Google Translate app 114
Gorbachev, Mikhail 32
Gould, Steven Jay 92
gross world product. *See* GWP
GWP 42

H

Harari, Yuval Noah 66
Hawking, Stephen 2, 119, 225-227,
       285
health technologies 58, 100, 120, 134
  disease management and human
       enhancement 178
Higgs, Peter 99
high net-worth individuals. *See*
       HNWIs
Hitler, Adolf 31
HNWIs 181, 182
Horowitz, Michael 31
Human 2.0 132
human enhancement 132, 133
Human Genome Project 112
human resources development 197

(The page numbers 227-285 in Index are from Endnotes.)